Mothers of Faith

MOTHERS OF FAITH

Motherhood in the Christian Tradition

WILFRED M. SUMANI, SJ

ORBIS BOOKS
Maryknoll, New York 10545

ORBIS BOOKS
Maryknoll, New York 10545

Fathers and Brothers
MARYKNOLL

Founded in 1970, Orbis Books endeavors to publish works that enlighten the mind, nourish the spirit, and challenge the conscience. The publishing arm of the Maryknoll Fathers and Brothers, Orbis seeks to explore the global dimensions of the Christian faith and mission, to invite dialogue with diverse cultures and religious traditions, and to serve the cause of reconciliation and peace. The books published reflect the views of their authors and do not represent the official position of the Maryknoll Society. To learn more about Maryknoll and Orbis Books, please visit our website at www.maryknollsociety.org.

Library of Congress Cataloging-in-Publication Data

Names: Sumani, Wilfred M., author.
Title: Mothers of faith : motherhood in the Christian tradition / Wilfred M.
  Sumani, SJ.
Description: Maryknoll : Orbis Books, 2017. | Includes bibliographical
  references.
Identifiers: LCCN 2017022186 | ISBN 9781626982574 (pbk.)
Subjects: LCSH: Mothers in the Bible. | Women in Christianity. |
  Motherhood—Religious aspects—Christianity.
Classification: LCC BS579.M65 S86 2017 | DDC 220.8/3068743—dc23
LC record available at https://lccn.loc.gov/2017022186

To Magrina and Lilian, mothers of faith

Contents

Part IV. Motherhood as Theological Analogy

Acknowledgments

"One head cannot carry a roof," says a Malawian proverb. A book, any book, is a product of many heads. I would like to register my gratitude to the many women and men who have contributed to the *birth* of this book.

First, I am indebted to my biological mother, Magrina, who, out of love, endured labor pains to bring me into this world. I also thank Lilian, my sister and adoptive mother, who took the baton of the relay race of motherhood from Magrina and brought me up with love and grace, instilling in me such values as hard work, loyalty, and integrity. I also remember with gratitude my father, Mathias, who inspired me with chivalrous stories of his journeys (on foot) to Mozambique and Zimbabwe, where he worked on farms and in mines. But it was my brother-in-law and adoptive father, Antonio, who saw to my daily needs from my childhood to the time my vocal cords broke. Our family was joyful, thanks to the friendship and bond I shared with my siblings Stella, Cornelia, Victor, Matilda, Cleopas, Monica, and Prisca. A hearty thank you to them all.

Special gratitude to Fr. Thomas Carroll, SJ, who went through the first draft of this book and made important stylistic corrections. Tom is by now familiar with my writing style, for when we were together in Collegio Bellarmino (Rome) he also edited my licentiate thesis and doctoral dissertation, in addition to a number of my articles. Words cannot express the depth of my gratitude for his unwavering generosity.

Fr. Agbonkhianmeghe E. Orobator, SJ, also deserves a special mention. When I completed the first draft of this book, I sent it to him for corrections and suggestions. Having gone through it, he suggested that I propose the manuscript to Orbis for publication. I was greatly humbled by his positive feedback, for I had never remotely imagined that an international publisher would be interested in the work of an unknown writer. It was a surreal experience when Jim Keane (from Orbis Books) sent me an e-mail letting me know that Orbis had decided to publish it. Like the proverbial Archimedes, I nearly jumped out of my room to proclaim the good news in the streets of Lusaka! I am grateful to Jim for trusting the intuitions of an upcoming writer.

Fr. Joseph Healey, M.M. (Maryknoll Fathers), is an indefatigable promoter of African theology and theologians. My thanks to you, Joe, for creating connections and networks among African theologians and artists.

Finally, I thank all my colleagues at Hekima University College for their support and encouragement: Fr. Festo Mkenda, SJ; Fr. Laurenti Magesa; Fr. Joachim Zoundi, SJ; Fr. John Ghansah, SJ; Fr. Kifle Wansamo, SJ; Fr. Jocelyn Rabeson, SJ; Sr. Ingrid Vorner, S.A.; Fr. Elisée Rutagambwa, SJ; Fr. Gaspar Sunhwa, SJ; Fr. Peter Knox, SJ; Fr. Francis Njuguna; Fr. Emmanuel Foro, SJ; Fr. Toussaint Kahfarire, SJ; and Fr. Elias Opongo, SJ.

I thank the following friends whose interest in the book kept me going even when the initial interest had waned: Samuel Satiele, S.M.M.; Likukela Mate; Alex Muyebe, SJ; Nicholas Penge, SJ; Ellen Maseve; Hector Mukwato, SJ; Lastone Lupupa, SJ, and Emmanuel Mumba, SJ (fellow ministers at Matero Parish); Dominic Liche; Diane Ndikuriyo (who recently became a mother to Eliana); Anna Yohane; Wilbroad Mubanga; Tendai Tafirei (proudly Zimbabwean!); Mai Malakata; Mai Mumba and Mai Banda (faithful sacristans at Matero Parish, Lusaka); and all members of the Integrated Young Innovators, Lusaka (Zambia).

One day, my niece Madalo and nephews Chikondi, Evans, George, and Stefano will grow up to read this book. May the collective wisdom contained herein inspire them all to become good mothers and fathers.

Last but not least, I thank you, dear reader, for picking up this book. May God bless you abundantly.

—WS

Abbreviations and Acronyms

Biblical Books

Gen	Genesis
Ex	Exodus
Lev	Leviticus
Numb	Numbers
Dt	Deuteronomy
Josh	Joshua
Judg	Judges
1Sam	1 Samuel
2Sam	2 Samuel
1Kg	First Book of Kings
2Kg	Second Book of Kings
1Chron	First Book of Chronicles
2Chron	Second Book of Chronicles
Neh	Nehemiah
Ps	Psalms
Prov	Proverbs
Eccl	Ecclesiastes
Song	Song of Songs
Wis	Wisdom
Sir	Sirach
Isa	Isaiah
Jer	Jeremiah
Ez	Ezekiel
Dan	Daniel
Hos	Hosea

Hab	Habakkuk
Zeph	Zephaniah
Zech	Zechariah
Mal	Malachi
1Macc	1 Maccabees
2Macc	2 Maccabees
4Macc	4 Maccabees
Mt	Matthew
Mk	Mark
Lk	Luke
Jn	John
Acts	Acts of the Apostles
Rom	Romans
1Cor	First Letter to the Corinthians
2Cor	Second Letter to the Corinthians
Gal	Galatians
Eph	Ephesians
Phil	Philippians
Col	Colossians
Heb	Hebrews
1Pt	First Letter of Peter
Ap	Apocalypse

Other Sources and Studies

ANF	Ante-Nicene Fathers
CCC	*The Catechism of the Catholic Church*. Nairobi, Kenya: Paulines Publications, Africa, 1994.
CCL	*Corpus christianorum series latina*. Turnhout, Belgium: Brepols, 1953–.
CSEL	*Corpus scriptorum ecclesiasticorum latinorum*. Berlin: De Gruyter, 1866–.
NPNF Series 1	*Nicene and Post Nicene Fathers*, Series 1. Edited by Philip Schaff. Grand Rapids, MI: Wm. B. Eerdmans, 1956–.

NPNF Series 2   *Nicene and Post Nicene Fathers*, Series 2. Edited by Philip Schaff and Henry Wace. New York: Christian Literature, 1890–.

PG   *Patrologia cursus completus series graeca*. Edited by J. P. Migne. Paris: 1857–1936.

PL   *Patrologia cursus completus series latina*. Edited by J. P. Migne. Paris: 1841–64.

SC   Constitution on the Sacred Liturgy *Sacrosanctum Concilium*. In *Vatican Council II: Conciliar and Post-Conciliar Documents*. Edited by Austin Flannery. Bombay, India: St. Paul Publications, 1992.

SCh   *Sources Chrétiennes*. Paris: Cerf, 1942–.

Introduction

"Every mother has a story." So goes an advertisement for a detergent in Zambia. But many stories about mothers remain untold and unread, though a mother plays the most crucial role in the lives of each of us from conception onward. The first intersubjective encounter of a human being begins in the mother's womb, where blood is exchanged between mother and child through the lifeline called the umbilical cord. Once the baby is born, he or she depends on the mother for warmth, acceptance, and nourishment. To a child, it does not matter whether the mother is tall or short, dark or pale, rich or poor, good natured or ill tempered; what matters first and foremost is that she is one's mother. The natives of the Trobriand Islands in British New Guinea are correct when they affirm the almost total dependency of the child on the mother: "The mother makes the child out of her blood."[1] An African proverb also goes, "Everyone knows a person's mother," and another is "Mother is Supreme."[2]

Mother is home. In the 2003 Peter Levin film entitled *Homeless to Harvard*, adapted from Liz Murray's autobiography *Breaking the Night*, Elisabeth "Liz" Murray becomes homeless at the age of fifteen. Her mother, a recovering drug addict, is dying. In one of her intense moments of reflection, Liz speculates: "What's home, any-

---

1. Bronisław Malinowski, *The Sexual Life of Savages in North-Western Melanesia: An Enthnographic Account of Courtship, Marriage and Family Life Among the Natives of the Trobriand Islands, British New Guinea* (New York: Harcourt, Brace & World, 1929), 4.

2. Chinua Achebe, *Things Fall Apart* (New Delhi, India: Allied Publishers, 2012), 122.

way? A roof? A bed? A place where, when you go there, they have to take you? If so then I was fifteen when I became homeless." Almost a minute later in the movie she says, "But sometimes I felt like I've never had a home in my life," and then adds, "And then, other times, I knew, wherever my mother was, that's where my home was." For Liz, it did not matter that her mum was a drug addict. What mattered was that she was her mum.

In the African context, mothers are among the busiest people in society. The Yoruba figure of *Obirin meta* (literally "three women") captures well the many tasks of an African mother. Sometimes the roles a mother plays would ordinarily require three women to undertake them. A. E. Orobator has used the image of a mother capable of balancing a big pot of water or a basket of farm produce on her head, at the same time carrying a baby strapped to her back and taking care of the needs of her family; and, as if that was not enough, she carries another baby in her womb.[3]

Motherhood is one of the most theologically fertile human and Christian experiences. To be a mother is to transmit and to nurture life. It is to ensure the continuity of a genealogy. It is to witness to the miracle of the beginning of life, its growth in the secrecy of the night—from the vulnerability of the fetus in the womb to the confidence of a full-grown man or woman. To be a mother is to be blessed by God, and to be blessed means to participate in the fecundity of God. When God created living things, God blessed them and gave them the power to multiply. In the same manner, when God created man and woman, God blessed them and commanded them to multiply and to fill the earth. Fecundity brings joy, sterility, sorrow. As Ben Sirach writes, one of the anxieties of a father is that his married daughter should be found sterile.[4]

Mothers encounter many joys and sorrows. To make sense of the challenges and opportunities, some fall back on traditional

---

3. Agbonkhianmeghe E. Orobator, *Theology Brewed in an African Pot* (Maryknoll, NY: Orbis Books, 2008), 31.

4. Sir 42:10.

wisdom, while others take recourse to insights from modern sciences such as psychology. And yet the Christian tradition also has its own valuable resources, because the tradition is full of stories of mothers of faith who became mothers in faith. As persons rooted in faith, they transmit faith to their children. This book explores the riches of the biblical and Christian tradition of faith-based motherhood.

The reflections in this book are partly a product of the many conversations I have had with mothers from a wide spectrum of sociocultural backgrounds: young and not so young; rich and not so rich; smiling, weeping; beaming with joy, writhing in pain; teeming with hope, wilting in the scorching sun of fate. Some mothers have approached me asking for prayers for their children about to cross an important threshold in life or stuck in the sticky mud of crises. These are mothers of faith who place their trust in God, knowing that God alone is the source of goodness and growth. I am grateful to all mothers who shared with me their personal experiences. The heart of a mother is full of prayers. May God be kind to all mothers and grant them their desires. But the immediate impetus to write the book came from a retreat I facilitated for the Legionaries of Mary at Kasungu Parish, Malawi, in 2012. This lay group of women and men approached me, rather at short notice, to offer some reflections on the motherhood of Mary. My tendency for meticulous preparation almost made me turn down the invitation for lack of adequate time to find enough meaningful material to offer to these women and men of faith. However, recalling the Ignatian principle of radical availability, I accepted to journey with them.

The evening before the beginning of the retreat, I took a long walk, during which I stumbled on the idea of inviting the women and men to pray with a select number of mothers in the Bible. When I went back to my room I drew up a list of mother figures from both Testaments. During the retreat, the participants shared their deep and down-to-earth reflections on the vocation of motherhood. After the retreat, I invited the participants to choose three people who would put together the insights we derived in a booklet to be published with a local religious publisher. However, the team found the task too difficult, and they threw the challenge back at me. Now, almost four years down the line, I agree with them that it is not an easy task to put together theological and practical reflections on motherhood. I am very grateful to all those who participated in the parish retreat.

I have no personal recollections of my biological mother. I learned her name only when it was time to register my name in the school books. It was then that I was told her name was Magrina. When I was barely ten months old, she had embarked on a long journey to the other side of life to join a throng of holy mothers who ceaselessly sing hymns of praise to the God of motherhood. May she rest in eternal peace! And then God sent a woman who courageously stepped in to assume the reins of motherhood for me and for my two elder sisters. Her name was Lilian. She was such an excellent mother that it took me many years to discover that she was not my biological mother, but rather my biological sister. By dint of some mystical intuition, she told me she would not be alive by the time I was ordained a priest. Sure enough, she passed on in 2003 while I was doing my third year of philosophical studies in Harare. Her last letter reached me after her demise. Lilian, thank you for your self-sacrificing love. May God grant you the joys of heaven.

This book is divided into four parts. The first presents portraits of select mothers in the Old Testament, while the second focuses on mothers in the New Testament, culminating in the longest chapter of all: Mary the Mother of Meditation. The third part takes a few samples of mothers from the Christian tradition. The fourth part articulates the sacramental character of motherhood, arguing, among other things, that motherhood mirrors important qualities of God. Thus, to borrow the expression of Margaret Hebblethwaite, one can find "God in motherhood" and "motherhood in God."[5] In this sense, the book is intended for a readership wider than mothers.

There is also a gradual progression in the book from narrative to more speculative theological engagement. The underlying conviction is that relevant and sound theology starts with human experience.

---

5. Margaret Hebblethwaite, *Motherhood and God* (London: Geoffrey Chapman, 1984), 1.

Part I

Mothers of the Old Testament

Chapter 1

Eve: Mother of All the Living

Introduction

The Christian imagination often associates Eve with temptation and sin. She is seen as the chief accomplice in the drama of the fall, the temptress that leads Adam to the original sin. She is seen as having betrayed the immortality of humanity, much as Delilah betrayed Samson to the Philistines.[1] Yet there is a way to reverse the power of that negative image. Eve also possesses qualities such as intellectual curiosity that lead her beyond the confines of what has been tried and tested. In a patriarchal society, such curiosity in women is proscribed, thereby casting a shadow of rebellion on Eve's exploration of what lies beyond the horizon of social and religious prescription.

Modesty in patriarchal societies, such as that from which the Genesis account emerged, would require women to wait at home for the fruits of the hunting or farming expeditions of their menfolk. Women's exploration of the unknown world is seen to be a kind of shredding of social norms. Eve, on the contrary, champions the discovery of novelty and shares it with her husband, Adam. Even more importantly, the biblical account presents Eve as the mother of all the living. In the Jewish pseudepigraphic *Apocalypse of Moses* (dating to between the second and fourth centuries), an

---

1. Judg 16:1–21.

imaginative retelling of the story of the fall of the first parents, Eve is the one who recounts to her children the story of the first couple's fall and expulsion from Paradise. She is the mother of tradition. Before Cain sheds Abel's blood, Eve receives a vision at night in which she sees the impending fratricide. After Adam's demise, Eve receives a revelation of the mysteries of the afterlife; she sees what happens to Adam after his death. All in all, Eve is portrayed as someone privy to the mysteries of life and death.[2]

Her Story

The story of motherhood starts on a painful note: Adam and Eve have transgressed the commands of the Lord and have eaten of the forbidden fruit. Their crime leads to a curse. Among other things, the woman is condemned to intense childbearing pain.[3]

Before the Fall, Adam names his wife "Woman," "for out of Man this one was taken."[4] But after the couple's fall from grace, Adam names his wife "Eve," "because she was the mother of all living."[5] The new name signals a new beginning, a return to life. It is possible that the name Eve is etymologically connected with "life."[6] In fact, John Chrysostom uses the Greek word *Zoe* (which means life) for Eve. Chrysostom further explains that Eve is the "source of all those who will come from her, the root and foundation of the future race."[7] The name Eve is an act of faith on the part of Adam: "Though threatened by death Adam does not believe that he and his wife are to be the first and last beings of the human race. Moth-

---

2. *Revelation of Moses*, trans. Alexander Walker, ANF, vol. 8 (New York: Charles Scribner's Sons, 1926), 565–70.

3. Gen 3:16.

4. Gen 2:23.

5. Gen 3:20.

6. Victor P. Hamilton, *The Book of Genesis: Chapters 1–17* (Grand Rapids, MI: Wm. B. Eerdmans, 1990), 205.

7. John Chrysostom, *Homilies on Genesis* XVIII, 3, trans. Robert C. Hill, The Fathers of the Church, vol. 82 (Washington, DC: Catholic University of America Press, 1990), 4.

erhood will emerge."[8] Motherhood holds the hope of the continuity of humanity threatened by death due to sin.

The woman's new name is prophetic of the birth of Cain and Abel narrated in the next chapter: "Now the man knew his wife Eve, and she conceived and bore Cain, saying, 'I have produced a man with the help of the LORD.'"[9] All along, Adam has been giving names to creatures, including his wife, Eve. But now it is Eve who gives a name to her firstborn son. The son's name is Eve's confession of faith: "I have produced a man with the help of the LORD." Eve interprets the birth of Cain as an act of God's providence. He is a godsend, a sign of hope.[10] As Ambrose of Milan says, Eve teaches humanity "not to claim our succession to ourselves, but attribute it entirely to God."[11]

The birth of Cain would seem to suggest that God is not angry with the sinful couple forever. In spite of Adam and Eve's disobedience, God is still their friend and helper. By attributing Cain's birth to God's help, Eve recognizes her participation in God's creative power. In childbirth, both the divine and the human are involved.[12] John Chrysostom surmises that the punishment incurred by Adam and Eve has brought Eve to her senses and now she "attributes the child she bore not to a natural process but to God, and displays her own gratitude . . . It is not nature, she is saying, that presented me with the child; instead, grace from above has given him to me."[13]

Eve gives birth to a second son, Abel. It is not clear who names the second son, nor is the etymology of the name given in the text. Some authors see some connection between the name Abel and the Hebrew word *hebel*, which can mean (among other things)

---

8. Hamilton, *The Book of Genesis*, 207.

9. Gen 4:1.

10. Allen P. Ross and John N. Oswalt, *Genesis, Exodus,* Cornerstone Biblical Commentary, vol. 1 (Carol Stream, IL: Tyndale House Publishers, 2008), 59.

11. Ambrose of Milan, *Cain and Abel* I, 2, trans. John J. Savage, Fathers of the Church, vol. 42 (New York: Fathers of the Church, 1961), 360.

12. Hamilton, *The Book of Genesis*, 242.

13. Chrysostom, *Homilies on Genesis* XVIII, 14.

"vanity," "wind," or "vapor," all of which point to the idea of being ephemeral or impermanent.[14]

Chrysostom attributes the birth of the second son to Eve's sense of gratitude to the Lord on the occasion of the birth of Cain:

> Since she proved to be grateful for the birth of the first child and acknowledged the former kindness, she enjoyed the good fortune of the second. Our Lord is like this, you see: when we display gratitude for previous good deeds and acknowledge the benefactor, he lavishes his gifts upon us more generously. Accordingly, because she attributed the birth to God, for that reason she receives another child.[15]

Chrysostom's remarks resonate with the now popular saying of the German-Canadian author Eckhart Tolle regarding the importance of gratitude: "Acknowledging the good that you already have in your life is the foundation for all abundance." Indeed, gratitude opens more taps of kindness and generosity.

Abel takes care of animals while Cain tills the land. Together, they represent the two communities of the ancient Near East: sedentary (agricultural) and nomadic (pastoral), respectively. The relationship between agricultural and pastoral communities was often characterized by conflict.[16] As the narrative states, Cain "built a city, and named it Enoch after his son Enoch."[17] Within this city, various professions developed such as musicians, ironsmiths, and coppersmiths. Abel's trade, instead, requires movement in search of pasture. His profession signals his impermanence: today he is here, tomorrow he is elsewhere; today he is alive, tomorrow he is dead.

Eve's joy on account of the gift of the two sons quickly turns into

---

14. Cf. Eccl 1:2; Hamilton, *The Book of Genesis*, 221.

15. Chrysostom, *Homilies on Genesis* XVIII, 15.

16. Ephraim A. Speiser, *Genesis: Introduction, Translation and Notes* (New Haven, CT: Yale University Press, 2008), 31.

17. Gen 4:17.

a sword that pierces her heart. The relationship between the brothers turns sour because God is pleased with the sacrifice of Abel, while Cain's offering is not acceptable to God. And so Cain kills his brother Abel. The death of Abel doubtless brings sorrow to Eve. Many scholars have speculated that the name Abel comes from the Hebrew root-verb *'abel,* which means to mourn or to lament, used especially in the sense of mourning the dead.[18] If one follows this meaning, then it is Eve who mourns and laments the death of her son Abel.

When God's blessings seem to be making a happy comeback in the form of the birth of the two sons, God's wrath rears its head again and strikes the family with yet another curse. Just as Adam and Eve were expelled from the Garden they were commissioned to till, Cain is removed from his land and is destined to be "a fugitive and a wanderer on the earth,"[19] because the land will no longer give him fruit. While the mother's womb is the cradle of life, the earth becomes the abode of the dead: it receives Abel's blood. The earth becomes a tomb, the antithesis of the womb. St. Ambrose addresses himself to Cain in the following words: "The earth, still wet with the blood of your slain brother, is a hostile witness. As a judge, the earth, befouled by such a crime, is even more antagonistic, inasmuch as she opened her mouth and received your brother's blood shed by your own hands ... You shed blood for which the earth in retaliation 'will not give her fruit to you.'"[20]

However, sorrow and shame are not the last word in the life of Eve: "Adam knew his wife again, and she bore a son and named him Seth, for she said, 'God has appointed for me another child instead of Abel, because Cain killed him.'"[21] Here, again, it is Eve who gives a name to the son. And she reads the event of the birth of Seth in the light of God's providence: God has given her Seth in

---

18. Cf. Gen 37:34; Isa 19:8; Amos 8:8.
19. Gen 4:12.
20. Ambrose, *Cain and Abel* II, 30.
21. Gen 4:25.

place of Abel, whom Cain has killed. Adam, who has named many creatures, including Eve, recedes into the background.

For her, God is one who replaces what is lost. God renews lost joy and compensates for human sorrow. Through the birth of Seth, God wipes away Eve's tears.

In Luke's account of the genealogy of Jesus, Seth is mentioned as one of Jesus's ancestors: "son of Enos, son of Seth, son of Adam, son of God."[22] The birth of Seth, thus, contains the promise of the Great Consolation from God, namely, Jesus Christ, who will transform the tomb into the womb of new life. Through the death and resurrection of Christ, the earth will recover its fecundity, for from its womb will emerge the Lord of life.

Reflection

Eve emerges as a woman of faith. She attributes the birth of her sons to divine intervention. She manifests and exercises her faith by naming her sons, at least Cain and Seth. The pain of childbirth does not embitter her and does not make her rebel against God who had placed the curse upon her. Nor does the murder of her second son, Abel, make her lose hope in life. While she does not simply sweep the tragedy of fratricide under the carpet of amnesia, she also does not allow the terrible event to condition her attitude to life. When Seth is born, the name she gives him shows that her attitude toward life remains positive. She does not remain wrapped in the mourning veil forever, nor does lament have the last word in her life.

The story of the motherhood of Eve shows the centrality of a mother in the household. While the Jewish society in which the story of Adam and Eve emerged was patriarchal, Eve takes center stage when it comes to naming the sons. To name is to exercise authority over what is named; but it is also a sign of affection. Adam names his wife "Woman" as an expression of intimacy with

---

22. Lk 3:38.

her, for she is "bone of my bones and flesh of my flesh."[23] In the nine months that a child spends in the womb of the mother, strong bonds between the two emerge. The mother can also say that the child is "bone of my bones and flesh of my flesh." Her blood flows into the baby. There is an intimate sharing between them, one that would mirror the *perichoresis* of the three Persons of the Holy Trinity. What Adam was to Eve is what Eve is to her sons.

The second account of creation narrates that God planted a Garden in Eden, and there he put the man he had fashioned. God gives man an orientation into the Garden, teaching him to distinguish between what would be good for him and what would destroy him.[24] In giving birth to a child, the mother *puts* the baby in the *garden* of the world, as it were. With her, the baby learns how to walk the *garden* of the earth, distinguishing what gives life from what deals death. With her, the baby learns that fire brings warmth, as long as one does not stay too close to it. The child understands that water quenches thirst and cleanses, but that too much of it kills. She imparts to her baby the practical lessons that God gave to the first human beings. In this regard, what God was to Adam and Eve is what Eve is to her sons.

Conclusion

Eve, the *mother of the living*, transmits and nurtures life in spite of the tragic beginning of her motherhood. She knows that fecundity is a gift from God. Thus, the names of her sons are an anamnesis of God's life-giving generosity. Naming in the Jewish culture to which the Genesis account was transmitted (and in many others) is such a powerful opportunity to manifest and transmit faith to one's children. Therefore, when choosing names for children, it is important to think carefully and diligently about it so that the name becomes a synthesis or summary of one's experience of God's providence. Sometimes people are so strongly impacted

---

23. Gen 2:23.
24. Gen 2:8, 17.

by negative experiences that they name their children, places, or things on the basis of those negative events. One's world is thus marked with negative memories. Children, places, houses, or trees become bearers of unhappy memories. Eve, on the contrary, does not let the unhappy circumstance of the death of Abel condition her worldview: she paints her world with happy colors, the colors of joy and gratitude to God who gives life and consoles the sorrowful. Eve shows that to be a mother is to give not only physical life but also to breathe into one's children the air of faith so that even the very names of one's children proclaim the wonders of the Lord.

Prayer

O God, out of your love for humanity, you gave us Eve to be the mother of all the living. In spite of her sin, she confessed you as the source of life and wellbeing. She grieved at the death of her son Abel, but you consoled her with the birth of Seth. Grant fecundity to all women yearning for the gift of children and console all mothers who have lost their beloved children. Through Christ our Lord. Amen.

Chapter 2

Sarah: Mother of the Promise

Introduction

One of the most prominent women in the history of salvation is Sarah, Abraham's wife. Bits and pieces of her journey of faith are scattered from the eleventh to the twenty-third chapters of the Book of Genesis. Her story is intertwined with Abraham's story. One of the words that best describe her journey of faith is *waiting*.

Her Story

Sarah is introduced in Genesis 11 as Sarai, Abram's wife. She is immediately presented as barren.[1] The departure of Abram from Haran is premised by God's promise to make Abram "a great nation."[2] Abram is seventy-five years old when he undertakes the journey. We are not told how old Sarai is at the time of departure. From the account of their sojourn in Egypt, it is clear that Sarai is so beautiful that even Pharaoh falls for her. To avoid trouble, Abram says that she is his sister. Sarai spends some time in the royal court as Pharaoh's wife, until God inflicts severe plagues on Pharaoh and his household, whereupon he returns Sarai to Abram and asks the

---

1. Gen 11:30.
2. Gen 12:1–2.

couple to leave Egypt, but not without giving them great wealth to carry with them.[3]

Sarai's experience in Egypt has some parallels with that of Moses and of the people of Israel. The latter ended up in Pharaoh's court as an adopted son, thanks to the ploy crafted by Moses's mother and sister. Moses is nursed by his own mother, who is paid for it, as the Pharaoh's daughter has mistaken her for a wet nurse. When he is weaned, Moses is brought to Pharaoh's daughter, who treats him like her son and names him Moses, because he was drawn out of the water.[4] Later, Moses becomes God's instrument for the liberation of Israel. To wrestle the people of Israel out of Pharaoh's strong hand, God brings ten plagues upon the land of Egypt, the last of which makes Pharaoh allow God's people to go.[5]

Another detail that buttresses the parallel between the Abram–Sarai and Moses–Israel experience is found in Genesis 15, where God says to Abram: "Know this for certain, that your offspring shall be aliens in a land that is not theirs, and shall be slaves there, and they shall be oppressed for four hundred years; but I will bring judgment on the nation that they serve, and afterward they shall come out with great possessions."[6] Thus, in a mysterious way, Sarai prefigures, on the one hand, the nation of Israel that is held captive in Egypt and, on the other, Moses, the captive turned liberator.

The liberation motif in the story of Sarai's sojourn in Egypt is underscored by the fact that, when a similar scenario happens at Beersheba, where Sarai (now Sarah) is taken in by King Abimelech—again under the pretext of being Abraham's sister—the dis-

---

3. Gen 12:10–20. Sharon P. Jeansonne makes a similar observation when she draws the reader's attention to the parallels between the famine that led the sons of Jacob to go to Egypt in search of food and the famine that forces Abram and his wife to turn to Egypt for help. In both cases, plagues play a crucial role in forcing Pharaoh's hand to release the people of God. Sharon P. Jeansonne, *The Women of Genesis: From Sarah to Potiphar's Wife* (Minneapolis: Fortress Press, 1990), 16.

4. Ex 2:1–10.

5. Ex 7:8–12:34.

6. Gen 15:13–14.

covery of the lie does not lead to the expulsion of Abraham and
Sarah from the land; rather, Abimelech invites Abraham to settle
wherever he pleases in the land.[7] Unlike Egypt, Beersheba is not
the land of slavery; therefore, Abraham and Sarah cannot be sent
away from this land.

Hope Tried and Tested

As years go by and the expected son does not come, God's promise
to Abram seems to turn into a folktale and a mockery of the aging
couple. The promise turns poetic when Abram is told to count the
stars if he can, for so numerous shall his descendants be.[8] While
Abram's faith in the promise of God is unwavering, Sarai wants to
be more realistic. She is well on in years, and the glimmer of hope
of bringing forth her own son is fading by the day. So she works out
a solution and says to her husband, "You see that the LORD has
prevented me from bearing children; go in to my slave-girl; it may
be that I shall obtain children by her."[9] The girl's name is Hagar,
an Egyptian slave-girl, whose experience of motherhood will be
discussed later in this book. Abram accepts the offer. There is no
case of immorality here, for such an arrangement was within the
acceptable practices in the ancient Near East.[10]

Instead of waiting upon the Lord to fulfill God's promise in
God's own time, Sarai becomes impatient and takes the initiative
to let Abram have a child through her slave-girl. While, according
to Chrysostom, Abram trusts in the "inventiveness of the Lord
and the fact that, being creator of nature, [God] is able to find ways
even where there are none,"[11] Sarai decides to take the matter into

---

7. Gen 20:1–18.

8. Gen 15:5–6.

9. Gen 16:2.

10. Victor P. Hamilton, *The Book of Genesis, Chapters 1–17* (Grand Rapids,
MI: Wm. B. Eerdmans, 1990), 444.

11. John Chrysostom, *Homilies on Genesis* XXXVIII, 2, trans. Robert C.
Hill, The Fathers of the Church, vol. 82 (Washington, DC: Catholic University
of America Press, 1990), 356.

her own hands and deploys what Chrysostom calls "good sense."[12] She concludes that God has prevented her from having her own children. Chrysostom interprets Sarai's decision as a gesture of affection for her husband: "Sensing his love she wanted to show how great was her affection for him, concerned not for herself but for a way in which she might devise some compensation for him for the lack of children."[13] The Antiochene Father sees in Sarai's gesture a sense of self-emptying and self-transcendence aimed at giving her husband joy and fulfillment. Chrysostom also describes Sarai as a person who humbly accepts the natural order of things, for she bears her condition of sterility nobly, without grumbling or lamenting. Her acceptance of her situation is rooted in her conviction that, "just as we close and open our house, so too the Lord works on our nature, turning the key by his personal command and then opening it whenever he wishes and bidding nature take its course."[14]

However, while she may be right in ascribing her sterility to God's will, since "everything comes from nature's Creator and that neither intercourse nor anything else is capable of ensuring succession unless the hand from above intervenes and prompts nature to birth,"[15] Sarai seems to have forgotten the promise of the Lord to Abram. She seems to have such an exhaustive knowledge of the Lord's will as not to expect any surprises at all. By giving Hagar to Abram, Sarai somehow becomes a self-appointed director of the drama of salvation.

But human solutions have their own limitations. Sarai's solution brings her pain and humiliation. Abram has intercourse with Hagar and she conceives, whereupon Sarai's humiliation begins: "When [Hagar] saw that she had conceived, she looked with con-

---

12. Ibid., 3.

13. Ibid., 4.

14. Ibid., 5.

15. Ibid., 4. Chrysostom, in fact, argues that men who recognize the divine cause of their wives' sterility will not despise their wives on account of their childlessness.

tempt on her mistress."[16] Hagar's conception gives her some power over her mistress Sarai. The tables of authority seem to turn: the slave becomes mistress, and the mistress pales into insignificance. Chrysostom's comment is apt:

> This, you see, is the way with servants; if they happen to gain some slight advantage, they can't bear to stay within the limits of their station but immediately forget their place and fall into an ungrateful attitude. This is what happened to this maidservant, too: when she saw the change in her figure, she gave no thought either to her mistress's ineffable forbearance, nor her own lowly station, but became arrogant and self-important, scorning the mistress who had shown such great regard for her as even to bring her to her husband's very marriage bed.[17]

Fecundity is a source and expression of power. In her anger, Sarai blames Abram for the situation. The helper has become the victim. She feels aggrieved because her gesture of generosity and self-abasement does not yield the sweet grapes of gratitude but instead the sour grapes of denigration. But Abram challenges her to overcome self-pity and assert her authority over Hagar.

New Names, New Fortunes

The birth of Hagar's son, Ishmael, does not mark the fulfillment of God's promise to Abram. God continues to promise Abram a son by his wife, Sarai. This promise is reinforced by the change of names: God changes Abram's name to Abraham: "No longer shall your name be Abram, but your name shall be Abraham; for I have made you the ancestor of a multitude of nations."[18] God's decision is definitive: "I *have* made you the ancestor of a multitude

---

16. Gen 16:4.
17. Chrysostom, *Homilies on Genesis* XXXVIII, 12.
18. Gen 17:5.

of nations." God no longer uses future tense. Though the child has not yet been born, Abraham has already become, in God's plan, the father of a multitude of nations. God tells Abraham to call his wife not Sarai but Sarah. God promises to bless her and to give Abraham a son by her. She "shall give rise to nations; kings of peoples shall come from her."[19]

Just as God gave a name to Adam and Adam in turn gave a name to his wife, Abram receives a new name from God, and God asks Abram to give a new name to Sarai. Eve is the mother of all living while Sarah is mother of *nations*. In spite of Sarai's hesitations, God's promise remains alive and well. She is the one through whom the promise God made to Abraham will be fulfilled. There will be neither shortcuts nor proxies.

By now Abraham has partly been infected with Sarah's *realism*. When God renews the promise of numerous progeny, Abraham laughs on account of the couple's old age. By now Sarah is eighty-nine years old, while he is ninety-nine. As Chrysostom humorously comments, promising children to Abraham and Sarah in their old age was like "promising to make people out of stones. After all, they were no different from stones as far as childbearing was concerned: the patriarch by this stage was impotent through old age and without the capacity to have children, and Sarrah [sic] in addition to her sterility had the extra handicap of extreme old age."[20] Here, again, Chrysostom argues that God deliberately delays the gift of children, allowing the couple to reach an age at which it is humanly impossible to expect the gift of children. On the part of Sarah, her sterility is now compounded by old age and her periods have already ceased to occur.[21] All these odds will make God's miracle shine forth with great splendor because it will be clear to all that the birth of the child is not within the matrix of human logic.[22]

God insists that Sarah will bear Abraham a son whom he must

---

19. Gen 17:16.

20. Chrysostom, *Homilies on Genesis* XL, 3.

21. Gen 18:10.

22. Chrysostom, *Homilies on Genesis* XL, 6.

name Isaac. God even specifies the time of his birth: "at this season next year."[23] This time frame is repeated when Abraham receives the three mysterious guests at Mamre: "I will surely return to you in due season, and your wife Sarah shall have a son."[24] When Sarah laughs at the promise of a son in her old age, the mysterious visitors retort, "Is anything too wonderful for the LORD?"[25] The New Jerusalem Bible renders this verse as, "Nothing is impossible for Yahweh," which words will be repeated to Mary during the Annunciation.[26]

Though assailed by doubt, Sarah already lives in her name what she will become. Like Eve who receives a new name before becoming a mother, Sarai is named Sarah even before the birth of Isaac. In name, she is already living the reality of motherhood. In name, the promise has come to pass.

Birth of Isaac

At long last Yahweh brings his promise to fulfillment: "The LORD dealt with Sarah as he had said, and the LORD did for Sarah as he had promised. Sarah conceived and bore Abraham a son in his old age, at the time of which God had spoken to him."[27] Those who receive the promise have to know how to wait for the right time. Abraham is a hundred years old when Isaac is born; Sarah is ninety. This is God's opportune moment, the *kairos.*

God brings God's own promises to fulfillment. The parallelism "as he had said / as he had promised" serves to underline the faithfulness of God. God who promises knows when to bring the promise to fulfillment. In the Lucan infancy narrative, Zechariah sings praise to God who has raised up a mighty savior "as he spoke through the mouth of his holy prophets of old."[28]

---

23. Gen 17:21.
24. Gen 18:10.
25. Gen 18:14.
26. Cf. Lk 1:37.
27. Gen 21:1–2.
28. Lk 1:70.

Of the two, it is Sarah who breaks into poetry (and perhaps dance): "God has brought laughter for me; everyone who hears will laugh with me."[29] She adds, "Who would ever have said to Abraham that Sarah would nurse children? Yet I have borne him a son in his old age."[30] With the birth of Isaac, the laughter of skepticism turns into the laughter of joy. The Lord has turned Sarah's mourning into dancing.[31] The mourning veil of her humiliation has been taken away. As the psalm says, "Weeping may linger for the night, but joy comes with the morning."[32] Those who used to laugh at her will now laugh with her. Sarah's neighbors rejoiced with her just as, later, Elisabeth's neighbors and relatives will rejoice with Elisabeth when in her old age she gives birth to a son. John Chrysostom imagines Sarah saying to herself, "The unusual character of the birth amazed everyone and gave everyone particular joy on learning that, after being no better than a corpse, I suddenly became a mother, I bore a child from a frozen womb, and was actually able to suckle it and release a flow of milk after having thus far no prospects of childbearing."[33] Chrysostom's images of *frozen womb* and *flow of milk* call to mind the beautiful lines of the hymn *Veni sancte Spiritus*: "*Riga quod est aridum*" (water that which is dry) and "*Fove quod est frigidum*" (warm that which is cold). God, in his ineffable wisdom and unfathomable power, warmed Sarah's womb and watered her breasts, even in her old age.

God on Her Side

After the birth of Isaac, Sarah begins to worry about the future of her son, especially with regard to the question of the inheritance. She is aware that Ishmael is as much Abraham's son as Isaac. Being the firstborn, Ishmael would naturally have the birthright. But Sarah does not want Ishmael to have a share in their father's inheri-

---

29. Gen 21:6.
30. Gen 21:7.
31. Cf. Ps 30:11.
32. Ps 30:5.
33. Chrysostom, *Homilies on Genesis* XLV, 25.

tance.[34] Abraham is indecisive because he treats Ishmael as his son too. But God is on the side of Sarah and tells Abraham to do what his wife says, because it is Isaac who is to inherit Abraham's name.[35] Sarah's initiative (to have Abraham have a child by a slave-girl) continues to haunt the family. In the interests of the divine promise, Ishmael must be sent away because God wants Isaac to inherit Abraham's name. Therefore, Abraham has to overcome his fatherly sentiments for Ishmael and send him away, knowing that God will also bless Ishmael, though in a different way.

After the sending away of Ishmael, Sarah recedes into the background and only resurfaces in Genesis 23, where there is a brief account of her death: "Sarah lived one hundred twenty-seven years; this was the length of Sarah's life. And Sarah died at Kiriath-arba (that is, Hebron) in the land of Canaan; and Abraham went in to mourn for Sarah and to weep for her."[36]

Reflection

Sarah comes across as a realistic and practical woman. When the prospects of bearing a child grow thin, she arranges to give her slave-girl to Abraham so the latter can bear him a child. She knows how to look for practical solutions to her problems. She does not spend her time lamenting her sterility. The only instance that points to a lament is when she attributes her barrenness to Yahweh.

Her realism is mingled with doses of humor. She laughs when, in her old age, God continues to promise that she will bear Abraham a son. Laughter is her way of coping with the painful reality of sterility. She is a woman who suffers in silence and does not make known to others her prayer of lament. Some of that pain surfaces when Hagar conceives and becomes arrogant to her; Sarah's heavy hand against Hagar could be a subtle manifestation of the anger

---

34. Gen 21:11.
35. Gen 21:12.
36. Gen 23:1–2.

and frustration the former has been experiencing because of her barrenness.

Before the birth of Isaac, Sarah seems to walk in the shadow of Abraham's faith, for it is Abraham who receives God's promises and follows the requisite instructions leading to the fulfillment of God's promises. An episode that typifies her withdrawn personality is the visit of the three mysterious figures; Sarah remains in the tent, perhaps in conformity with the prescriptions of the ancient Near Eastern culture, while Abraham entertains the visitors. In the tent, she feels protected, as it were, from the unpredictable winds of divine intervention. In the tent, she feels in charge of her life and of her household. In the tent, she is hidden from the prying eyes of those prone to mocking her on account of her barrenness. But the word of God breaks the barrier of the tent and pierces her ears with the prophecy of her impending conception. She is challenged to go beyond the *tent*, the safe and predictable environment, and to venture into the uncharted territory of God's plans. All along, she has exercised control over her household, but now she is invited to surrender that control to God. She is reminded that *nothing is impossible for Yahweh*.

Sarah's openness to God's plan is shown in that she accepts going wherever Abraham goes. She accepts the name Sarah, which speaks of the advance fulfillment of God's promise. Her faith actively shines forth when Isaac is born; her poetry to celebrate the event is a clear testimony of her belief in God as the source of blessings. She is the mother of the promise who travels the length and the breadth of the earth in search of its fulfillment. But she does so with laughter, both in moments of pain and of joy.

Conclusion

Barrenness is a cross carried by many women. The stigma that goes with the inability to bring forth a child adds salt to the injury. Some marriages break down on account of the absence of the fruit of the womb in the family. In many cases, the blame is laid at the woman's door. In some African communities, "a woman's inability to bear children, especially frequent miscarriages, is blamed on her; she is accused of harboring in her belly a form of witchcraft."[37]

Like Sarah, consequently, some couples resort to arrangements that bring in a third party in order to give the family a child. Modern science also provides solutions to barrenness, often by involving a surrogate father or mother. Such scientific or cultural interventions, however, do not truly bring the satisfaction and joy of fathering or mothering a child by one's own husband or wife. Fathers and mothers would like to call their children bone of my bone and flesh of my flesh. Sarah suffered the humiliation of being barren. God consoled her with the birth of Isaac. In her faith, she praised God for his marvelous deed (*mirabilia Dei*), the unexpected gift of a child.

Prayer

O God of old, you promised to Sarah that even in her old age she would bear a son. Many times you visited her and renewed the promise until she brought to light Isaac your servant. Grant that we may trust in your faithful word and wait patiently for its fulfillment, for nothing is impossible with you. Grant the laughter of joy all those women who suffer the laughter of scorn on account of their barrenness. Through Christ our Lord.

---

37. Ludovic Lado, *Catholic Pentecostalism and the Paradoxes of Africanization: Processes of Localization in a Catholic Charismatic Movement in Cameroon* (Leiden, Germany: Brill, 2009), 48–49.

Chapter 3

Hagar: Mother in the Desert

Introduction

When we speak of households, we usually mean those comprised only of family members. However, rich households are often comprised also of various servants, including maids. Many of these maids live in the shadows of the family life, so much so that the stories of their joys and sorrows are largely untold. While some enjoy the privileges of the family, others are subjected to ignominious treatment at the hands of their masters and mistresses. But domestic servants play an important role and need to be celebrated.

Mary Sibande, a South African artist, whose mother, grandmother, and great-grandmother were maids, has undertaken the noble task of celebrating these unsung heroes in her sculptures that feature her alter ego called Sophie, represented as a domestic mother. In one representation, she dresses the maid figure with sumptuous and overflowing gowns that have become run-of-the-mill in the contemporary red-carpet fashion world. Nonetheless, the material of the maid's gown is the usual rustic blue cotton fabric worn by house helps. In another representation, the maid is shown riding on a horse performing airs above the ground (front legs in the air), portraying the adventurous side of the life of a maid. In both these images, the maid wears her apron and headgear, both of which speak of her domestic chores. The sequence of the images betokens progress toward emancipation, for in the third and fourth

22

representations the maid is decked in purple (royal color), and the apron and the headgear are unfastened (in the third) and completely removed (in the fourth).[1]

The story of Hagar, one of Sarah's domestic servants, is perhaps well captured by Mary Sibande's visual characterization of house helps: confident, courageous, and resilient. Hagar is a woman who starts off as a house servant and eventually not only attains her freedom but also receives a share of God's promise to her master Abraham. Her name has been emblazoned on the pavement of history, and her story can inspire mothers who find themselves in the predicament of having to raise their children in difficult conditions of social subjugation and material want.

Her Story

When Abram and Sarai leave Egypt, they take with them their flocks, oxen, donkeys, men and women slaves, she-donkeys, and camels. It is probable that Hagar is one of the female slaves taken from Egypt. Due to Sarai's barrenness, Hagar is given to Abram as a concubine. In Sarai's view, this is the only way God's promise to Abraham can be fulfilled. The slave-girl is "taken" and "given"[2]; she is treated as an object.[3] She is a woman with "little control over her destiny and therefore is required to do the bidding of her mistress."[4] The slave-girl is enlisted in her master's quest for descendants. Commenting on the condition of Hagar, Judette A. Gallares recalls that in the patriarchal world of the Old Testament, to be a female foreign slave was a triple tragedy, for, first, women were considered inferior to men; second, foreigners did not have legal rights

---

1. "South African Artist Mary Sibande: 'Why I Want to Celebrate Maids,'" http://www.bbc.com/news/world-africa-37935319.

2. Gen 16:3.

3. Victor P. Hamilton, *The Book of Genesis: Chapters 1–17* (Grand Rapids, MI: Wm. B. Eerdmans, 1990), 446.

4. Sharon P. Jeansonne, *The Women of Genesis: From Sarah to Potiphar's Wife* (Minneapolis: Fortress Press, 1990), 43.

and suffered discrimination; third, slaves enjoyed neither freedom nor the right of self-determination.[5]

Hagar seems passive in the narrative until she conceives, whereupon she asserts her identity as a subject. All along, she has been acted upon, but now she has discovered that she has the power to act, the faculty to nurture life. On her womb depends, at least as things stand now, the continuity of Abram's name. Henceforth, she demands her place as Abram's wife, no longer as a slave-girl. She no longer recognizes Sarai as her superior.

But Sarai refuses to be intimidated by her own slave-girl, though the latter carries in her womb Abram's seed. Hagar suffers mistreatment during her pregnancy and runs away into the desert. She is threatened with the forces of death. The arid relationship with her mistress is but a foretaste of the dryness of the desert. She seeks refuge by a spring, the source of life and sustenance for herself and for the baby in her womb. The desert is a place of temptation; is she tempted to take her own life? Is she tempted to terminate her pregnancy, especially considering that the father of the baby within her is a man who has failed to defend her against her heavy-handed mistress?

The angel of the Lord meets her in the desert and says to her, "Hagar, slave-girl of Sarai, where have you come from, and where are you going?"[6] The angel reminds her of her identity as a slave-girl. He further tells her to "return to your mistress, and submit to her."[7] As Chrysostom writes, "See how even the angel's words made her mindful of her proper station . . . He reminded her of her mistress, so that she might know that even if she shared her mistress's marriage bed countless times, she still ought acknowledge Sarah as her mistress."[8] In other words, God does not sanction

---

5. Judette A. Gallares, *Images of Faith: Spirituality of Women in the Old Testament* (Maryknoll, NY: Orbis Books, 1992), 7.

6. Gen 16:8.

7. Gen 16:9.

8. John Chrysostom, *Homilies on Genesis* XXXVIII, 16, trans. Robert C. Hill, The Fathers of the Church, vol. 82 (Washington, DC: Catholic University of America Press, 1990), 368.

the exploitation of fertility to undermine social institutions. Sarai cannot lose her place in society simply because she is barren. The angel invites Hagar to respect Sarai, even as the latter is incapable of conceiving.

Hagar knows her past but does not know her future; she can only answer the angel's first question: "Where have you come from?" But she cannot answer the second question: "Where are you going?"[9] She is wandering in the desert; it is God who gives her a sense of direction by revealing what the future holds in store for her. The angel of the Lord reveals to her that she is not simply a "slave-girl of Sarai." She too is a subject of God's promise. By carrying in her womb the seed of Abram, Hagar participates in the promise given to the patriarch. She becomes a member of Abram's household. God promises to make her descendants too numerous to be counted,[10] the same promise made to Abram. As a participant in the history of salvation, she will exercise the right to name her son Ishmael, which means "may God hear," just as Abram will name his son Isaac.

Hagar is privy to God's revelation, and this "sets her apart from the matriarchs of Israel,"[11] because promises of descendants are normally made to patriarchs. Hagar is a recipient of the word of the Lord in the wilderness, just like Moses,[12] Elijah,[13] and John the Baptist.[14] The birth of her son is a sign that Yahweh has heard Hagar's cry of distress.[15] This prophecy illumines her path and relativizes her present hardships, even the difficult prospect of returning to her heavy-handed mistress.

---

9. Gen 16:8.

10. Gen 16:10.

11. Hamilton, *The Book of Genesis*, 452.

12. Ex 3:1.

13. 1Kg 19:4.

14. Lk 3:2. Cf. Hamilton, *The Book of Genesis*, 453.

15. Some parallels have been noted between Hagar's story and that of Elijah: both are found alone in the wilderness having fled persecution, the angel of the Lord meets them and instructs them to return where they came from. Cf. 1Kg 19; Hamilton, *The Book of Genesis*, 449.

John Chrysostom remarks that God shows favor to Hagar on account of her connection with Abram: "See once more in this incident . . . how much favor from on high the maidservant also enjoyed on account of the esteem for the just man [Abraham]: since she carried with her the just man's seed, accordingly she was accorded also the vision of the angels."[16] Though God's love is universal and goes beyond considerations of people's status but rather focuses on the disposition of their soul, Chrysostom is convinced that in the case of Hagar, God's providence is in view of God's solicitude for Abram.[17]

In her response to the divine revelation, Hagar confers a name on God: "You are El Roi," she says, by which she meant, "Have I really seen God and remained alive after seeing him?"[18] Another translation has, "Have I really seen the back of him who sees me?" And yet another has, "Have I really looked upon the one who sees me?"[19] The sense here is that God sees the human condition first, before human beings see God's presence in their lives. God has not been blind to Hagar's misery; nor has God left her alone in the wilderness. Indeed, "although Hagar is in barren territory, she is at a life-giving source."[20] Though Ishmael's future is not all roses,[21] Hagar finds reassurance in God's promise to be with her in the wilderness of her life. What matters, in the final analysis, is not prosperity or renown but that one's life lies within the circumference of God's plan.

Hagar is the only mortal in the Old Testament to give a name to a deity, for normally it is the deity who confers a name on the

---

16. Chrysostom, *Homilies on Genesis* XXXVIII, 16.

17. Ibid., 17.

18. Gen 16:13–14.

19. Hamilton, *The Book of Genesis*, 455.

20. Jeansonne, *The Women of Genesis*, 45.

21. These details are partly meant to serve aetiological purposes, namely, to account for the origins of the place of the Ishmaelites (the Bedouins) on the border between the desert and the cultivated area. Cf. Ephraim A. Speiser, *Genesis: Introduction, Translation and Notes* (New Haven, CT: Yale University Press, 2008), 121.

mortal.[22] Contrary to her condition as a slave, which reduces her to passivity, Hagar assumes an active role in her relationship with God and takes the initiative to give God a name in view of God's action on her behalf.

The well at which Hagar encountered God is named Lahai Roi—"well of the living sight"[23]—to commemorate her theophanic experience. Again, in the Old Testament, it is patriarchs who give names to places in commemoration of their encounter with God.[24] Hagar thus has a place of her own among the matriarchs, for she names a place after her experience of God. Though a slave woman, she has immense authority in the history of salvation, paralleling that of the patriarchs.

In the Old Testament, encounters at the well or spring often have nuptial connotations. Abraham's servant meets Isaac's wife Rebekah by the spring[25]; Jacob meets his future wife Rachel at the well;[26] Moses encounters his future wife Zipporah at the well in Midian.[27] In the New Testament, Jesus the true bridegroom meets the Samaritan woman at the well.[28] Could Hagar's encounter with God by the spring also suggest that Yahweh is the true bridegroom, the true father of all offspring? Sharon Jeansonne's observation is poignant: "Forced out of the household and driven to the threshold of death, this woman who has no advocate is addressed by God."[29] God, as it were, adopts her and becomes her defender.

John Chrysostom observes that the difficulties and hardships Hagar has been subjected to have helped her to mature in faith: "Do you see the maidservant becoming gradually wiser from the

---

22. Gen 17:5; 32:28; 35:10; Hamilton, *The Book of Genesis*, 455; Alice O. Bellis, *Helpmates, Harlots, and Heroes: Women's Stories in the Hebrew Bible* (Louisville, KY: Westminster John Knox Press, 2007), 64.

23. Speiser, *Genesis*, 119.

24. Cf. Gen 22:14; 28:19; Ex 17:15.

25. Gen 24:1–27.

26. Gen 29:1–14.

27. Ex 2:16–22.

28. Jn 4.

29. Jeansonne, *The Women of Genesis*, 44.

hardship affecting her, giving evidence of deep gratitude for the kindness done her and acknowledging as far as in her lay the great care that had been accorded her."[30] Her faith has been tested in the fire of desert hardship, and she has grown humbler in the sight of the Lord. In the face of affliction, counsels Chrysostom, those who trust in God ought to approach God "with anguish of spirit and warm tears," instead of grieving in their afflictions.[31]

Single Mother

When Sarah eventually gives birth to Isaac, Sarah asks Abraham to send Hagar and her son away; Sarah does not want Ishmael to share the inheritance with her son Isaac. Abraham is distressed about Sarah's request, but God assures him that God will take care of Hagar and her son Ishmael. God promises to make the slave-girl's child into a great nation, because Ishmael, too, is Abraham's son. Abraham thus dismisses Hagar and her son early in the morning, giving them some bread and a skin of water. Hagar wanders off into the desert of Beersheba, and soon the skin of water runs dry. Unable to face the death of her son, she abandons him under a bush, and she goes to sit down at a distance. She sobs.[32] The clouds of death seem to be descending on her. The dry and deadly desert is about to consume her baby's life. She is all alone in the wilderness. She is confronted with the experience of single motherhood. The father of the child is nowhere to be seen. She has to fend for herself and for the baby.

Then suddenly God comes onto the scene. God hears the boy crying, and the angel of God calls to Hagar from heaven: "What troubles you, Hagar?" the angel asks and adds, "Do not be afraid; for God has heard the voice of the boy where he is. Come, lift up the boy and hold him fast with your hand, for I will make a great nation of him."[33] While the text says that it is Hagar who sobs, it is the

---

30. Chrysostom, *Homilies on Genesis* XXXVIII, 20.

31. Ibid., 22.

32. Gen 21:1–16.

33. Gen 21:17–18.

cry of the child that prompts God to act. Implicitly, both the child and the mother are crying, but it is the cry of the weaker party that prompts God to act. Jürgen Moltmann says it well: "The beginning of every experience of divine salvation is a cry from the creaturely depths."[34]

The "God-who-sees" opens Hagar's eyes to see a well, and she fills the skin with water and gives some to the boy.[35] It is at the well that God gives salvation to her and to the boy. The story says that God opens Hagar's eyes to see a well as if the well has always been there, except that Hagar does not see it. Perhaps sorrow and fear overwhelm her and blind her to the resources available in the desert of her single motherhood. But God opens her eyes to the wellspring of salvation present in her condition of need. God never abandons his own: "God was with the boy"[36] is a statement reminiscent of God's presence with Jesus: "And God's favor was with him."[37]

The boy grows up in the desert, and the mother eventually gets him a wife from Egypt.[38] While it is Abraham who arranges his son Isaac's marriage,[39] Hagar, being a single mother, takes up the responsibility to find a wife for her son.

Abraham's blood is fused with Egyptian blood in a twofold sense: first, Hagar is from Egypt and gives birth to Abraham's son; second, Ishmael's wife comes from Egypt. This implies that God's promise now extends to the people of Egypt. The universalism of God's Kingdom is already present through Hagar, the slave-girl turned sharer in the divine promise. Isaiah's prophecy is fulfilled, albeit proleptically:

---

34. Jürgen Moltmann, *The Source of Life: The Holy Spirit and the Theology of Life*, trans. Margaret Kohl (Minneapolis: Fortress Publishers, 1997), 111.

35. Gen 21:19.

36. Gen 21:20.

37. Lk 2:40.

38. Gen 21:21.

39. Cf. Gen 24.

> On that day there will be an altar to the LORD in the cen-
> ter of the land of Egypt, and a pillar to the LORD at its
> border. It will be a sign and a witness to the LORD of hosts
> in the land of Egypt; when they cry to the LORD because
> of oppressors, he will send them a savior, and will defend
> and deliver them. The LORD will make himself known to
> the Egyptians; and the Egyptians will know the LORD on
> that day, and will worship with sacrifice and burnt offer-
> ing, and they will make vows to the LORD and perform
> them.[40]

Hagar becomes the bridge between slave and master in the history
of salvation. She who was a slave becomes a member of Abraham's
household. Later, when the people of Israel end up in Egypt as
slaves, they will already have *relatives* among the Egyptians. Thus,
the people of Israel are not total strangers in the land of Egypt. The
blood of the chosen nation has been mingled with the blood of the
Egyptians. Later, Esau (Isaac's elder son) marries Mahalath, Ishmael's daughter.[41]

Hagar settles in the desert, a halfway house between Egypt and
the Promised Land. Though presented as a dry and barren place
infested with evil spirits, the desert was to be a key rendezvous for
the encounter between God and the people of Israel. She, as it were,
prepares Israel's way in the desert en route to the Promised Land.
The desert is the place where ex-slaves go after their liberation. To
win the battle of liberation one has to be *weaned* from the status
quo of servitude in order to face the unpredictable experience of
freedom that starts with a desert experience of penury and hardship. When Hagar leaves Abram's house, she is only given a loaf of
bread and a skin of water. It is likely that at some point, when the
bread finishes and the water is used up, she looks back with nostal-
gia to the relative comfort of her former slave condition. But she
does not return to her master and mistress. The umbilical cord of

---

40. Isa 19:19–21.
41. Gen 28:9.

servitude has been severed definitively. The people of Israel would later go through a similar experience, having been weaned from slavery in Egypt. In spite of the hunger, thirst, and disease suffered in the desert, none of the Hebrews decided to return to Egypt. The Promised Land was ahead of them, not behind. The Red Sea could not be crossed twice.

Reflection

Hagar's story of motherhood is as intriguing as it is mystifying, for it oscillates between subjugation and self-assertion, despair and hope, abandonment and election, dependency and sovereignty. Most likely Hagar is not the only slave-girl in Abraham's household. The fact that she is selected to bear Abraham a son suggests that she possesses some qualities suitable for the role. And it is Sarah, a fellow woman, who selects her for the role, meaning that Hagar is endowed with some maternal merits. She is the favored one among Abraham's handmaids.

Yet, her blessing turns into a curse when a conflictual relationship emerges with her mistress. She has to defend herself and her child from the powers of death. In her struggle, she experiences God's saving presence and receives God's promise. She develops a personal spirituality, as evident in the name she gives to God, which helps her to cope with difficulties in life. She is a mother whose faith has matured through difficulties. She remains a mother, even as she is subjected to conditions of slavery. In this sense, Hagar is a model for single mothers who have to raise their children under difficult circumstances.

Conclusion

Motherhood and childhood come in different shades. Some are mothers in freedom, while others are mothers in slavery. Some children are born in peace, while others begin their earthly life in war. Some are born to rich families, while others find themselves *thrown*, to borrow Heidegger's term, into poor families. In all these circumstances, God has a plan both for the mother and for the children. When conditions are tough, God extends his saving hand and provides for the struggling mothers, just as God came to the aid of Hagar in the desert. In the midst of life's struggles, especially those associated with single motherhood, God sends his angels to mothers and confirms them with the words, "Do not be afraid."

Prayer

Lord God, your mysterious plans surpass our understanding. Of old you chose Hagar to be a mother of Ishmael, Abraham's first-born son. In this way, you made her partake of your promise to Abraham. In the desert you heard the cry of her son and came to his rescue. Grant, we pray, your help to all mothers tempted to abandon their children due to difficulties. Lead all struggling mothers, especially single mothers, to the waters of hope and renew their confidence in you, who live and reign forever and ever. Amen.

Chapter 4

Rebekah: Mother of the Struggle

Introduction

Literature is replete with stories of sibling rivalry. In William Shakespeare's *King Lear* (c.1606), the homonymous king sets in motion a rivalry among his three daughters by throwing them into a competition consisting of describing how each one of them loves him. The Cain–Abel rivalry is mirrored in John Steinbeck's *East of Eden* (1952). Adam and Charles ("A" for Abel, "C" for Cain) end up falling in love with the same woman, Cathy. When she conceives twins, it is difficult to determine who the father is. Another rivalrous set are Caleb ("C" for Cain) and Aron ("A" for Abel), Cathy's twins. As regards character, the two are polar opposites, the latter being dutiful and virtuous, the former wild and rebellious. In John W. Gwengwe's *Sikusinja ndi Gwenembe* (1970), a Chewa novel, the Cain–Abel rivalry is equally reproduced in the shooting contest between the brothers Sikusinja and Gwenembe, which competition leads to fratricide: the loser (Sikusinja) kills the winner, just as Cain, the loser of the sacrificial contest, killed Abel. The enmity between siblings may reach exasperating proportions between twins. The desire for the same object (mother's love, family inheritance, or esteem) may engender conflict between children of the same family.

In the drama of sibling rivalry, mothers are perhaps the most affected—now refereeing the contest, now taking sides with the

33

weaker side. This is the story of Rebekah, mother of the twins Esau and Jacob, who are locked in a struggle even as they are in their mother's womb.

Her Story

Rebekah, daughter of Bethuel, is the wife of Isaac. She is immediately introduced as a barren woman: "Isaac prayed to the LORD for his wife, because she was barren; and the LORD granted his prayer, and his wife Rebekah conceived."[1] Abraham's servant travels a long distance to look for the right wife for Isaac and prays that God may show him the right woman. God answers the servant's prayer and shows him Rebekah as the chosen woman to continue Abraham's lineage through Isaac. But the announcement of Rebekah's sterility puts everything into question: how can a barren woman be the vessel through which to carry forward the promise of descendants as numerous as the stars of heaven?[2] Since the choice of Rebekah is directed by God, God's very intervention will be necessary to overcome the obstacle of her sterility.

Regarding the sterility of Rebekah and other prominent women in the Bible, John Chrysostom poses an important question: why is it that these women, wives of virtuous men, are stricken with sterility? Chrysostom is aware that some people attribute barrenness to the sins of the woman or her husband. But such a theological caricature cannot be applied to Abraham or Isaac and their wives, for the virtues of these biblical figures are greatly commended in both the Old and New Testaments. In Chrysostom's view, such sterility is God's way of preparing humanity for the great miracle of the virginal conception of Jesus Christ. In other words, the aforementioned women were barren "so that when you see the Virgin giving birth to our common Lord you may not be incredulous. Exercise your mind, it is saying, on the womb of these sterile women so that

---

1. Gen 25:21.

2. Victor P. Hamilton, *The Book of Genesis: Chapters 18–50* (Grand Rapids, MI: Wm. B. Eerdmans, 1995), 175.

when you see an infertile and sealed womb opened for childbearing by God's grace, you may not be surprised to hear that a maiden gave birth."[3] Those who question how the Virgin could give birth ought to be reminded of the women in the Old (and New) Testament who gave birth in their old age. The "barren woman prepares the way for the Virgin," argues Chrysostom.[4]

Isaac prays for his wife, but the couple has to wait about twenty years before receiving the gift of children. Here again, John Chrysostom underscores the virtue of patiently waiting upon the Lord. Isaac, man of faith, intercedes for his wife so that the Lord might untie the knot of her barrenness. Isaac's supplication, however, does not yield immediate results. In fact, as Chrysostom finds, Isaac prays for twenty years, beseeching the Lord to open Rebekah's womb.[5] Sometimes the prayer of those who believe in God may take time to be answered. The apparent delay of God's answer should therefore not be occasion for discouragement or despair, as the Antiochene Father counsels.

At long last, Yahweh hears Isaac's prayer, and his wife Rebekah conceives.[6] But Rebekah's pregnancy is problematic. In medical parlance, one might say she develops complications. This pain leads her to the brink of despair, so much so that she loses the appetite for life: "If it is to be this way, why do I live?"[7] The pain results from the struggle between the children within her womb. Rebekah consults Yahweh about her condition, and Yahweh tells her that she carries in her womb two nations that will become rivals; one nation will subjugate the other, and the elder will be subservient to

---

3. John Chrysostom, *Homilies on Genesis* XLIX, 7, trans. Robert C. Hill, The Fathers of the Church, vol. 87 (Washington, DC: Catholic University of America Press, 1992), 45.

4. Ibid.

5. Ibid., 12–13.

6. Gen 25:21.

7. Gen 25:22.

the younger.[8] The "uterine struggle is but an anticipation of a much more difficult situation."[9]

John Chrysostom praises Rebekah for turning to the Lord in her moment of distress, instead of taking "recourse to any human assistance or to those prepared to judge such things by guessing and observations of their own reasoning."[10] In her trials she does not consult any self-styled prophet or healer. Instead, she addresses herself to the Lord, who had opened her womb and rendered it fruitful. She consults the priest of God, "minister of divine things,"[11] who reveals to her the plan of God with regard to the twins in her womb. Rebekah thus becomes privy to God's plan. Thanks to the revelation through the mouth of the priest, she now knows that the younger of the twins will dominate the elder.

When time comes for her to deliver, she gives birth to twins, the first of whom has an excess of red hair on his skin. He is named Esau.[12] The second is named Jacob, because his hand grasps Esau's heel.[13] According to Chrysostom, it is Rebekah who names the two sons.[14] The names of the twins reflect the prophecy about the destiny of each one of them, as revealed through the mouth of the priest whom Rebekah consulted. Chrysostom writes, "Notice the keen perception of the people of old, or rather God's great wisdom, in that women did not see to the naming of their children idly or by chance, but by the child's name they gave a forecast of what would

---

8. Gen 25:23.

9. Hamilton, *The Book of Genesis*, 177.

10. Chrysostom, *Homilies on Genesis* L, 2.

11. Ibid., 3.

12. "Red" is meant to serve as an aetiology for Edom, while "hairy" is connected with Seir, Esau's home. Cf. Hamilton, *The Book of Genesis*, 178.

13. Here, again, there is a play on words: Jacob ($ya^{ca}q\bar{o}\underline{b}$) is etymologically connected with $^{c}\bar{a}q\bar{e}\underline{b}$, Hebrew for "heel." The denominative verb $^{c}\bar{a}qa\underline{b}$—meaning "follow closely, pursue, or overtake"—is formed from the noun $^{c}\bar{a}q\bar{e}\underline{b}$. Jacob follows his brother closely and eventually overtakes him. Cf. Hamilton, *The Book of Genesis*, 178.

14. "Since this had been promised earlier in an oracle, hence Rebecca gave him that name by calling him Jacob"; Chrysostom, *Homilies on Genesis* L, 3.

later happen."[15] Chrysostom's singling out of Rebekah as the giver of the names is interesting given that the biblical text seems to suggest that both parents were involved in the naming of the twins. By making Rebekah the name-giver, Chrysostom throws into high relief the role of Rebekah in the history of salvation, which agency is informed by her godliness.

From the description of their characters, one understands that Esau and Jacob live in two different worlds. Esau has prominent masculine features (outdoor life, hunting, hairy skin), while Jacob has some feminine qualities (indoor life, smooth skin, cooking). Naturally, Rebekah prefers (loves) Jacob, while Isaac prefers (loves) Esau. Esau is cut out for outdoor life, a skilled hunter, while Jacob likes to stay at home; he is described as being wholesome, which adjective may connote innocence or moral integrity, that is, blamelessness. But, as the story develops, it will become clear that Jacob is far from blameless. His very name contains irony.[16]

Trading the Birthright

Esau goes out and interacts with untamed realities, such as unfavorable elements of weather (sun, rain), dangerous animals, bush, hunger, and thirst. Every time he goes out of the house, he puts his life in danger. As Yves Congar would say,

> The man is intended for the hazards of the struggle outside, where he may receive wounds and be at the mercy of adventure and inconstancy. In the woman he finds again

---

15. Ibid., 5. He further chides people of his time for their tendency to name children after the parents instead of conferring a name that serves as a constant reminder of some significant event.

16. Such a positive evaluation of Jacob is probably meant to reinforce the biblical tradition's preference for a domesticated way of life, over against nomadic lifestyle. Hamilton, *The Book of Genesis*, 181.

the one who waits, keeping intact the warmth and intimacy of the home.[17]

Jacob instead remains within the tamed environment of the homestead. He is protected from harmful elements and helps the mother with the administration of the household. One day Esau comes back home hungry, and he sees the red stew his brother Jacob has prepared. Esau asks for some, but Jacob wants Esau's birthright in return. Esau agrees to forfeit his birthright, and loses the rights of the firstborn son.

On this score, John Chrysostom enjoins his listeners never to trade God's gifts for worthless things, just as Esau traded his birthright for stew. Esau forfeited the particular privilege and distinction accorded to those who opened their mother's womb. It is pointless, therefore—argues Chrysostom—to hanker after wealth all the while neglecting the Kingdom of God. Such wealth is useless and only breeds anxiety, sleepless nights, and worry in the life of the owner. In the depth of his heart, the rich man who neglects the Kingdom of God admires the poor man behind the shop counter who "prepares his own meals by hand."[18]

It is not clear whether Jacob shares this development with the mother. The father, however, remains in the dark about it, for when time comes for him to impart the final blessing, Isaac wants Esau to receive the blessing due to the firstborn. It is also not clear whether the idea of constraining Esau to sell his birthright originates with the mother, who prefers Jacob to Esau. Nonetheless, when time comes for the two sons to receive the final blessing from their father, Rebekah plays an active role in ensuring that Jacob receives the blessing. Esau's marriage to two Hittite women, Judith and Basemath, does not help matters either, for both Isaac and Rebekah are bitterly opposed to the two women.[19]

---

17. Yves Congar, *The Meaning of Tradition*, trans. A. N. Woodrow (San Francisco: Ignatius Press, 2004), 25.

18. Chrysostom, *Homilies on Genesis* L, 7.

19. Gen 26:34–35.

Before giving the blessing, Isaac asks his son Esau to hunt him some game and to prepare his favorite dish. Rebekah eavesdrops on the conversation between Isaac and Esau, and she plots to overtake Esau's hunting expedition. She tells Jacob to bring her two good kids so she can make the kind of special dish Isaac likes. Then Jacob will take the dish to his father so the latter may bless the younger son. Jacob is scared about his mother's scheme, for should the father discover the plot, Jacob risks receiving a curse instead of a blessing. But the mother cannot be dissuaded by Jacob's fear: "Let your curse be on me, my son," she allays his fears.[20]

To disguise Jacob as Esau, the mother takes Esau's best clothes and puts them on Jacob, covering all the smooth parts of the latter's body. Jacob musters up the courage to present the dish to Isaac, though Jacob's voice makes Isaac hesitate as to which of the two sons has presented himself. Isaac is not satisfied with Jacob's claim to be Esau, so the blind father seeks further proof by feeling his son's skin. Isaac observes, "The voice is Jacob's voice, but the hands are the hands of Esau!"[21] After some moment of hesitation, Isaac eventually gives the blessing to Jacob. In the blessing, Isaac asks God to give the son dew from heaven, the richness of the earth, abundance of grain and wine, and that peoples and nations may serve him; may the son be master of his brothers.[22]

By the time Esau returns from the hunt, it is too late, the deed has been done. The blessing given to Jacob is irrevocable. When Esau insists that the father blesses him, Isaac's blessing is less than favorable: "See, away from the fatness of the earth shall your home be, and away from the dew of heaven on high. By your sword you shall live, and you shall serve your brother; but when you break loose, you shall break his yoke from your neck."[23]

The fraud gives rise to deep hatred between Esau and Jacob, so much that the former contemplates killing Jacob after their father's

---

20. Gen 27:13.
21. Gen 27:22.
22. Gen 27:27–28.
23. Gen 27:39–40.

death. Rebekah gets wind of it and warns her son Jacob to take refuge with her brother Laban in Haran.[24] With Jacob's flight, Rebekah disappears from the stage.

John Chrysostom presents Rebekah as the agent of the fulfillment of God's will. While Isaac acts according to natural affection and cultural conventions regarding the firstborn son, Rebekah directs the events according to the prophecy she received through the mouth of the priest. She is not merely acting out of a mother's affection, but rather follows God's design. In other words, "she was not concocting this only out of her own thinking but was also implementing the prediction from on high."[25] However, Rebekah and Jacob need to do their part to ensure that God's plan is realized. The mother prepares tasty food while the son wears the skins of animals so as to resemble Esau's hairy body. Chrysostom insists that Jacob's words are not to be considered deceitful: "rather, consider that God wanted his prediction to take effect and so arranged everything to happen this way,"[26] and this is why the old man was unable to detect the deceit, but rather believed Jacob and gave the latter the blessing.

Reflection

What image of motherhood does Rebekah portray? First, she represents mothers whose children end up being locked in conflict, sometimes over trivial interests, such as the red stew. She carries right in her womb the conflict between Esau and Jacob, which rivalry robs her of her peace. Her life is implicated in the conflict right from the beginning. Her heart is pierced by the sword of fraternal division. Being a woman of faith, she consults God about it. It is in prayer that she finds the strength to endure her pain until the children are born.

In the conflict between children, mothers sometimes take sides,

---

24. Gen 27:41–45.
25. Chrysostom, *Homilies on Genesis* LIII, 5.
26. Ibid., 10.

though they may wish both warring parties well. Often mothers side with the weaker party. Jacob, being the younger of the two, with decidedly feminine features, wins Rebekah's favor. The mother plays the role of Jacob's protector in many ways: she seeks to empower the younger son with the father's final blessing; she covers him in Esau's clothes, as if to lend Jacob the very strength of the elder son. As it were, she takes Esau's *royal* vestments and gives them to the younger son; henceforth, Jacob will lord it over Esau. Finally, she protects Jacob from Esau's murderous wrath by sending the former away to her brother in Haran.

During a workshop given to members of the Legion of Mary a few years ago at Kasungu Parish, Malawi, some participants suggested that Rebekah was an accomplice in Jacob's fraudulent conduct. They called her the origin of the conflict, the *mother of the struggle*, for she engineers Jacob's fraud. However, some others in the room were quick to defend Rebekah, arguing that it is the mother who knows best the character of her children. They stay in her womb nine months, feed on her breasts and grow under her watchful eye. Therefore—the women argued—it is only right that Rebekah should play a role in choosing the one to assume the leadership position in the family. They cited African traditions whereby a chief or king is never elected without the consent of mothers, for the latter know who is worthy to take up the mantle. Perhaps it is that maternal *knowledge* of children that pushes Rebekah to take sides with the younger son.

Conclusion

Some women have pregnancy complications that make the experience of motherhood less than pleasant. In some cases, women lose lives during or after delivery. Caesarean sections are not uncommon either. Twins can also be a mixed blessing. Sometimes they bond so well that they become inseparable. At times, however, rivalry characterizes their relationship. Rebekah's twins were unfortunately pitted against each other right from their time together in her womb. Strong forces of mimesis, where one imitates the desires of another, were at work; one brother coveted what the other had. Esau desired to have Jacob's soup, while the latter eyed Esau's birthright. Families with twins often avert rivalry by trying to give the twins exactly the same things, but this can sometimes be impossible. Rebekah had to manage the relationship between the two sons, occasionally acting as an arbiter. In an attempt to prevent a repetition of the primordial fratricide, she had to send Jacob away to her brother Laban. Sometimes peace can be obtained only by separation. Distance weakens mimetic forces, for each is given the space to develop his or her personality and potential in a unique environment. All in all, Rebekah's motherhood was not an easy one.

Prayer

Lord God, you supported Rebekah in her trials while expecting her two sons. In her pain, she turned to you, and you strengthened her faith in your help. In your unfathomable wisdom you showed her the one to inherit the blessing of your servant Isaac, in accordance with your mysterious plan of salvation. Look with pity upon your expectant daughters facing various problems; let your healing hand raise them up and lead them safely to their delivery. Through Christ our Lord. Amen.

Chapter 5

Leah and Rachel: Mothers of the Twelve Tribes

Introduction

What is more advantageous to possess: beauty or fecundity? While in modern times, beauty might seem to override child-bearing capacity, traditional communities would have preferred fecundity, for it guaranteed respectability in society. The story of Leah and Rachel is the story of two sisters engaged in a relentless competition for their husband's love. Rachel's strength is beauty; however, her Achilles' heel, at least initially, is barrenness. Leah is not so beautiful but has the gift of fertility. The plot of the story becomes even more complex when Leah's childbearing prowess does not succeed in monopolizing Jacob's love. Another unexpected turn of events is that God eventually opens Rachel's womb. In the rivalry between brothers or sisters, there are mechanisms of compensation that alleviate the grief of the (apparent) loser. Even more importantly, beneath the tumultuous waves of human passions and struggles are the quiet undercurrents of the history of salvation leading humanity to its consummation. Unbeknownst to them, Leah and Rachel are actually in the process of constituting the twelve tribes of Israel.

Their Stories

Having received Isaac's blessing, Jacob leaves for Haran and lives with his maternal uncle Laban. Jacob falls in love with Laban's younger daughter, Rachel. However, on the wedding night, Laban cheats Jacob and gives him the elder daughter, Leah, instead. He who obtained Isaac's blessing by disguising himself as his elder brother Esau is now cheated into marrying a woman disguised as his bride Rachel. Jacob has to labor for Laban another seven years to get Rachel, the love of his life. Clearly, Leah, being a woman forced upon Jacob, receives less love from her husband.

Fruitful Competition

Yahweh sees that Leah is unloved and, in what could be seen as God making a fundamental option for the poor, *opens* her womb, while Rachel remains barren. Chrysostom looks at Leah's fertility as God's way of compensating for the little love she receives from Jacob:

> See God's creative wisdom: whereas one woman by her beauty attracted her husband's favor, the other seemed to be rejected because she lacked it. But it was the latter he awoke to childbirth while leaving the other's womb inactive. He thus dealt with each in his characteristic love so that one might have some comfort from what was born of her and the other might not triumph over her sister on the score of charm and beauty.[1]

Chrysostom's sentiments would seem to echo a proverb from the African Chewa people: *Ukaipa dziwa nyimbo* ("those who are ugly ought to know how to sing well"). Thus, Leah conceives and gives birth to a son whom she names Reuben. The name Reuben liter-

---

1. John Chrysostom, *Homilies on Genesis* LVI, 14, trans. Robert C. Hill, The Fathers of the Church, vol. 87 (Washington, DC: Catholic University of America Press, 1992), 125.

ally means "Look, a son"; in this context, however, its meaning is extended to include the hope that the birth of the son will make Jacob love Leah. "The LORD has looked on my affliction; surely now my husband will love me,"[2] she exults. The birth of Reuben assuages Leah's pain on account of her not being Jacob's beloved wife.

Leah conceives again and gives birth to a second son whom she names Simeon, "Because the LORD has heard that I am hated, he has given me this son also."[3] The birth of the third son, Levi, bolsters Leah's hope that "this time my husband will be joined to me, because I have borne him three sons."[4] Judah is Leah's fourth son, and in gratitude Leah exclaims, "This time I will praise the LORD!"[5] After these four children Leah is granted a reprieve from childbearing.[6]

At the heart of Leah's experience of bearing children is the hope that her fecundity will make her husband love her. Leah's thanksgiving prayers to God for the first four sons underline the desire to be loved by her husband. She expects Jacob to reward her for having ensured the continuity of his name.

Meanwhile, Rachel remains barren. Though she is Jacob's beloved wife, happiness eludes her, and she becomes jealous of her elder sister. Rachel becomes desperate for a child and threatens Jacob, "Give me children, or I shall die!"[7] Jacob confesses his inability to grant Rachel her desire, for it is God who has denied her the gift of motherhood. Chrysostom imaginatively addresses himself to Rachel in the following terms: "Why do you demand from your husband what is beyond the power of nature and, while ignoring the Lord of nature, accuse your husband, who is incapable

---

2. Gen 29:32.
3. Gen 29:33.
4. Gen 29:34.
5. Gen 29:35.
6. Gen 29:31–35.
7. Gen 30:1.

of doing anything to solve this problem?"[8] Children are a gift from the Lord, as the psalmist says.[9]

In her desperate quest for a child, Rachel resorts to an arrangement her ancestress Sarah once adopted: Rachel gives her slave-girl Bilhah to her husband. The difference, though, is that while Sarah wanted the slave-girl to give Abraham a son in order to facilitate the fulfillment of God's promise to Abraham, Rachel wants children so she can receive some respect from her sister and the community at large. When Bilhah gives birth to a son, Rachel names him Dan, because "God has judged me, and has also heard my voice and given me a son."[10] Bilhah's second son is named Naphtali, because Rachel sees herself in a contest with her sibling, and "With mighty wrestlings I have wrestled with my sister, and have prevailed!"[11] The birth of the two sons gives her a sense of victory and vindication. Unfortunately, she remains a mother by proxy. Her womb remains dry. Legally, she is a mother, but deep within her she still feels that gnawing anguish of emptiness and deprivation.

Leah aggravates the competition between the two sisters by hiring her slave-girl to obtain more children. Her maid Zilpah is given in concubinage to Jacob, and she gives birth to Gad ("Good fortune")[12] and then Asher ("Happy am I! For the women will call me happy!").[13] Because of her children, women will call Leah blessed, reflecting the reality that in that culture, it was a blessing to have many children.

Later, Leah resumes her own child-bearing adventure. One day, during the wheat harvest, Reuben finds some mandrakes in the field, which he brings to his mother Leah. The mandrake is a plant believed to have aphrodisiac properties, so much that it is also

---

8. Chrysostom, *Homilies on Genesis* LVI, 18.

9. Ps 127:3.

10. Gen 30:6.

11. Gen 30:8.

12. Gen 30:11.

13. Gen 30:13.

called the "love plant."[14] Rachel asks for some, but Leah is not willing to give her any, because Rachel has monopolized their husband Jacob. Desperate to have the mandrakes, Rachel enters into a bargain with Leah, an arrangement redolent of the trade-off between Esau and Jacob: Rachel allows Leah to sleep with Jacob that night in return for the mandrakes. When she sleeps with Jacob, Leah conceives and gives birth to a son whom she names Issachar, saying, "God has given me my hire because I gave my maid to my husband."[15] Leah does not attribute the recovery of her fecundity to the power of the mandrakes; rather, it is God who rewards her for having given her maid to Jacob. When she gives birth to a sixth son, Leah names him Zebulun and declares, "God has endowed me with a good dowry; now my husband will honor me, because I have borne him six sons."[16] The birth of her daughter Dinah does not seem to make headlines, and there is no specific praise motif associated with her name.[17] No doubt the insignificance attributed to the birth of the daughter reflects the patriarchal worldview of the people of Israel.

Finally, it is Rachel's turn to shine:[18] "Then God remembered

---

14. Cf. Ephraim A. Speiser, *Genesis: Introduction, Translation and Notes* (New Haven, CT: Yale University Press, 2008), 231.

15. Gen 30:18.

16. Gen 30:20.

17. Gen 30:21. Footnote *g* in the *New Jerusalem Bible* (1985) notes that, in this passage, Dinah completes the number twelve of the children of Jacob, but she is later replaced by Benjamin born in Canaan to Rachel. When Levi becomes a priestly family, the lacuna is filled in by dividing the tribe of Joseph into his sons Ephraim and Manasseh. The list of the twelve sons of Jacob in Genesis 35:23–26 does not mention Dinah, while that in Genesis 46:8–25 mentions her. Though the list in Genesis 49:1–28 speaks of twelve tribes of Israel, those mentioned are actually eleven, Dinah being omitted.

18. Ironically, the name Rachel (*rāḥēl*) comes from the same root as the word for "ewes" (*reḥēleykā*). While her name connotes offspring, she remains barren; yet, her name contains the promise of fecundity. Cf. Victor P. Hamilton, *The Book of Genesis: Chapters 18–50* (Grand Rapids, MI: Wm. B. Eerdmans, 1995), 306.

Rachel, and God heeded her and opened her womb."[19] She conceives and gives birth to a son. She praises God who has taken away her disgrace and then adds a prayer, "May the LORD add to me another son!"[20]

There is an interlude before another son is added to Rachel. Jacob parts ways with Laban; as they head for Ephrath, Rachel goes into labor. Unfortunately, she develops complications and, before her death, gives birth to a boy whom she names Ben-Oni, because he is born just before she breathes her last. Rachel dies and is buried on the way to Ephrath, probably the present-day Bethlehem. Jacob later renames the last son Benjamin.[21] It is likely that Ben-Oni means "son of my misfortune" or "son of wailing,"[22] a choice that speaks for itself within the context of his birth. Women who undergo difficult birthing experiences can identify with Rachel's sentiments of despair. The name Benjamin, instead, means "son of good fortune."

Of all the children, the last born risks being the only one carrying a name with a negative reading of history. It is Jacob who rereads the birth of the last born in the light of God's providence: in spite of the difficult birthing experience, leading to the mother's death, the birth of a son is presented as a grace-filled moment. Jacob does not allow the unfortunate circumstances surrounding his last son's birth to condition forever the family's reading of history. Names are carriers of memories. Negative names evoke negative memories. The last-born cannot be "son-of-wailing" forever. That is why Jacob gives him a new name in order to give a positive interpretation to the story of the child's birth. Of all the sons of Jacob, Benjamin is the only one who receives a name from the father.[23]

---

19. Gen 30:22.
20. Gen 30:24.
21. Gen 35:16–20.
22. Cf. Hamilton, *The Book of Genesis*, 384.
23. Ibid.

Reflection

The story of Leah and Rachel reveals a number of aspects about motherhood in the Old Testament. First, motherhood is seen as a booster of self-worth. Both Leah and Rachel draw consolation and strength from the experience of motherhood. They are locked in a childbearing contest and do not hesitate to take recourse to mechanisms that will increase the number of their children. For Leah, having children gives her the hope of winning the husband's love, since the latter prefers Rachel. Rachel, however, does not feel secure with the love she receives from Jacob. She knows that sooner or later barrenness will be her Achilles' heel in marriage and in society.

Second, children (especially sons in that culture) are seen as a blessing from God. The birth of a child is a sign that God has looked kindly on one's misery and answered one's prayer. Accordingly, thanksgiving motifs underlie the names given to the children. Of the twelve children born to Jacob through the two women and their slave-girls, only the last one receives a name that describes his birth as a moment of misfortune (Ben-Oni). By changing the son's name to Benjamin, Jacob transforms the moment of the son's birth from misfortune to fortune. Thus, the birth of all the children of Jacob is a moment of grace.

Though these sons (and daughter) legally belong to the two wives of Jacob,[24] the role of the slave-girls in completing the number twelve of Israel's eponymous tribes cannot be lost sight of. The list of the twelve sons of Jacob given in Genesis 35:23–26 places the sons with their mothers, including the slave-girls. Therefore, the *birth* of the nation of Israel is a synergy of free and slave women. Unlike Hagar's son Ishmael who is sent away from Abraham's household, the sons born of the slave-girls become part and parcel of Jacob's family. In the slave-girls is placed the seed of the promise to be reaffirmed in the New Testament:

---

24. The sense of *ownership* is alluded to by the fact that it is Leah and Rachel who give names to the children born of the slave-girls.

For in Christ Jesus you are all children of God through faith. As many of you as were baptized into Christ have clothed yourselves with Christ. There is no longer Jew or Greek, there is no longer slave or free, there is no longer male and female; for all of you are one in Christ Jesus. And if you belong to Christ, then you are Abraham's offspring, heirs according to the promise.[25]

Though born of slave women, Dan, Naphtali, Gad, and Asher are entitled to enjoy all the rights of being Jacob's sons. This is possible because their biological mothers are part and parcel of Jacob's household. It is the *household* that gives birth to them.

Conclusion

The rivalry between Esau and Jacob takes a new form in the competition between the sisters, Leah and Rachel, who seek to outdo each other in winning their husband's love. They know that childbearing is the surest and shortest way to the husband's heart. Their sense of self-worth and dignity in society would appear to depend on their fecundity. That is why Rachel is not content with her husband's love. Unbeknownst to them, their competition leads to the building up of the twelve tribes of Israel. Indeed, God writes straight with crooked lines, as the proverb says. In polygamous societies, the fecundity of the wives endears them to their husband. It is not uncommon for women to be turned out by their husbands on account of barrenness. The pressure to bear children sometimes leads women to resort to unpalatable solutions that may jeopardize their dignity as daughters of God.

One of the undercurrents of the story of this competition is that only God can quench one's thirst for love. Leah thinks that childbearing will guarantee her husband's love; but having born many sons for Jacob, she still struggles to win her husband's heart. Chasing human love can be as futile as trying to catch a mirage in the

---

25. Gal 3:26–29.

desert. As Augustine would say, our heart is restless until it rests in God. Deep beneath Leah's longing for Jacob's love is a quest for God's love. Behind Rachel's yearning for social esteem is a desire to be esteemed by the Lord. While she thinks she is wrestling with her elder sister, Rachel, as her husband will later do,[26] is actually wrestling with God. She wants God's blessing, and she obtains it.

Prayer

Lord God, you are the source of fecundity. To some you give physical fertility and to others spiritual productivity. Look with favor on your daughters reeling from the burden of barrenness and open their eyes to the many blessings that you have lavished on them. May they use them to build your Kingdom, for your love is worth much more than a thousand children. You who live and reign forever and ever. Amen.

---

26. Gen 32:22–32.

Chapter 6

Hannah: Mother with a Song

Introduction

If there are people who can accept sterility with an apparently matter-of-fact attitude, there are others for whom the torment of not being able to have children is visible on the surface, especially in the face of social stigma. In the biblical tradition, as in many other societies, lack of fertility is considered a *privatio boni*, a serious deficiency of good.[1] Hans Wilhelm Hertzberg calls it "the most bitter misfortune possible for an Eastern woman."[2] Hannah, Elkanah's first wife, is an example of women who do not suppress their bitterness and frustration on account of their sterility. Her sorrow is aggravated by the humiliation she suffers at the hands of her co-wife Peninnah, whom the Lord has blessed with children. In the usual rivalry between co-wives, Hannah's *dry womb* becomes a soft spot for Peninnah's merciless punches.

Sacrifice of Lips

Hannah has a yearly reminder of her barrenness. Every year, Elkanah takes his whole family to Shiloh to sacrifice to Yahweh.

---

1. Cf. Martin Ott, *African Theology in Images*, Kachere Series, vol. 12 (Blantyre: Christian Literature Association in Malawi, 2000), 499.

2. Hans W. Hertzberg, *I & II Samuel*, trans. John S. Bowden (London: SCM Press, 1964), 23.

Elkanah gives portions of the sacrifice to Peninnah and her children but, according to the *New Revised Standard Version* (NRSV), he gives a double portion to Hannah, "because he loved her, though the LORD had closed her womb."[3] The *New Jerusalem Bible* (NJB), instead, says that Elkanah gives only one portion to Hannah for "though he loved Hannah more, Yahweh had made her barren." While it is easy to understand why, according to NJB, Elkanah would give a single portion to Hannah (namely, distributive justice), NRSV's explanation for her receiving a double portion (that is, because Elkanah loved her) would seem to suggest that Hannah was loved more than the rest of the family. A possible solution to this enigma is given by Hans Wilhelm Hertzberg, who gives the meaning of the Hebrew word *'appāyim* as "portion of the face," signifying "a particularly large piece, a portion of honor."[4] That is, though Hannah receives a single portion, her piece is special. This preferential treatment would exacerbate Peninnah's harshness toward Hannah. Indeed, she "used to provoke her severely, to irritate her, because the LORD had closed her womb. So it went on year by year; as often as she went up to the house of the LORD, she used to provoke her."[5]

Hannah cannot take the blows anymore, so she weeps and refuses to eat. Her husband Elkanah tries to console her, assuring her that she means to him more than ten sons, but Hannah refuses to be consoled. One day, after supper, Hannah goes to pray to Yahweh and throws a challenge at him:

> She was deeply distressed and prayed to the LORD, and wept bitterly. She made this vow: "O LORD of hosts, if only you will look on the misery of your servant, and remember me, and not forget your servant, but will give to

---

3. 1Sam 1:5.

4. Hertzberg, *I & II Samuel*, 24. Another instance of preferential treatment can be found in Genesis 43:34, where Benjamin receives portions that are five times as large as those of his brothers.

5. 1Sam 1:6–7.

your servant a male child, then I will set him before you as a nazirite until the day of his death. He shall drink neither wine nor intoxicants, and no razor shall touch his head."[6]

Hannah can no longer stand the taunts she suffers on account of her barrenness. So she decides to engage in a kind of Freudian *free association* with God. She feels secure and uninhibited in the presence of the Lord. In her prayer, Hannah asks the Lord to remember her. The Hebrew verb remember (*zakar*) also speaks of salvation. To be remembered by God is to be saved. In the religious terminology of Israel and her neighboring nations, remembering "referred to the benevolent treatment of an individual or group by a god, often, as in this case, in response to a specific plea."[7] To be forgotten is to be damned. In fact, in Hebrew imagination, *Sheol*, the abode of the dead, is the land of the forgotten. Barrenness is an experience of death, while fecundity is participation in the fruitfulness of God. Those who do not have children will be forgotten very quickly, while the names of those with progeny are immortalized in their children.

Eli the priest thinks Hannah is intoxicated, especially given that drinking was not unusual at sacrificial meals.[8] So he accosts her and reprimands her: "How long will you make a drunken spectacle of yourself? Put away your wine."[9] Hannah's experience is redolent of the Pentecost event, where the disciples were suspected of having had too much wine that morning.[10] Only Yahweh can understand the state of Hannah's mind; only Yahweh can allow her to express herself with full spontaneity. The temple functionary, on the contrary, cannot stand such comportment in the sacred space mystified by taboos and decorum.

---

6. 1Sam 1:10–11.

7. P. Kyle McCarter, *I Samuel: A New Translation with Introduction, Notes and Commentary* (New Haven, CT: Yale University Press, 2008), 62.

8. Cf. Hertzberg, *I & II Samuel*, 25.

9. 1Sam 1:14.

10. Cf. Acts 2:13.

Hannah has to explain herself to Eli and convince him she is not under the influence of alcohol: "No, my lord, I am a woman deeply troubled; I have drunk neither wine nor strong drink, but I have been pouring out my soul before the LORD. Do not regard your servant as a worthless woman, for I have been speaking out of my great anxiety and vexation all this time."[11] Eli is touched by her response and adds his intercessory voice to her prayer: "Go in peace; the God of Israel grant the petition you have made to him."[12]

After that moment of honest and profound prayer before the Lord, Hannah begins to eat, and her dejection vanishes. In her prayer, she has had a true experience of faith, which the letter to the Hebrews defines as "the assurance of things hoped for, the conviction of things not seen."[13] Her prayer is a mystical moment in which Hannah receives in her soul what she has asked for. She is like a drowning person whose fears dissipate simply upon hearing the voice of a rescuer. After her prayer, she develops a sense of tranquility and confidence that Peninnah can no longer puncture. Hannah is now a joyful woman; one can picture her laughing and even playing with the children of her rival Peninnah. Hannah has been liberated; the yoke of sadness has been lifted from her shoulders. The *piece of meat*[14] on which she has been choking for years has been dislodged from her throat. Like Job, she can be heard exclaiming, "I will forget my complaint; I will put off my sad countenance and be of good cheer."[15]

When Elkanah and his family return home to Ramah, Elkanah sleeps with Hannah, and she conceives and gives birth to a son, whom she names Samuel. Hannah's explanation of the choice of

---

11. 1Sam 1:15–16.

12. 1Sam 1:17.

13. Heb 11:1.

14. Verecundus explains the Latin word *obprimebat* used for Peninnah's attitude toward Hannah in the sense of choking on a piece of meat one has regurgitated. Cf. Verecundus Iuncensis, *Commentarii super cantica ecclesiastica* XXII, 8, ed. Roland Demeulenaere, CCL, vol. 93 (Turnhout, Belgium: Brepols, 1976), 38–39.

15. Job 9:27; cf. McCarter, *I Samuel*, 55.

the name is that, "I have asked him of the LORD."[16] Another possible meaning of Samuel is "name of God" or "His-name-is-El."[17] In the Old Testament, the *name* of God refers to God's wonderful deeds for the salvation of his people.[18] The birth of Samuel is thus interpreted as one of the marvels of the Lord, the *magnalia Dei*, which are the object of people's joyful praise. Some biblical scholars hold that the word Samuel (*Šemū'ēl*), being a combination of *šēm* (name) and *'ēl* (God), means "he over whom the name of God has been said."[19] However, the root *sha'al* (to ask) would give *sha'ul*, Saul, which makes some scholars imagine that the meaning of Samuel in this context is influenced by elements of the account of Saul's birth. To be consistent with Hannah's etymology of the name Samuel, the son's name would have to be *šemē'ēl*, "He-who-is-from-God."[20]

Origen notices a pattern in biblical narratives regarding barren women: they are often the first or beloved wives of the biblical figures. Strangely, the first or beloved wives are initially unable to bear children for their husbands, and the latter have to take recourse to other (less loved) wives to have children before the Lord opens the wombs of the beloved spouses. In the case of Elkanah's wives, Origen's figurative reading of the order of child-bearing focuses on the meaning of the names of the two women: Hannah means grace and Peninnah conversion. According to Origen, the first fruits of a Christian come through conversion, just as Peninnah was the first to bear children for Elkanah; only after conversion can Christians bear the fruits of grace, for grace and truth came to us through

---

16. 1Sam 1:20.

17. McCarter, *I Samuel*, 62.

18. Cf. Friedrich V. Reiterer, "*šēm*," in *Grande lessico dell'Antico Testamento*, vol. 9, ed. Heinz J. Fabry and Helmer Ringgren, trans. Pier G. Borbone (Brescia, Italy: Paideia, 2009), 469–70; Walther Eichrodt, *Theology of the Old Testament*, vol. 2, trans. John A. Baker (London: SCM Press, 1967), 40.

19. Hertzberg, *I & II Samuel*, 25.

20. Cf. McCarter, *I Samuel*, 62, 65.

Jesus Christ.[21] In other words, God seems to give the best things last, for it is the child of grace who is consecrated to God and to the word of God, as will be seen in the following section. Significantly, while the names of Peninnah's children are not given, the name of Hannah's son is mentioned, that is, Samuel, which, according to Origen, means "God is here" (*Ibi ipse Deus*).[22]

Remembering and Offering

After weaning the son, Hannah goes up to Shiloh again, bringing with her a three-year-old bull, half a bushel of flour, and a skin of wine. The bull is sacrificed, while the child is led to Eli. The encounter between Hannah and Eli is a moment of anamnesis, remembering. Hannah reminds Eli who she is: "Oh, my lord! As you live, my lord, I am the woman who was standing here in your presence, praying to the LORD. For this child I prayed; and the LORD has granted me the petition that I made to him."[23] Hannah helps Eli to remember the woman who has now been remembered by Yahweh.

In their first encounter, Hannah did not tell Eli exactly what she was praying for. She only mentioned that she was a woman in distress and that she was pouring out her soul before the Lord. In the second encounter the object of her prayer is made known. Now it is her time to remember the Lord's deeds in her favor. The sanctuary is transformed from being the place of lament to the space of gratitude. It is *here* that she stood beside Eli praying to God. Her anamnesis has a spatial dimension to it, because there is no remembrance detached from space. God's favors are received in space and time.

In her acknowledgment of the Lord's wonders, Hannah offers material gifts, such as a bull, wine, and flour, but the ultimate offering comes last: her only son! In the history of salvation, the sacrifice

---

21. Origen, *Homélies sur Samuel* I, 5, 48–58, ed. Pierre Nautin and Marie-Thérèse Nautin, SCh, vol. 328 (Paris: Cerf, 1986), 112.

22. Ibid., 78.

23. 1Sam 1:26–27.

of bulls and grain was but a shadow of the ultimate sacrifice: the only-begotten Son of God!

By way of diversion, it can be remarked that nowadays many preachers of the gospel of prosperity seek to impress upon their followers that to be blessed, one must first offer something—a seed—to the Lord, as if to suggest that the Lord cannot give gratuitous blessings to those who humble themselves before the throne of God. Hannah did not offer any *seed* to ask for the child, save if one regards her prayer of supplication as a sacrifice of her lips;[24] it is only after receiving God's favor that she comes with gifts to the Lord in thanksgiving for the marvels of the Lord. Significantly, she offers to the Lord the very gift she received. In fact, every gift, every offering, every sacrifice made over to the Lord is already an acknowledgment of the fact that every good thing comes from the Lord. One cannot give what one has not received. One does not have to go to the bank and borrow money to be offered to the Lord.

She who was suspected of acting under the influence of wine now offers wine to the Lord. She who did not have a son now offers her only son to the Lord. Her anamnesis leads to a kenotic moment, a moment of self-emptying before the Lord, because she knows that all she is and possesses comes from the Lord. She risks appearing childless to her neighbors again, but what matters to her is fidelity to her promise to the Lord. She is like her ancestor Abraham, who did not withhold Isaac, his only son, from the Lord.[25] Her action is prophetic of God's very action: "For God so loved the world that he gave his only Son, so that everyone who believes in him may not perish but may have eternal life."[26]

Hannah's Magnificat

Having offered her son to the Lord, Hannah breaks into song.[27] For Origen, Hannah's song of praise is the prayer with which she con-

---

24. Cf. Heb 13:15.
25. Gen 22.
26. Jn 3:16; Rom 8:32; 1Jn 4:9–10.
27. 1Sam 2:1–10.

secrates her son to the Lord.[28] "My heart exults in the LORD," she sings, "The barren has borne seven, but she who has many children is forlorn."[29] It is a song she has probably borrowed from the repertoire of Israel's songs of praise. Perhaps several other women before her have sung this song, and several others after her will sing it to celebrate the Lord's salvation. In the New Testament, for instance, Mary will take up these lyrics and adapt them to her experience of God's favorable visit manifested in the promise of the birth of Jesus. Indeed, "the song as a whole, therefore, belongs to a fairly large category of biblical psalms which elaborate the declaration of a specific instance of God's beneficence with a general celebration of his sovereignty and grace."[30] The song celebrates more events than the birth of a son. However, "the song is not wholly unsuited to its secondary context. The central theme is joy over an elevation in condition, quite possibly the birth of a child understood as a divine gift of posterity."[31] Hannah's song of praise is an intelligent borrowing of traditional hymns of praise to celebrate her own experience of God's visitation.

Hannah's is a foretaste of the eschatological joy, when the Lord "will wipe every tear from their eyes. Death will be no more; mourning and crying and pain will be no more, for the first things have passed away."[32] In Hannah's life, the sorrowful things of old have passed away and have given way to the joy of God's new things. Her experience is antithetical to Amos's prophecy: "I will turn your feasts into mourning, and all your songs into lamentation";[33] Hannah has placed her trust in the Lord her rock, unlike the sinful nation of Israel that counted on human strength and despised the Lord.

Hannah offers a threefold sacrifice: material goods (bull, flour

---

28. Cf. Origen, *Homélies sur Samuel* I, 9, 1–4.
29. 1Sam 2:5.
30. McCarter, *I Samuel*, 74.
31. Ibid., 76.
32. Rev 21:4.
33. Amos 8:10.

or bread, and wine), her only son, and the sacrifice of praise.[34] The woman who walks onto the stage weeping makes her exit singing a song of praise, her face beaming with joy. She gives to God without counting the cost, because God has given to her without measure. In her song of praise, her words of lament are transformed into words of gratitude for what the Lord has done not only in her life but also in the universe. Her fast is turned into a feast. Hers is the essence of the joy of believing.

The gift of Samuel becomes an occasion, a veritable *sacrament*, of the human-divine exchange. As divine providence would have it, Samuel becomes one of the prominent prophets in the history of Israel and anoints Saul, the first king of Israel. Later he anoints David, "the singer of the songs of Israel,"[35] the ancestor of Joseph the foster father of Jesus. Her tears cleanse her eyes, and now she can see more clearly God's footprints in the history of salvation.

Like Anna, the aged widow in Luke's infancy narrative, Hannah has seen the salvation of the Lord. In his letter to Proba on the importance of prayer, Augustine beautifully weaves the connection between these two women:

> There were two women with the honored name of Anna: one married, who gave birth to holy Samuel; the other a widow, who recognized the Saint of saints when he was still an infant. The married one prayed with grief of soul and affliction of heart, because she had no sons. In answer

---

34. In liturgical circles, the notion of prayer as sacrifice has been amply developed by the following: Goffredo Boselli, "*Sacrificium laudis*. La preghiera come sacrificio," *Rivista Liturgica* 95 (2008): 943–45; Geoffrey G. Willis, "*Sacrificium laudis*," in *The Sacrifice of Praise: Studies on the Themes of Thanksgiving and Redemption in the Central Prayers of the Eucharistic and Baptismal Liturgies in Honour of Arthur Hubert Couratin*, ed. Bryan D. Spinks, BELS, vol. 19 (Rome: C.L.V. Edizioni Liturgiche, 1981), 86–87; Edward J. Kilmartin, "*Sacrificium laudis*: Content and Function of Early Eucharistic Prayers," *Theological Studies* 35 (1974): 275–87.

35. 2 Sam 23:1.

to her prayer Samuel was given to her, and she offered him
to God as she had vowed in her prayer to do.[36]

In both instances, the presentation of the child becomes an occasion for praising God for the wonders of salvation. Further, both Hannah and Anna pray and fast in preparation for their experience of God's salvation. Hannah refuses to eat and retreats into prayer, just as Anna "never left the temple but worshiped there with fasting and prayer night and day."[37]

A Full Measure, Pressed Down . . .

Having offered Samuel to the Lord, Hannah continues her annual visits to the sanctuary. In addition to materials for sacrifice, she carries a little coat for her son Samuel. Each time they go up to the shrine, Eli blesses her together with her husband, saying, "May the LORD repay you with children by this woman for the gift that she made to the LORD."[38] The prayer no longer comes from Hannah's lips. She is content with the gift she has received from Yahweh.

God hears Elkanah's prayer and visits Hannah; she conceives and gives birth not only to one child but to three sons and two daughters.[39] In return for the one son she gave to the Lord, Hannah receives five children. As Jesus would say, "Give, and it will be given to you. A good measure, pressed down, shaken together, running over, will be put into your lap; for the measure you give will be the measure you get back."[40] It is impossible to outdo God in generosity. God will always give more than we do. God pours the gift of five children into Hannah's lap. St. Jerome observes in his letter to Laeta (a mother anxious to know from Jerome how she ought to bring up her daughter Paula as a virgin consecrated to Christ)

36. Augustine, *Letter CXXX*, trans. Wilfrid Parsons, The Fathers of the Church, vol. 18 (New York: Fathers of the Church, 1953), 399.

37. Lk 2:37.

38. 1Sam 2:20.

39. 1Sam 1:21.

40. Lk 6:38.

that, since "[Hannah] had borne her firstborn for God, she was given five children for herself. Do you marvel at the happiness of that holy woman? Imitate her faith."[41] She kept her promise to offer her son, and now God reveals himself to be more than faithful to his promise: "Sing, O barren one who did not bear; burst into song and shout, you who have not been in labor! For the children of the desolate woman will be more than the children of her that is married, says the LORD."[42]

Hannah, an Example to Emulate

Many Fathers of the Church hold up Hannah as an example Christians have to imitate. Tertullian exalts the power of fasting manifested in the spiritual experience of Samuel's mother. Her fasting creates space in Hannah's belly, so to speak, which then becomes the abode of her son.[43] To receive God's grace, one has to empty oneself before God; and fasting is an important gesture of self-emptying. Chrysostom, instead, fixes his attention on her tears of prayer. He compares the tears to rainstorms that moisten and soften even hard ground and make it ready for the seed; likewise, Hannah's tears moisten her dry womb and make it ready for a child.[44] Elsewhere he writes, "Where tears are, there is always affliction also; where affliction is, there is great wisdom and attentiveness," and a few paragraphs later he affirms, "Nothing renders the heart so wise as affliction."[45]

Caesarius of Arles uses the example of Hannah's silent prayer to chide those inclined to chatter in their prayer, thereby disturbing

---

41. Jerome, *Letter* CVII, 13, trans. William H. Fremantle, NPNF, Series 2, vol. 6 (New York: Christian Literature, 1893), 195.

42. Isa 54:1.

43. Tertullian, *On Fasting* VII, trans. Sidney Thelwall, ANF, vol. 4 (Grand Rapids, MI: Wm. B. Eerdmans, 1979), 106.

44. John Chrysostom, *Homilies on Hannah* I, trans. Robert C. Hill, Old Testament Homilies, vol. 3 (Brookline, MA: Holy Cross Orthodox Press, 2003), 77.

45. John Chrysostom, *Homilies on Ephesians* XXIV, trans. Gross Alexander, NPNF, Series 1, vol. 13 (New York: Christian Literature, 1889), 170.

others who also want to pray. Caesarius advises that one should pray in silence and quiet, allowing only "moans and sighs and groans" to be heard. Indeed, "our prayer ought to be like that of holy Anna, the mother of blessed Samuel . . . Let everyone hear and imitate this, especially those who pray aloud without any embarrassment and in such a chattering fashion that they do not allow those near them to pray. Therefore, let us pray, as I said, with sighs and moans and groans."[46]

Cyprian of Carthage agrees with Caesarius: God hears the prayer of the heart. Hannah "prays to God not with a noisy petition but silently and modestly within the very recesses of her heart. She spoke with a hidden prayer but with manifest faith; she spoke not with the voice but with the heart, because she knew that so the Lord hears, and she effectually obtained what she sought, because she asked with faith."[47]

The third Church Father to enjoin silent prayer is Cyril of Jerusalem, who takes the precedent of Hannah to encourage those awaiting exorcisms (part of the catechumenate), especially virgins and married women, to follow the example of Hannah, that is, to pray with their lips without letting anyone hear what they say, for God hears prayers even if they are not said aloud.[48] These exhortations may console those who attend prayer sessions and are tempted to be overcome with anxiety on account of their inability to pray with loud voices and bodily exertions, as others do.

---

46. Caesarius of Arles, *Sermon* LXXII, 2, trans. Mary Magdalene Mueller, The Fathers of the Church, vol. 31 (New York: Fathers of the Church, 1956), 339.

47. Cyprian, *The Lord's Prayer* V, trans. Roy J. Deferrari, The Fathers of the Church, vol. 36 (New York: Fathers of the Church, 1958), 130.

48. Cf. Cyril of Jerusalem, *Procatechesis* 14, trans. Anthony A. Stephenson, The Fathers of the Church, vol. 61 (Washington, DC: Catholic University of America Press, 1969), 81.

Conclusion

The motherhood of Hannah is preceded by the excruciating pain of barrenness, which John Chrysostom describes thus: "Extreme the pain, great the length of grief—not two or three days, not twenty or a hundred, not a thousand or twice as much; instead, 'for a long time,' it says, for many years the woman was grieving and distressed."[49] But, knowing that God holds the keys to fertility, she pours out her heart to God in prayer. Hannah does not hold onto the child but offers him back to God whence the child came. Hannah's gesture illustrates the *exitus* (origin) and *reditus* (return) dynamics inscribed in the whole creation: all things come from God and have to return to God. There are many mothers who have given their children to serve as ministers or religious in the church. This is no mean sacrifice. But such mothers do so knowing that God is the source of fertility. Giving one's children to the church is not a waste; it is rather a gesture acknowledging God as the origin of children. Human generosity is a response to God's generosity, and when human beings respond to God's giving with giving, God gives even more. Giving is a supreme gesture of love.

Prayer

Almighty God, you are the source of everything that we are and have. You never despise the tears of those who come to you seeking help. Long ago, you heard the prayer of Hannah your servant and dried her tears with the consolation of a son. Kindly listen to the prayers of your sons and daughters who find themselves deprived of various things and visit them with a basket full of your graces, so that they may praise your holy name, through Christ our Lord. Amen.

---

49. Chrysostom, *Homilies on Hannah* I, 74–75.

Chapter 7

Widow of Zarephath: Mother of Hospitality

Introduction

In a world characterized by mass migrations, the *other*, the *foreigner*, is often treated with suspicion and disdain. In various countries, the shouts of those agitating for the closure of national or regional borders to migrants are escalating to a deafening pitch, thereby drowning the cries of those in need of hospitality. But an ancient African proverb affirms that it is the visitor who comes with a sharp knife, a knife that can cut the Gordian knot of society's intractable problems. Hospitality is not a preserve of the rich. Even the poor can exercise this virtue using the limited resources at their disposal. For instance, many poor countries in Africa host millions of refugees from war-torn countries. The story of the widow of Zarephath is a story of how the virtue of hospitality can open the floodgates of God's grace.

Her Story

In the time of Elijah, God strikes Israel with drought for three years. During those years, there is neither dew nor rain. Yahweh's punishment is announced by Elijah the prophet, which omen provokes public ire. Elijah's life is in danger. King Ahab is determined to kill the prophet for having brought drought upon Israel. Yahweh thus directs the prophet to hide by the torrent of Cherith, east of the Jordan. There, the prophet finds water and Yahweh orders the ravens to bring Elijah food. In the morning the ravens bring him bread and in the evening meat.[1] Elijah's is an experience reminiscent of God's providence to the people of Israel in the desert, where God gave them manna in the morning and quails in the evening.[2] When the stream dries up, Yahweh instructs Elijah to relocate to Zarephath in Sidon and to stay with a widow whom Yahweh has ordered to provide bread for the prophet. The widow is clearly non-Jewish since Sidon is in pagan territory.

Gathering Sticks

When he reaches the city, Elijah meets the widow gathering sticks by the city gate. The prophet is thirsty, and the first thing he asks for from the widow is water: "Bring me a little water in a vessel, so that I may drink."[3] As the widow goes to fetch the water, Elijah makes an additional request: "Bring me a morsel of bread in your hand."[4] The widow does not have problems with Elijah's first request, but the second one is beyond her means. Politely but honestly she replies, "As the LORD your God lives, I have nothing baked, only a handful of meal in a jar, and a little oil in a jug; I am now gathering a couple of sticks, so that I may go home and prepare it for myself and my son, that we may eat it, and die."[5] Yahweh has sent Elijah to a poor woman who is herself threatened with death from hunger. As Cogan observes, "widowhood was a mark of dependency, since

---

1. 1Kg 17:1–6.
2. Ex 16:1–16. Cf. John Robinson, *The First Book of Kings* (Cambridge: Cambridge University Press, 1972), 200.
3. 1Kg 17:10.
4. 1Kg 17:11.
5. 1Kg 17:12.

such women often lacked the means to support themselves, even more so in times of famine."[6]

The widow is evidently not a worshipper of Yahweh ("the LORD your God"[7]). Yet, the story says that God has instructed a widow to provide for Elijah. Her reference to "the Lord" as the God of Elijah may presuppose some background knowledge of the prophet's deity. From a narratological point of view, one may wonder whether she has already received God's instruction even prior to meeting Elijah. If she has, is she still struggling to accept the mission she has received from this strange God, especially given her meager means? As the saying goes, one cannot give what one does not have.

Elijah insists and asks her to make a little scone for him before baking some for herself and for her son. The prophet seems to be a selfish guest who demands to be served first. Then Elijah makes known to her what Yahweh, the God of Israel, says: "The jar of meal will not be emptied and the jug of oil will not fail until the day that the LORD sends rain on the earth."[8] Elijah announces an imminent miracle. Yahweh does not choose to "turn stones into bread,"[9] but rather promises to multiply the little food the widow has. It is in sharing that the bread is multiplied.[10]

The widow goes and does as Elijah has instructed her. The miracle comes to pass: they all eat, but the flour and the oil are not emptied, just as Elijah had told her.[11] The apparent burden of hosting a man (a foreigner) has turned into an occasion for experiencing the power of the God of Israel who gives bread to the hungry.[12] Elijah's

---

6. Mordechai Cogan, *I Kings: A New Translation with Introduction and Commentary* (New Haven, CT: Yale University Press, 2008), 427.

7. The name "Elijah" is said to mean "Yahweh is my God." The widow's speech therefore involves a play on words. Cf. ibid., 425.

8. 1Kg 17:14.

9. Cf. Mt 4:3; Lk 4:3.

10. Cf. Mt 14:13–21.

11. 1Kg 17:15–16.

12. Ps 146:7.

material need opens the window for sharing his faith with the widow.

The Taste of Sorrow

However, something terrible happens while Elijah stays with the widow: her son is taken ill and dies. The widow is devastated and lays the blame at Elijah's door: "What have you against me, O man of God? You have come to me to bring my sin to remembrance, and to cause the death of my son!"[13] For her, the death of the son is God's punishment for her sins. The wheels of fortune have changed, and the pendulum swings from providence to punishment, miracle to malediction. The death of a son pierces the heart of the mother. As Robinson observes, her hospitality to the man of God should have brought her blessings from God, and the "clearest form that blessing could take was immunity from the natural disasters of life. The opposite proved to be the case."[14]

Elijah responds with a mixture of guilt and compassion. The woman who has looked after him has not only lost her son but is blaming it on him and his God. No theological discourse can soothe her; no metaphysical disquisition can exculpate him. Therefore, Elijah does what he knows best: prays to his God. The prophet asks the widow to *give* him her son. The prophet takes the deceased child to the upper chamber. There he cries out to God: "O LORD my God, have you brought calamity even upon the widow with whom I am staying, by killing her son?"[15] His prayer of lament is accompanied by a gesture: he stretches himself on the child three times and adds a prayer of petition: "O LORD my God, let this child's life come into him again."[16] Yahweh hears Elijah's prayer and restores the child to life. Elijah takes the child from the upper room and *gives* him to his mother, saying to her, "See, your son is

---

13. 1Kg 17:18.
14. Robinson, *The First Book of Kings*, 202.
15. 1Kg 17:20.
16. 1Kg 17:21.

alive."[17] The widow responds with a confession of faith: "Now I know that you are a man of God, and that the word of the LORD in your mouth is truth."[18] The episode thus progresses from lament (on the part of the mother and Elijah) to petition or epiclesis (to God), then God's comforting intervention or paraclesis (bringing the child back to life) and, finally, praise or doxology (widow's recognition of the power of God).

While in the first part of the story the dominant verb in the exchange between Elijah and the widow is *bring* (bring a little water; bring a scrap of bread), in the second part, the dominant verb is *give*. Elijah asks the widow to give him her son and, when the child's life is restored, Elijah gives him back to the mother. As it were, God brings Elijah to her in order to give her the gift of faith in the one God who knows no geographical or ethnic boundaries. This faith is life-giving, as symbolized by the return to life of the son. The confession of her sin ("You have come to me to bring my sin to remembrance") turns into the confession of faith ("Now I know . . . that the word of the LORD in your mouth is truth"). Elijah's mission has been accomplished. He has brought a gentile to the recognition of the power and providence of the only true God. Cogan puts it well:

> There in Zarephath, Elijah proved YHWH's omnipotence; he was not limited to one land, because it was he who had brought the drought upon Israel just as he had upon Tyre; and it was he who provided food to those who believed in him.[19]

God walks into the widow's life as a beggar, asking her to provide for his servant Elijah. But in the end, it is God who gives her new life. She is like the Samaritan woman whom Jesus meets at Jacob's

---

17. 1Kg 17:23.

18. 1Kg 17:24. A similar story, this time concerning Elisha, is narrated in 2Kg 4:8–37.

19. Cogan, *I Kings*, 432.

well. Jesus approaches her as a person in need of help: "Give me a drink."[20] Just as the widow is quick to dissociate herself from Elijah by referring to the God of Israel as "the LORD your God," the Samaritan woman reminds Jesus that they do not belong to the same nation: "How is it that you, a Jew, ask a drink of me, a woman of Samaria?"[21] Then Jesus reveals to her that he who is asking for water is in fact offering something greater: living water that quenches thirst forever. The end of their long conversation is an inchoate confession of her faith in Christ: "Come and see a man who told me everything I have ever done! He cannot be the Messiah, can he?"[22]

Another significant verb in the story is *order* or *command*. God orders the ravens to bring Elijah bread and meat. When the brook dries up, God orders the widow of Zarephath to provide for the prophet. The Hebrew verb employed here is *ṣavah* (command, appoint), from which is derived *miṣvah* (commandment). It is striking that in both cases, God directs the command to one who will be an instrument of God's providence. God's commandments (including the Ten Commandments) are ministerial in character, for they are meant to place the recipient of the command at the service of God's people, particularly those in need. To obey God's commands is to discern their ministerial content. It is not by coincidence that in the New Testament Jesus bases the final judgment on one's ability to heed God's commands to minister to those in need.

For the widow of Zarephath, hospitality becomes an occasion and mediation (*sacrament*) of God's visitation. In the New Testament, Zacchaeus welcomes Jesus into his home and receives the gift of salvation: "Today salvation has come to this house, because he too is a son of Abraham,"[23] Jesus declares. Jesus's visit is not primarily meant to remind Zacchaeus of his sins, but rather to help

---

20. Jn 4:7.
21. Jn 4:9.
22. Jn 4:29.
23. Lk 19:9.

him to remember that he, too, is a son of Abraham. Similarly, Elijah does not go to the widow's home to remind the widow of her sins, but rather through the seemingly unfortunate event of the death of the widow's son, to reveal to her the true God, the Lord of life.

Reflection

The story of the widow of Zarephath can be brought to bear on the question of hospitality in our time. The increasingly diminishing economic resources make it difficult for communities to open their doors to those in need, especially when the latter are from countries stigmatized by terrorism. Thousands of vulnerable children, women, and men find themselves stranded at borders, unable to secure entry into safer zones. Immigration regulations are growing more stringent and stultifying, while security checks are becoming more detailed and demeaning. The *other* has become a dreaded beast. Yet, more often than not, the needy foreigner needs nothing more than a slice of bread, a glass of water, and a roof over the head. It is paradoxical that communities engaged in what Pope Francis calls the throwaway culture should fail to offer these basic amenities to needy strangers. The generosity of the widow of Zarephath challenges Christian communities today to see Elijah in the many hungry and destitute people knocking at the door.

The story of the widow of Zarephath also partly justifies the growing fear of the *other*. Having welcomed Elijah into her home, the widow's only son falls sick and dies, which development the widow interprets as the visitation of God's wrath upon the household. It sometimes happens that communities open their arms and hearts to welcome those from the other side of the world. Unfortunately, such hospitality is sometimes reciprocated with acts of violence and destruction. Visitors, thus, morph into the Trojan horse and destroy the hosting community from within. Such acts are reminiscent of the proverbial porcupine that on a rainy day sought refuge in the hare's cave, but, alas, the guest started unleashing his quills upon the host and boisterously decreed, "Whoever is uncomfortable with my quills may leave the cave." Elijah was aware of the gravity of the widow's lament regarding the death of her only son; that is why he did everything he could to bring the child back to life. He became the intercessor of the house. It is beautiful when guests contribute to the progress and prosperity of host nations—fixing what is broken and reviving what is dead—as Elijah did.

Conclusion

In the New Testament, Jesus alludes to the widow's openness to receive the good news when he reminds his fellow Galileans that "There were many widows in Israel in the time of Elijah, when the heaven was shut up three years and six months, and there was a severe famine over all the land; yet Elijah was sent to none of them except to a widow at Zarephath in Sidon."[24] She who initially distances herself from the God of Israel eventually accepts Yahweh as the true God and Elijah as his messenger. Through giving she receives not only food but also eternal life that consists in believing in the God of Israel, creator of heaven and earth. Yahweh seems to take things away from her (food, her son's life), only to give her more abundantly. It is in giving that one receives.

Prayer[25]

O Divine Master,
Grant that I may not so much seek
To be consoled, as to console;
To be understood, as to understand;
To be loved as to love.
For it is in giving that we receive;
It is in pardoning that we are pardoned;
And it is in dying that we are born to eternal life.

---

24. Lk 4:25–26.
25. Part of the prayer for peace attributed to St. Francis of Assisi.

Chapter 8

Mother of the Maccabean Brothers: Mother of the Resurrection

Introduction

Few mothers would be able to bear the sight of the torturous death of their own children. A mother would prefer to die first so as not to see the death of her own sons or daughters. But faith can embolden the soul of a mother and give her the courage not only to witness the gradual loss of her children's lives but even to encourage them not to flinch in the face of martyrdom. As Paul says in the Letter to the Philippians, "I can do all things through him who strengthens me."[1] Such boldness makes sense only when informed by a higher cause. Such is the story of the mother of the seven Maccabean brothers who accepted to die rather than transgress the Law of Moses. Galvanized by hope in the resurrection, the mother provided spiritual support to her sons so they could witness to the Lord even unto death.

Historical Context

The second Book of Maccabees tells the story of the trial of the Israelites living in Palestine during the reign of the pagan king

---

1. Phil 4:13.

Antiochus IV from 167 to 164 B.C. The temple in Jerusalem was dedicated to the Greek god Zeus Olympios, and all Jewish observance was forbidden. Many Jews were under pressure to embrace the Greek way of life (Hellenistic culture), which was seen as a sign of progress and integration in the sociopolitical establishment. Some Jews, called Hellenizers, bought into the Hellenizing agenda of the government and invited fellow Jews to become Antiochene citizens, which citizenship promised privileges. Unfortunately, some of the pagan practices were at variance with the Jewish monotheistic faith. That is why Jews who cared about their faith refused to abandon the traditions of their ancestors. The drive to impose Hellenistic culture even in Palestine resulted in a terrible conflict between the political establishment and Jews. The latter mounted a political and religious resistance to the machinations of foreign powers. Jews who resisted the Hellenistic agenda of these pagan kings were persecuted.[2]

Gallant Mother and Intrepid Sons on Death Row

Among those who embrace martyrdom in defiance of King Antiochus is a family consisting of a mother and her seven sons. It is probable that the mother is a widow. She and her seven sons are arrested because of their refusal to eat pork, which is forbidden by the Jewish law.[3] The spokesperson of the group declares, "We are ready to die rather than transgress the laws of our ancestors."[4] In his fury, the king orders that the spokesperson's tongue be cut out. He is tortured to death. The mother and the other brothers look on and encourage one another to die nobly rather than break the law. They are sure that the Lord is taking notice of their faithfulness and will take pity on his servants, as it stands written in Deuteronomy

---

2. Cf. 2Macc 6:1–11; Jonathan A. Goldstein, *II Maccabees: A New Translation with Introduction and Commentary* (New Haven, CT: Yale University Press, 2008), 3–8.

3. Cf. Dt 14:8.

4. 2Macc 7:2.

32:36: "The LORD will vindicate his people, have compassion on his servants."

The second brother is brought forward and ordered to consume pork, but he stands his ground, citing belief in the resurrection as the basis for his willingness to face martyrdom: "You accursed wretch," he says to the king, "you dismiss us from this present life, but the King of the universe will raise us up to an everlasting renewal of life, because we have died for his laws."[5] The second brother contrasts the limited power of the earthly king with the universal power of God, King of the universe. By implication, the earthly king falls under the authority of God. The speaker also contrasts earthly life (which is transient) and life after death, which is everlasting. Being dismissed from this brief life, which burns away as fast as a candle, is no cause for great anxiety, because the next life is more glorious than the present life. Thus, the second son is submitted to death.

Then the third son is brought forward and tortured like the two before him. Before expiring, he declares, "I got these [limbs] from Heaven, and because of his laws I disdain them, and from him I hope to get them back again."[6] The third son recognizes God as the source of life. He is therefore confident that God who gave him limbs cannot fail to give them back after they have been destroyed. As Paul will later say in the Letter to the Philippians, "I regard everything as loss because of the surpassing value of knowing Christ Jesus my Lord. For his sake I have suffered the loss of all things, and I regard them as rubbish, in order that I may gain Christ."[7] The Maccabean brother is willing to suffer loss of his limbs on account of his obedience to God.

When the third son is killed, the fourth one is brought forward to be tested so he too can give a worthy testimony of his faith. In his speech, he explicitly mentions faith in the resurrection: "One cannot but choose to die at the hands of mortals and to cherish the

---

5. 2Macc 7:9.

6. 2Macc 7:11.

7. Phil 3:8.

hope God gives of being raised again by him. But for you there will be no resurrection to life!"[8] He clearly states that resurrection is reserved for those who are faithful to God. The impious king cannot hope to be raised from the dead.

Then follow the fifth and sixth sons, who also make known their determination to die rather than to break the law of the Lord. They attribute their suffering to the sinfulness of the people of Israel and not to the power of the king. God, they affirm, is punishing them on account of their infidelity to God.[9] By reading the persecution in the light of the sin of the people of Israel, the Maccabean brothers relativize, if minimize, the power of the temporal king, who is simply an instrument in the hands of God for exacting punishment on the sinful nation of Israel.

Before the torture of the last son, the text introduces the mother of the seven sons in the following words:

> The mother was especially admirable and worthy of honorable memory. Although she saw her seven sons perish within a single day, she bore it with good courage because of her hope in the Lord. She encouraged each of them in the language of their ancestors.[10]

According to the text, her heroism is twofold. First, she witnesses the torture and death of her sons and yet is not tempted to intervene to save the lives of her children. Any mother would understand how trying and excruciating it can be to watch helplessly one's own beloved children be subjected to torture and death. One immediately thinks of the courage of Mary who watched every detail of the passion and death of her son.

Second, the mother of the Maccabean brothers gives them the strength to face death because of her hope in the Lord. In her encouraging remarks, she helps them to remember that God is the

---

8. 2Macc 7:14.

9. 2Macc 7:15–19.

10. 2Macc 7:20–21.

true source of life; her womb was only a vessel of God through which the sons received life. She confesses:

> I do not know how you came into being in my womb. It was not I who gave you life and breath, nor I who set in order the elements within each of you. Therefore the Creator of the world, who shaped the beginning of humankind and devised the origin of all things, will in his mercy give life and breath back to you again, since you now forget your-selves for the sake of his laws.[11]

The mother acknowledges the miracle of life. Though she carried them in her womb, she does not know how it is that they ended up there, for she did not give them the breath of life herself. She is not the one who fashioned their being. Maybe she has Psalm 139 in mind: "I praise you, for I am fearfully and wonderfully made. Wonderful are your works; that I know very well. My frame was not hidden from you, when I was being made in secret, intricately woven in the depths of the earth."[12] In the second creation story, God is said to have fashioned man out of dust and then breathed into his nostrils the breath of life.[13] The mother of the Maccabean brothers is therefore aware that the origins of human life cannot be reduced to biological processes. There is a supreme power that sets in motion all these processes. Self-preservation cannot be sought at the expense of the principles of the supreme giver of life. She is aware that human beings were created to praise and glorify God so as to inherit eternal life.

From her bold speech, it is clear that the relationship between God and humanity is thus characterized by the verb *give*. God gives life to people so they can give praise to God. To the extent that human beings use the gift of the God-given life to praise and glo-rify God, the latter will glorify them with the gift of eternal life. In

---

11. 2Macc 7:22–23.
12. Ps 139:14–15.
13. Cf. Gen 2:7.

the New Testament, Jesus's priestly prayer captures this exchange in the discourse on glory: "Father, the hour has come; glorify your Son so that the Son may glorify you."[14] The relationship between the Father and the Son consists in reciprocal glorification. Jesus's obedient death on the cross glorifies the Father, and the Father glorifies the Son by raising the latter from the dead. By the same token, the Maccabean brothers glorify God by offering their lives in obedience to God, and God will glorify them by giving them new life.

The mother of the Maccabean brothers shows special solicitude for the youngest son, who is paraded last for the torture. The king wants to take advantage of two weaknesses of human nature. First, he wants to exploit the ambition of youth by promising the lad riches and happiness if he accepts to abandon the traditions of his ancestors. In fact, the king goes as far as promising to number the Jewish boy among the king's friends and to reward him with public office. Second, the king knows the mother's affection for the youngest son and wants to take advantage of the affection of the mother to persuade the youngest son from resisting the king's command to consume forbidden food.

The mother seems to pander to the king's desires. She bends over her son but chooses to speak in her ancestral tongue instead of Greek. She tells him,

> My son, have pity on me. I carried you nine months in my womb, and nursed you for three years, and have reared you and brought you up to this point in your life, and have taken care of you. I beg you, my child, to look at the heaven and the earth and see everything that is in them, and recognize that God did not make them out of things that existed. And in the same way the human race came into being. Do not fear this butcher, but prove worthy of your brothers. Accept death, so that in God's mercy I may get you back again along with your brothers.[15]

---

14. Jn 17:1.
15. 2Macc 7:27–29.

The mother acknowledges having played a role in the birth and upbringing of the son: she carried him in her womb for nine months; she suckled him for three years; she fed him and provided for him. Yet, she is aware that God is the ultimate source of life, for God created everything, visible and invisible. She appeals to the first creation account (Genesis 1), where God is said to have created the world simply with the *fiat*: "Let there be." In theological parlance, God is said to have created the world *ex nihilo*. Human life, too, was created out of nothing. As the Psalmist says, "It was you who took me from the womb; you kept me safe on my mother's breast."[16]

With this awareness of the supremacy and primacy of God's love, the mother of the Maccabean brothers relativizes her own importance as a mother and points to God as the source of all being. Therefore, it is right and just to accept death in order to remain faithful to God, the giver of life, and not to the king.

If God can create the universe out of nothing, God cannot fail to restore to life those who remain faithful to him. The God who gave the breath of life to the children in the womb will also give breath to their bones: "I will lay sinews on you, and will cause flesh to come upon you, and cover you with skin, and put breath in you, and you shall live; and you shall know that I am the LORD."[17] The torturers have stripped the skin from the heads of the seven sons, but God will restore it; their breath has been taken, but God will breathe new life into their lifeless bodies.

In 4 Maccabees 8, the king is presented as claiming to have

---

16. Ps 22:9.

17. Ez 37:6. Leila Leah Bronner lists Ezekiel 37 as one of the pre-Exilic texts that point to the existence of belief in the resurrection among the Jews. This is contrary to the common opinion that belief in the resurrection is a late (post-Exilic) development in the Jewish tradition, beginning with Daniel 12. Cf. Leila L. Bronner, "The Resurrection Motif in the Hebrew Bible: Allusions or Illusions?" *Jewish Bible Quarterly* 30 (2002): 143–54. Desmond Alexander also defends the existence of belief in the resurrection even before the Exile; cf. Desmond Alexander, "The Old Testament View of Life after Death," *Themelios* 11 (1986): 41–46.

the power to execute those who do not obey his commands and the power to be a benefactor to those who follow his orders.[18] The king arrogates to himself the power that does not belong to him. As Jesus would later say to Pilate, "You would have no power over me unless it had been given you from above."[19] The executioner is impotent and is not to be feared. Jesus once advised his disciples: "Do not fear those who kill the body but cannot kill the soul; rather fear him who can destroy both soul and body in hell."[20] This is the kind of faith the Maccabean mother instills in her son.

With that spiritual conversation between mother and son, the latter is ready to face martyrdom, and he does it with a sense of urgency: "What are you waiting for? I will not obey the king's command, but I obey the command of the law that was given to our ancestors through Moses."[21] After receiving the faith tradition from his mother, the son is ready to profess it publicly: "For we are suffering because of our own sins. And if our living Lord is angry for a little while, to rebuke and discipline us, he will again be reconciled with his own servants."[22] The people of Israel are suffering not because of the pagan king's power but because of Israel's unfaithfulness to God. This is the faith that has been handed on from generation to generation.

A similar confession of sin is found in the prayer of Azariah, who, in his intercession for the people of Israel undergoing persecution, acknowledges that they are suffering on account of their sin. Azariah prays, "You have executed true judgments in all you have brought upon us and upon Jerusalem, the holy city of our ancestors by a true judgment you have brought all this upon us because of our sins. For we have sinned and broken your law in turning away from you; in all matters we have sinned grievously."[23] Azariah's prayer ends on a petitionary note, asking God to be reconciled with his

---

18. 4Macc 8:6.
19. Jn 19:11.
20. Mt 10:28.
21. 2Macc 7:30.
22. 2Macc 7:32–33.
23. Dan 3:28–29.

people.[24] The God who inflicts pain can also heal. As Job observes, God "wounds, but he binds up; he strikes, but his hands heal."[25] In a way, the persecution they suffer is a process of purification. They are being tested like gold in a furnace.[26] And it is God, not the pagan king, testing them.

The last son's confession of faith takes on a tone of evangelization: "I, like my brothers, give up body and life for the laws of our ancestors, appealing to God to show mercy soon to our nation and by trials and plagues to make you confess that he alone is God."[27] By saving Israel from these trials, God's glory will be made manifest beyond the confines of the nation of Israel. Even the pagan king will confess that the God of Israel alone is God. This doxological motif is also seen in Azariah's prayer cited above: "Let them know that you alone are the Lord God, glorious over the whole world."[28] And when God saves the three Hebrews from the fire, King Nabuchodonosor promulgates a decree that outlaws any form of blasphemy against the God of the Hebrews.[29]

Like the three Hebrews, the youngest Maccabean brother knows that his true promotion comes from the Lord, not from the earthly king. Because of his boldness, the youngest brother is treated worse than his elder brothers.

After the seventh son, the mother is also put to death.[30] The text does not report what the mother says before her death. But it is clear that she has been the strength of the seven sons. She does not need to profess[31] her faith again, because she has already done so through her children.

---

24. Dan 3:39–45.

25. Job 5:18.

26. Cf. Isa 48:10.

27. 2Macc 7:37.

28. Dan 3:45.

29. Cf. Dan 3:96.

30. 2Macc 7:39–41.

31. This word comes from the Greek *proferō*, meaning "bring forward," "bring before," "bring in front of." To "profess" one's faith is therefore to bring it before or in front of someone.

At the center of the courage of the seven brothers is the faith of their mother. Though she speaks only toward the end of the story, it is clear that she is the one who has nurtured in her children the uncompromising faith in a God who never abandons his own people but raises them up to new life. God's love is greater than a mother's love for her baby: "Can a woman forget her nursing child, or show no compassion for the child of her womb? Even these may forget, yet I will not forget you."[32] This is the faith that sustains the mother and her seven sons in their struggle against the temptation to conform to pagan practices.

Reflection

On a human level, the mother of the Maccabean sons stands as a pillar of support for all mothers who have to witness the torture and death of their children, especially in war-torn countries. Harrowing stories are told of mothers in some countries who watch soldiers nail their babies to the trees or sever their limbs. One cannot imagine the horror of seeing fetuses removed from their mothers' wombs and then having their throats cut open.[33] The mother of the Maccabean brothers can console such mothers with her firm belief in the resurrection.

Conclusion

Through her faith, the mother of the seven Maccabean brothers transcends her biological motherhood and generates her sons in the spirit. Her bodily gesture of bending over the youngest son symbolizes her effort to bring him up to spiritual maturity, just as a mother bends over her child in order to lift him/her up. Her action is prophetic of the Johannine rebirth: "Very truly, I tell you, no one can enter the kingdom of God without being born of water and Spirit. What is born of the flesh is flesh, and what is born of the

---

32. Isa 49:15.

33. Cf. Allan D. Grimshaw, "Genocide and Democide," in *Stress of War, Conflict and Disaster*, ed. George Fink (San Diego, CA: Elsevier, 2010), 293.

Spirit is spirit."[34] She is aware that she gave birth to the sons in the flesh but now allows them to be reborn in Spirit through death and resurrection.

Prayer

Almighty and ever living God, your promise of new and eternal life sustained the faith of the Maccabean brothers and their mother, who did not fear bodily death out of their love for your law. Strengthen the faith of mothers who experience various temptations to renounce their faith in you as the source of life and joy; give consolation to those who mourn due to the suffering and death of their children, for yours is the life and the resurrection. Amen.

---

34. Jn 3:5.

Part II

Mothers of the New Testament

Chapter 9

Elisabeth: Mother of Prophesy

Introduction

On May 10, 2016, the British newspaper *The Telegraph* published a story about an Indian woman who gave birth to her first child at the age of seventy-two. Daljinder Kaur conceived with the help of fertility treatments. The article lists a few other women who, with the help of modern technology, have managed to beat the odds of barrenness and have tasted the joy of childbirth long after menopause. As Dr. Aniruddha Malpani comments in the same article, with modern science even a ninety-year-old woman can conceive and give birth to a child.[1] Such technology, however, was not available two thousand years ago, when in her old age Elisabeth conceived and gave birth to John the Baptist. Her conception was without the assistance of an egg donor. It was a pure miracle, God's own work, an answer to the prayer of the aged couple.

Elisabeth's Faith Journey

Of the four gospel accounts, only Luke furnishes information about Elisabeth. The name Elisabeth means "God is my

---

1. Cf. Andrew Marszal, "Indian Woman Gives Birth at 70 With Help of IVF," *The Telegraph*, May 10, 2016, http://www.telegraph.co.uk/news/2016/05/10/indian-woman-gives-birth-at-70-with-help-of-ivf/.

oath."[2] She is introduced as a descendant of Aaron. Her husband, Zechariah, also belongs to the priestly section of Abijah, the eighth division of the twenty-four classes of the priesthood. Zechariah is a simple priest, not a member of the more prestigious classes of Jewish priesthood. The fact that Elisabeth descends from Aaron is a guarantee that she is of genuine Hebrew origin, and this is the only regulation concerning the wife of a priest.[3]

Both Zechariah and Elisabeth are described as "righteous before God, living blamelessly according to all the commandments and regulations of the Lord."[4] However, in spite of their righteousness, they are childless. The difficulty is on Elisabeth's side, for she is barren.[5] Sterility "is grievous to all Orientals, and specially grievous to Jews, each of whom is ambitious of being among the progenitors of the Messiah. It was commonly believed to be a punishment for sin."[6]

But Elisabeth's sterility is not God's punishment for sin, as was the case with the women at Gerar, where God made all the women of Abimelech's household sterile because Abimelech had taken Sarah, Abraham's wife.[7] In this paradoxical situation of the faithfulness of the couple and their childlessness lies the promise of God's intervention. In other words, by delaying, so to speak, the gift of a child until Zechariah and Elisabeth get on in years, God wants to show that the birth of John the Baptist is not to be attributed to human faculties.

Like Sarah, Elisabeth's story begins in the shadows of her husband's faith experience. It is Zechariah who is the beneficiary of the vision of an angel in the temple. It is Zechariah who receives the promise of a son, just as it was to Abraham that the promise

---

2. Alfred Plummer, *A Critical and Exegetical Commentary on the Gospel According to S. Luke* (London: T&T Clark International, 1896), 6.

3. Cf. François Bovon and Helmut Koester, *Luke 1: A Commentary on the Gospel of Luke 1:1–9:50* (Minneapolis: Fortress Press, 2002), 33.

4. Lk 1:6.

5. Lk 1:7.

6. Plummer, *A Critical and Exegetical Commentary*, 10.

7. Cf. Gen 20:18.

of the child (Isaac) was given. The angel says that it is Zechariah's prayer that has been heard and that Elisabeth "will bear you a son, and you will name him John."[8] Luke makes a slight distinction between Zechariah's personal intercessory prayer[9] and the prayer of the nation.[10] In the birth of the child, an answer to personal prayer becomes a promise and an assurance of God's response to national prayer. This is clear in the description of the destiny, character, and mission of Zechariah's son:

> He will be great in the sight of the Lord. He must never drink wine or strong drink; even before his birth he will be filled with the Holy Spirit. He will turn many of the people of Israel to the Lord their God. With the spirit and power of Elijah he will go before him, to turn the hearts of parents to their children, and the disobedient to the wisdom of the righteous, to make ready a people prepared for the Lord.[11]

First, the child is to be named John, which means Yahweh is merciful. On a personal level, God's mercy is shown in the gift of a son to an old couple. On an institutional level, God's mercy is manifested in God's readiness to forgive and take back the strayed sons and daughters of Israel. On the basis of Malachi 3:23,[12] it was expected that Elijah would return and prepare the way for the coming of the Messiah. In the Gospel of Matthew, Jesus presents John as Elijah, whose return would announce the coming of the Messiah.[13]

Second, the birth of the child will bring joy to many. According to Plummer, this joy stems from the fact that prophets had become

---

8. Lk 1:13.

9. Here given as *he deēsis*.

10. Here designated by the term *proseuchē*.

11. Lk 1:14–17.

12. "Lo, I will send you the prophet Elijah before the great and terrible day of the LORD comes. He will turn the hearts of parents to their children and the hearts of children to their parents, so that I will not come and strike the land with a curse." In NRSV, this verse appears as Mal 4:5–6.

13. Cf. Matt 17:12.

rare in Israel, and the appearance of one was certain to bring joy and consolation to many people in Israel.[14] But it is also possible that the joy of the people emanates from the fact that the child is born to a couple already beyond the childbearing age; thus, the birth of John is a clear sign of God's favorable visitation of his people.

Third, the child is not to take any strong drink. This prescription is reminiscent of the prophecy about the birth of Samson, a great judge through whom God would save Israel from their enemies. An angel of the Lord appeared to Manoah's barren wife and said to her that she would conceive and bear a child. The angel advised her to be careful in matters regarding drink, for the child would be a nazirite to God from birth.[15] Thus, John is walking in the footsteps of two great Old Testament figures, namely, Samson and Elijah, just as Elisabeth shares the faith experience of Sarah, Manoah's wife, and other great matriarchs. Elisabeth has ancestresses to relate to and to learn from.

Elisabeth Takes the Word

Thus far, Elisabeth has been passive in the story of the prophecy about John's birth. Even after conceiving, she remains secluded for months. While it is possible that Elisabeth's reclusion is meant to protect herself from public reproach or mockery until her pregnancy is visible to all,[16] it is also possible that Elisabeth spends these early months of her pregnancy in meditation of the marvels of the Lord. Later, she confesses God's miracle: "This is what the Lord has done for me when he looked favorably on me and took away the disgrace I have endured among my people."[17]

Like her ancestresses in the Old Testament, Elisabeth is aware that her conception is the work of the Lord, who has deigned to take away her humiliation and suffering, for "childlessness was felt to be a humiliation in a society in which motherhood was the wom-

---

14. Plummer notes that the word *agalliasis*, used rarely though classic, means "extreme joy, exultation." Plummer, *A Critical and Exegetical Commentary*, 13.

15. Judg 13:3–4.

16. Cf. Plummer, *A Critical and Exegetical Commentary*, 19.

17. Lk 1:24–25.

an's raison d'être."[18] Sterility was like a bad spell cast on her, but now the Lord has removed the spell and replaced it with the blessing of a Spirit-filled child. It can be assumed that "Zechariah and Elizabeth prayed earnestly to the Lord that he would grant them a child."[19] Her conception is a sign of God's merciful condescension in response to their humble prayer. God's merciful love leads the beneficiary to praise God. The beneficiary cannot keep God's favor a secret forever. In other words, human experience of salvation is incomplete without doxology. That is why the psalmist invites all who have tasted the fruits of salvation to proclaim the wonders of the Lord.[20]

Elisabeth breaks her silence again when she receives a visitor, a young woman from Nazareth, her cousin, who has also been visited by the Lord. Her name is Mary. The greeting between the two graced women becomes a sign of God's presence: "When Elizabeth heard Mary's greeting, the child leaped in her womb. And Elizabeth was filled with the Holy Spirit."[21] Mary's greeting has a special power and energy to it. She received from the angel the sign of Elisabeth's pregnancy, and now Mary has seen with her own naked eyes the pregnancy of an old woman whose chances to be a mother had faded into the realm of wishful thinking. Mary is moved by what she sees, and her sense of wonder moves Elisabeth in turn, so much that even the child within the latter leaps. It is a spirited encounter, a moment of the Holy Spirit, for both John and Jesus are full of the Spirit of God. It is a mini-Pentecost. An African reading of this encounter cannot help picturing the two women dancing together to celebrate the marvels of the Lord.

Just as the Spirit gives utterance to the apostles on the day of Pentecost, Elisabeth, inspired by the Spirit, also opens her mouth and exclaims:

---

18. Bovon and Koester, *Luke 1*, 40.

19. Victor H. Prange, *Luke* (Milwaukee, WI: Northwestern Publishing House, 1988), 9.

20. Cf. Pss 105:1; 40:5; 71:15; 145:11.

21. Lk 1:41.

Blessed are you among women, and blessed is the fruit of your womb. And why has this happened to me, that the mother of my Lord comes to me? For as soon as I heard the sound of your greeting, the child in my womb leaped for joy. And blessed is she who believed that there would be a fulfillment of what was spoken to her by the Lord.[22]

In her Spirit-inspired words, Elisabeth no longer focuses on her own blessedness; she has already done that in a pithy praise sentence: "This is what the Lord has done for me." She now looks at the bigger picture of which her own experience is but a significant part: the baby in her womb is a precursor of someone greater—the Messiah, the promise of Israel. Elisabeth is not narcissistic, absorbed in and limited to her own experience. She knows that narcissism kills,[23] while altruism opens one's eyes to the flowers blossoming in the fields yonder. So she lifts her head and sees the wider horizon of the fulfillment of God's salvation plan, which has its new beginning in Mary's pregnancy.[24] Her attitude is prophetic of her son's humility, for John the Baptist will point away from himself and recognize Jesus as the Lamb of God, the promised Messiah, whose sandals the Baptist is not worthy to untie.[25] In a similar manner, Elisabeth expresses her unworthiness to receive a visit from the mother of the Lord. She is aware that the visit is purely the grace of God, not something she can lay claim to.

---

22. Lk 1:42–45.

23. The word "narcissism" comes from a Greek myth about one Narcissus, son of river god Cephissus. Narcissus was known for his beauty and fell in love with a reflection of himself in the water, until one day, apparently seeking to embrace the image, he fell into the water and died.

24. It has been observed that Luke's infancy narrative begins and ends in the temple (Lk 1:8; 2:41–51), just as the Gospel of Luke begins and ends in the temple; after the ascension of the Lord, the disciples go back to Jerusalem, "and they were continually in the Temple praising God" (Lk 24:53). Cf. John Nolland, *Luke 1:1–9:20*, Word Biblical Commentary, vol. 35A (Dallas, TX: Word, 2002), 23.

25. Cf. Jn 1:27–35.

Mother of a prophet, Elisabeth is prophetic herself and discerns what God is doing in the world through the young woman who has come to visit her. She utters the first beatitude in the gospel: "Blessed is she who believed that there would be a fulfillment of what was spoken to her by the Lord." Though she is addressing Mary, Elisabeth is herself blessed, for she too believed the word of the Lord spoken to her through Zechariah, and now she is in her sixth month of pregnancy. Mary's blessedness is but a reflection of Elisabeth's own beatitude. As Paul says, citing Psalm 116:10, "I believed, and so I spoke."[26] Elisabeth's beatitude anticipates the last beatitude in the gospels: "Blessed are those who have not seen and yet have come to believe."[27] In both beatitudes, blessedness is predicated on belief. Those who believe in God do not doubt God's promise even if it takes time to come to pass. They abide by God's word even when circumstances seem least propitious. On the journey of faith, the footsteps of believers are guided by the lamp of God's promises, because believers are always walking toward God, the Promise of promises.

Elisabeth speaks again on the occasion of the circumcision and naming of the child. The people want to name the child after his father, Zechariah, but Elisabeth intervenes and tells them that the child is to be called John. The people hesitate, because in Zechariah and Elisabeth's family, there is no one who bears that name. Zechariah then in writing confirms the child's name. The naming of the child departs from the ancestral tradition. In the birth of John the Baptist, God is doing something new. Elisabeth is faithful to what her husband intimated to her after his religious experience in the temple. She could have chosen to take advantage of her husband's momentary muteness to name the child as she pleased. But she chooses to be faithful to the word of God so that God's plan may be realized. She plays a prophetic role, speaking on behalf not only of the husband but also of God who chose to name the child John.

The gospel account then adds that when Zechariah writes

---

26. 2Cor 4:13.

27. Jn 20:29; cf. Plummer, *A Critical and Exegetical Commentary*, 29.

down the name of the child, his speech returns, and he praises God.[28] Doubting the word of God ties one's tongue, while fidelity to the word of God loosens one's tongue. One who always doubts has little to say. One who doubts God's word cannot praise God. Zechariah *writes* the good news of God's mercy (for that is what the name John means) way before the evangelists do it. The child's name speaks about Elisabeth's own faith experience just as much as it points to John's role in the history of salvation.

Reflection

In the gospel, Elisabeth is presented as someone surrounded with friends and relatives. When the neighbors and relations hear that the Lord has been merciful to her, they share her joy.[29] This is a sign that she, too, shared their joy when they and their daughters gave birth or received various signs of God's mercy. Though she did not have a child, she clearly was a woman who knew how to transcend her own sorrow and find comfort in the shade of the blessings received by other people. Her barrenness had not turned her into a bitter recluse. She does not allow the shame and stigma of childlessness to compromise her relatability. Now she receives back the fruits of friendship.[30] One can imagine long processions of friends and relations snaking down the narrow road to her house, hearts beating fast in anticipation of their own confirmation of the miracle. One can see with the eyes of the imagination women and children gathered in her compound to share her joy.

The gospel also says that all who heard of the event of John's birth treasured it in their hearts.[31] To treasure something in the heart is not simply to commit it to memory. It is to find spiritual warmth and encouragement in it. It is to be confident that nothing is impossible with God. The birth of John is a sign that God had visited his people with the gift of salvation. One can imagine bright-

---

28. Lk 1:64.
29. Lk 1:58.
30. Lk 1:65.
31. Lk 1:66.

faced people returning home engaged in animated conversations about what they have seen, quite the opposite of the depressed conversation of the disciples of Emmaus.[32] One can imagine their backs hunched by heavy burdens of too many unfulfilled promises as they pick homeward steps with a surer hope in God's providence. If God could make Elisabeth's womb fruitful in her old age, how can God not heal my less serious forms of impotence? If an old dumb man could speak again, can God not heal my spiritual dumbness? If . . . ? If . . . ?

God's marvelous deeds in the house of Zechariah have pushed back the ever-constricting frontiers of possibility. The onlookers treasure the event in their hearts because they have been edified and confirmed in their faith. They walk back with renewed confidence in the power of God to level the mountains of barrenness and to let waters of salvation spring forth out of the rock of human limitations. It is such a blessing to be the one through whom God strengthens the faith of the people.

Conclusion

In her old age, Elisabeth's faith is rejuvenated, her hope renewed. She is spared the pain of growing into a disgruntled and cynical old woman for whom realism takes on the aspect of nihilism. God has made sweet wine out of her sour grapes. She who was surrounded by the darkness of despair has seen the light of God's salvation prepared for all people.

Prayer

Almighty God, you consoled Elisabeth in her old age with the conception and birth of John your servant; she rejoiced to see the mother of your Son and confirmed the faith of her cousin Mary. Grant, we pray, that we too may believe in your power to turn our barren lives into fertile vineyards of your Kingdom. Through Christ our Lord. Amen.

---

32. Lk 24:13–17.

Chapter 10

The Widow of Nain: Finding a New Husband

Introduction

Widow. The word itself conjures up images of pain and tears, loss and loneliness, marginalization and disenfranchisement. In her novel *So Long a Letter*, the Senegalese writer Mariama Bâ describes the pain of a Senegalese widow called Ramatoulaye, who not only undergoes demeaning widowhood rituals but also loses her hard-won property to in-laws. Understandably, every Senegalese woman dreads widowhood because it is "the moment when she sacrifices her possessions as gifts to her family-in-law; and, worse still, beyond her possessions she gives up her personality, her dignity, becoming a thing" completely at the mercy of in-laws and society at large.[1] In some African cultures, widows are "subjected to a whole gamut of obnoxious widowhood rites aimed at making her die within the mourning period of about one year."[2] Philip Jenkins also finds that in many traditional cultures, especially in Africa, widows may be subjected to rituals involving intercourse with their brothers-in-

1. Mariama Bâ, *So Long a Letter*, trans. Modupé Bodé-Thomas (Nairobi: Heinemann, 1981), 4.
2. Rose Acholonu, "Women in the African Novel and the Quest for Human Rights," in *Beyond the Marginal Land: Gender Perspective in African Writing*, ed. Chioma Opara (Port Harcourt, Nigeria: Belpot, 1999), 97.

law, so as to exorcise the spirit of the deceased husband, thereby protecting the community from the malevolent presence of the spirit of the defunct husband. The burdens widows sometimes carry "amount almost to a kind of social death."[3]

In the midst of various trials, widows often find consolation in their children. Ramatoulaye's sorrows, for instance, are allayed by her twelve children who show great devotion and loyalty to her. In John Munonye's novel *The Only Son*, Chiaku loses her husband, Okafo, barely six moons after the birth of their first-born child, Nnanna. Henceforth, Chiaku devotes her love and attention to Nnanna, whom she fondly calls "my husband's father," because Nnanna was believed to be a reincarnation of Okafo's father. In fact, when she returns to her people, having run away from the harshness suffered at the hands of her in-laws, Chiaku is welcomed home with a song that encourages her not to lose heart on account of the loss of her husband: "You have a husband / He is Nnanna / Who is also your son."[4] Because of her great devotion to him, Chiaku remains unmarried for about fifteen years. She lives for him. To her, he is everything. She spoils him with many praise titles so much that her brother Oji warns her that "a big name kills a puppy." Chiaku is so protective of her son that her brother Oji cautions her against entertaining too much attachment to the boy, because "anything that breathes is, by and large, an uncertain possession and one mustn't put one's heart too much in it."[5]

Such may have been the relationship between the widow of Nain and her only son, and one can understand the depth of her pain when the son succumbs to the "dark miracle of death,"[6] as Mariama Bâ would call it. Unlike other mothers in the Bible, the name of the widow is withheld; she is just a widow. She is a woman who lives in the shadows of anonymity. Nor does she say a word, except

---

3. Philip Jenkins, *The New Faces of Christianity: Believing the Bible in the Global South* (Oxford: Oxford University Press, 2006), 173.

4. John Munonye, *The Only Son* (London: Cox & Wyman, 1966), 22.

5. Ibid., 27.

6. Bâ, *So Long a Letter*, 3.

for mourning. Only the city of her provenance is mentioned: Nain, a village believed to be the modern Arab village of Nein, located circa five miles southeast of Nazareth.[7] Though the word Nain probably means pleasant, since the village afforded a pleasant view of the Plain of Esdraelon,[8] the widow's experience is initially far from pleasant, for her only son is dead. It only becomes pleasant when Jesus shows up.

Encounter with Jesus

The encounter between Jesus and the widow of Nain lends itself to the imagination. Having cured a centurion's servant, Jesus flows with the tide of consolation. The centurion had shown great faith in asking Jesus to cure the centurion's servant even without having to enter the pagan's house but only to say the healing word.[9] After that, Jesus goes to a town called Nain, in the company of his disciples and a great number of people. Luke reports, "As he approached the gate of the town, a man who had died was being carried out. He was his mother's only son, and she was a widow; and with her was a large crowd from the town."[10]

Jesus's crowd flows into another crowd processing from the land of the dead, Hades. The two crowds are charged with opposite energies, positive and negative, respectively. Jesus's crowd is energized by Jesus's miracle of the "remote" healing of the centurion's servant, while the other crowd is charged with the negative energy of sorrow on account of the demise of the only son of the widow. The two groups are approaching each other. Which energy will neutralize the other? Which current will overpower the other? Will the joy and enthusiasm of Jesus's crew fade into the tide of sorrow of the crowd of Nain? Will sorrow be stronger than joy? Will Jesus's team pass on the energy of consolation to the grieving throng?

---

7. Cf. David C. Pellett, "Nain," in *The Interpreter's Dictionary of the Bible*, vol. 3, ed. George A. Buttrick (Nashville: Abingdon Press, 1962), 500.

8. Ibid.

9. Cf. Lk 7:1–10.

10. Lk 7:12.

Jesus's eyes land on the widow. He sees how she weeps, weeping for her only son.[11] He hears her silent prayers of lament, perhaps of petition or of confidence in God. As the first Letter to Timothy says, "The real widow, left alone, has set her hope on God and continues in supplications and prayers night and day."[12] Jesus can almost feel the warmth of her tears running down her cheeks. Each one of those drops tells a story of hope tested, faith tried, love purified. It is not clear how the widow of Nain interprets the death of her only son. Does she take it as a curse from God? Perhaps she accepts the death of the son with the faith of Job: "The LORD gave, and the LORD has taken away; blessed be the name of the LORD."[13] Whatever may be her reaction, her grief is unmistakable. She is a woman of sorrows.

First, she lost her husband. That was no insignificant loss. In the highly patriarchal Jewish society, to be a widow rendered a woman defenseless; it exposed her to all forms of vulnerability. Widows belonged to the same class as orphans and strangers. That is why prophets insist on the need to defend widows: "Learn to do good; seek justice, rescue the oppressed, defend the orphan, plead for the widow."[14] Deuteronomy equally insists on the need to respect the rights of widows: "You shall not deprive a resident alien or an orphan of justice; you shall not take a widow's garment in pledge."[15] Further, "When you reap your harvest in your field and forget a sheaf in the field, you shall not go back to get it; it shall be left for the alien, the orphan, and the widow, so that the LORD your God may bless you in all your undertakings."[16] Widows, like orphans and strangers, need special protection.

As a widow, she not only struggles to meet her daily needs but also loses the prospects of bearing more children, unless another

---

11. Cf. Jer 6:26; Zech 12:10.
12. 1Tim 5:5.
13. Job 1:21.
14. Isa 1:17.
15. Dt 24:17.
16. Dt 24:19.

man marries her and gives her children. With the death of the only son, she goes back to the stigmatized status of childlessness, not to mention the loss of her only possible source of financial support.

The widow, like Rachel of Ramah, weeps for her only son: "A voice is heard in Ramah, lamentation and bitter weeping. Rachel is weeping for her children; she refuses to be comforted for her children, because they are no more."[17] Jesus is deeply moved by her sorrow: "When the Lord[18] saw her, he had compassion for her and said to her, 'Do not weep.'"[19] Just as Yahweh told Rachel to "keep your voice from weeping, and your eyes from tears,"[20] Jesus consoles the widow and tells her to stop weeping.

This is not the only occasion when Jesus tells mourners not to weep anymore. When Jesus went to Jairus's house, he also found people mourning for Jairus's daughter, and he said to them, "Do not weep; for she is not dead but sleeping."[21] Then Jesus raised the little girl from the dead. Again, when Jesus rose from the dead, Mary Magdalene went to the tomb weeping, but Jesus rhetorically told her to stop weeping: "Woman, why are you weeping?"[22] In all these instances, Jesus plays the role of the comforter, the paraclete.

In Scripture, when God tells a troubled person not to cry or weep, that is an indication that God is about to console the person in sorrow with a saving intervention. The divine voice of comfort answers the human voice of mourning. This exchange is typical of the theandric (God-human) movement exemplified in prayer. The cry of anguish does not simply fade in the noise of the crowd but goes up to heaven, to him who alone knows how to console and to save.[23]

---

17. Jer 31:15.

18. It is to be noted that, from this point on, Luke frequently makes use of the term "*Lord*" (in Greek, *Kyrios*) in his narratives.

19. Lk 7:13.

20. Jer 31:16.

21. Lk 8:52.

22. Jn 20:15.

23. Cf. Ex 3:7–10; Walter Brueggemann, "From Hurt to Joy, From Death to Life," *Interpretation* 28 (1974): 3.

In the widow's cry is hidden a prayer for God's salvation,[24] and God, through Jesus Christ, responds with a saving act. As St. Ambrose remarks, because of her tears, she has merited the resurrection of her son. Accordingly, the Lord asks her not to weep for someone destined for the resurrection. Ambrose imaginatively speaks of the bier on which the dead son was carried as being made from wood, which evokes the wood of the cross that became the source of eternal life on account of the Lord's crucifixion. Ambrose further compares, in a figurative manner, the tears of the widow to the tears of mother church for her sinful children, for the church suffers when she sees her children go to perdition because of their sins. Even when individual sinners cannot wash themselves clean by their tears, continues Ambrose, they can count on the efficacy of the tears of their mother, the church.[25]

The phrase "only son" has two other parallels in the Gospel of Luke. Jairus's daughter is also described as "an only daughter."[26] The second parallel is found in the story about a man whose "only child" had an unclean spirit that the disciples were unable to drive away.[27] Therefore, the idea of "only son" or "only child" speaks of endearment, which leads to great sorrow when the child dies. Already, one can anticipate the sorrow of Mary when her only son dies on the cross.

The tears of the widow move Jesus to compassion. The Greek verb *splagchnizomai*—to have compassion—is also used in Luke 10:33 (the Samaritan had compassion on the man who had been left for dead) and 15:20 (the father's compassion for the returning prodigal son).[28] Its Hebrew equivalent is the adjective *raḥum*—compassionate.[29] In both cases, the recipient of compassion is a

---

24. Cf. Ex 3:9.

25. Ambrose of Milan, *Traité sur l'Evangile de s. Luc* V, 89–92, ed. Gabriel Tissot, SCh, vol. 45 (Paris: Cerf, 1956), 214–16.

26. Lk 8:42.

27. Lk 9:37–40.

28. R. Alan Culpepper, *The Gospel of Luke*, The New Interpreter's Bible, vol. 9 (Nashville: Abingdon Press, 1995), 159.

29. Cf. Ex 34:6; Deut 4:31; 2Chron 30:9; Neh 9:17, 31, etc.

vulnerable and defenseless person. The widow for whom Jesus has compassion belongs to this category of people. Like the man left for dead, the death of her only son is, so to speak, her own death sentence. Like the prodigal son, the death of her only son leaves her bereft of any mechanisms for sustaining herself.

Having ordered the pallbearers to stop, Jesus ignores Jewish regulations regarding ritual purity[30] and touches the bier.[31] Then Jesus says to the dead man, "Young man, I say to you, rise."[32] Immediately, the dead man sits up and begins to speak. Jesus's life-giving word revives the young man and gives back to him the very breath God breathed into the first man.[33] This breath supports human speech[34] and allows the speechless man to speak again. In Ambrose's spiritual imagination, the young man begins to speak words of life, words of praise.[35]

Then Jesus takes the young man and gives him to his mother.[36] Of old, God, through Elijah, performed a similar miracle for the widow of Zarephath. Elijah is reported to have taken the widow's son to the upper room and then, having revived him, gave him back to the mother.[37] Biblical scholars agree that the story of the raising of the son of the widow of Nain is deliberately meant to provide an "echo effect"[38] of the resuscitations accomplished by Elijah and Elisha in 1 Kings 17 and 2 Kings 2, respectively.

Elijah was a visitor through whom God provided relief to the widow and brought her son back to life. Likewise, Jesus is the visitor through whom God "has visited his people" with the gift of consolation. But Jesus is not any other visitor; he is the true bride-

---

30. Cf. Numb 19:11–16.

31. Lk 7:14.

32. Ibid.

33. Cf. Gen 2:7.

34. Cf. André Wénin, *D'Adam à Abraham ou les errances de l'humain. Lecture de Genèse 1, 1–12, 4* (Paris: Cerf, 2007), 59.

35. Cf. Ambrose of Milan, *Traité sur l'Evangile de s. Luc* V, 92.

36. Lk 7:15.

37. 1Kg 17:23.

38. Cf. Culpepper, *The Gospel of Luke*, 159.

groom who gives children to a childless woman. In her sorrow, the widow of Nain has been consoled with a great gift: she has a new husband—God himself, of which Jesus is the embodiment. Indeed, by giving the child back to the widow, Jesus acts like a husband who gives a child to the widow and takes away the sorrow and shame of her childlessness. For her, the words of the prophet Isaiah come alive:

> Do not fear, for you will not be ashamed; do not be discouraged, for you will not suffer disgrace; for you will forget the shame of your youth, and the disgrace of your widowhood you will remember no more. For your Maker is your husband, the LORD of hosts is his name; the Holy One of Israel is your Redeemer, the God of the whole earth he is called.[39]

Though the widow's reaction to the raising of her only son is not recorded, one can imagine the immensity of her joy at Jesus's saving intervention. Her reluctant graveyard-bound steps must have turned into vigorous dance steps! Her loud wailing is changed into a vociferous song of praise. Her arms flailing in the air in indistinct gestures of lamentation are now raised up to heaven in conscious prayer of thanksgiving and adoration. Life is back. God has come to her defense. Jesus has transformed the *dark miracle of death* into the glorious miracle of resuscitation. What was prophesied by the Prophet Jeremiah comes to pass in her life: "I will turn their mourning into joy, I will comfort them, and give them gladness for sorrow."[40]

The event edifies the onlookers: "Fear seized all of them; and they glorified God, saying, 'A great prophet has risen among us!' and 'God has looked favorably on his people!'"[41] The "fear" here is that of reverence; it is the sense of awe that grips mortals when

---

39. Isa 54:4–5.
40. Jer 31:13.
41. Lk 7:16.

they find themselves standing in the presence of what Rudolf Otto (1869–1937) calls the *mysterium tremens et fascinans*—mystery that is at once fearful and fascinating. The resuscitation of the widow's son moves the onlookers to glorify God. The glory of God is manifested when "the blind receive their sight, the lame walk, the lepers are cleansed, the deaf hear, the dead are raised, the poor have good news brought to them."[42]

The relevance of the miracle is not limited to the widow's household. The people of faith recognize that the miracle is a sign of God's favor on his people. In other words, each one of them is impacted by the miracle. It strengthens their faith and hope in God. Henceforth they can face the death moments of their lives with a renewed confidence in divine assistance. If God can bring a dead person back to life—one can imagine them saying—can God not bring back to life my dead marriage? If God can revive the dead, can God fail to heal me of my illness? If God can restore the dead to life, can God fail to restore my lost job?

The miracle marks the end of the funeral procession. The food prepared at the funeral home turns into a feast, while dirges give way to festal music. As they walk back to their respective homes, they do so with bold steps, knowing that God's favor is upon them, upon their families, upon their nation. If God can vanquish death, then there is no problem in this world that can withstand the finger of the *rahumic*, compassionate God.

Widow's Silent Faith

The evangelist does not report a single word from the mouth of the widow. While it is normal for the evangelist to focus on the reaction of the crowd after a miracle has occurred (and in this the crowd resembles the *chorus* in Greek literature), it is strange that the miracle takes place without the widow's petition for help. In the miracle of the raising of Jairus's daughter, the father approaches Jesus with a request. Accordingly, Jesus often commends the faith of the ben-

---

42. Lk 7:22.

eficiaries, for instance, the woman with hemorrhage.[43] E. Arle Ellis thus argues that "in contrast to the previous episode [healing of the centurion's servant], the faith of the woman plays no role."[44]

The question, however, is, could Jesus have performed this miracle without the widow's faith? In Matthew 13:58, we are told that Jesus did not perform many miracles in his hometown because of their unbelief. Before raising Lazarus from the dead, Jesus asks Martha whether she believes that Jesus is the resurrection and the life and that whoever believes in him will rise from the dead.[45] Since Jesus's miracles are not simply humanitarian actions, but rather signs of faith, it is not unreasonable to conjecture that Jesus would have seen the widow's faith in God. To paraphrase Jesus's sermon in the synagogue (Luke 4:24–25), there must have been many widows in Israel who lost their only sons, but Jesus raised the son of this particular widow, though she is clearly a socially obscure person, for her name is not even mentioned. It is not unlikely that in her mourning she addressed a prayer of supplication to God, and Jesus, God incarnate, heard that prayer from the depth of her heart and answered it by raising the widow's son from the dead. Hers was a silent but deep faith in God who saves (which is the meaning of the name Jesus).

Reflection

Among the Chewa of Malawi and neighboring countries, when a woman lost a husband, the brother to the deceased was supposed to sit within sight of the widow and console her: "As you mourn, look at me." The idea was that the brother would inherit the widow and look after her. If necessary, he would give her children. Thus, the widow's sorrow occasioned by the demise of her husband was partly allayed by the assurance that she would not be left alone; she would have a pillar to support her in the person of the

---

43. Lk 8:48.

44. Edward A. Ellis, *The Gospel of Luke*, The New Century Bible Commentary (London: Marshall, Morgan & Scott, 1974), 118.

45. Jn 11:23–28.

brother-in-law. Jesus, as it were, tells the widow of Nain to look at and up to him as she mourns, that is, to place her confidence and hope in Jesus, who is the "resurrection and the life."[46]

The story of the widow of Nain is an encouragement to all mothers who have lost their beloved husbands or children, for it instills and buttresses the Christian faith that the dead shall live again. God, from whom the breath of life originates, will speak the deceased brothers and sisters back to life. God, the husband of all believers, will fill their houses with the gift of life.

Prayer

Lord God, from whom no suffering is concealed and whose ears are deaf to no cry for help, your Son raised the widow's only son and gave him back to the mother. Look with favor upon the many mothers who have lost their husbands and children to various diseases, wars, drugs, and accidents. May their tears move you to compassion so that you may raise them up from the dungeon of sadness to the light of faith in the Risen One, who alone can console them and give them the fullness of joy. Through Christ our Lord. Amen.

---

46. Jn 11:25.

Chapter 11

Zebedee's Wife: Mother of the Kingdom

Introduction

Every parent knows the anxiety that can come with ensuring that one's sons and daughters have places in good schools or find secure jobs and positions in society. Those in charge of renowned educational institutions are often inundated with phone calls from anxious and caring parents determined to secure a place for their children. Instinctively, a mother wishes the very best for her sons and daughters. Some mothers are prepared to risk derision and scorn to obtain what they desire for their children. Such is the story of the mother of James and John, two of the disciples of Jesus. She wants places for her two sons in the Kingdom of God.

Her Story

One bright afternoon, the wife of Zebedee brings her two sons to Jesus and bows low (or kneels) before him. Jesus, familiar with the comportment of people in need, notices that she has a request to make: "What do you want?"[1] Jesus's is a familiar question. When two of John the Baptist's disciples followed Jesus, he turned around

---

1. Mt 20:20.

and asked them, "What do you want?"[2] When the blind man at Jericho invoked Jesus's pity, Jesus also asked him, "What do you want me to do for you?"[3] In all these cases, the suppliants show a sign of faith in Jesus. The disciples of John the Baptist followed Jesus because John had told them that Jesus was the Lamb of God. The blind man of Jericho called Jesus son of David, clearly a Messianic title. Though the man could not see Jesus, he believed that the man passing by was the Messiah. The mother of James and John *bows* before Jesus. This gesture[4] points to the mother's faith in Jesus as someone who possesses great authority.

Her request is even more indicative of her faith in Jesus's authority, for she asks him to "declare that these two sons of mine will sit, one at your right hand and one at your left, in your kingdom."[5] Apparently, it is a selfish request. Some exegetes blame her request on "parental affection" and "excess of love."[6] The mother's petition provokes the ire of the other disciples: "When the ten heard it, they were angry with the two brothers."[7] This could be the reason why Matthew, perhaps intent on saving the good name of the two disciples, one of whom was a hero of the Jewish Christians,[8] puts the request in their mother's mouth.[9] He does not even mention their

2. Jn 1:38.

3. Lk 18:40; Mt 20:29–34.

4. The Greek verb used here is *proskynéō*, meaning "worship" or "make obeisance." Such a gesture points to the 'church's adoration of the Risen Lord. Cf. *The Complete Word Study Dictionary: New Testament*, ed. Spiros Zodhiates et al. (Chattanooga, TN: AMG Publishers, 1993), 4352.

5. Mt 20:21.

6. William D. Davies and Dale C. Allison, *A Critical and Exegetical Commentary on the Gospel According to Saint Matthew*, vol. 3: *Commentary on Matthew XIX–XXVIII* (Edinburgh: T&T Clark, 1997), 87.

7. Mt 20:24.

8. Cf. Benedict T. Viviano, "The Gospel According to Matthew," in *The New Jerome Biblical Commentary*, ed. Raymond E. Brown et al. (London: Geoffrey Chapman, 1990), 663.

9. Cf. Ulrich Luz, *Matthew 8–20*, trans. James E. Crouch (Minneapolis: Fortress Press, 2001), 542.

names. In Mark, on the contrary, it is the two disciples themselves who make the request:

> James and John, the sons of Zebedee, came forward to him and said to him, "Teacher, we want you to do for us whatever we ask of you." And he said to them, "What is it you want me to do for you?" And they said to him, "Grant us to sit, one at your right hand and one at your left, in your glory."[10]

Is there something about this request that smacks of egoism and vanity on the part of the two disciples or their mother? An anonymous ancient commentator on Matthew thinks that in making this request the two disciples covet places of honor in the Kingdom; and that coveting is vanity, an attempt to usurp the judgment of God, who alone has the prerogative to allot such places.[11]

Some discern parallels between Zebedee's wife's request and the political maneuvering of Bathsheba, Solomon's mother, who wanted to make sure that her son became the next king over against Adonijah, another contender to David's throne.[12] It is reported that Bathsheba went to King David, "bowed and did obeisance to the king, and the king said, 'What do you wish?'"[13] The gesture of Mrs. Zebedee is similar to that of Bathsheba—bowing or prostrating oneself before the king. Jesus's question is also similar to David's question. Bathsheba approached David to remind him about the promise he had made that Solomon, not Adonijah, would inherit the throne. Solomon's mother did not want anyone to usurp her son's throne.

The case of the impropriety of the request of the mother of Zebedee's sons would seem to be strengthened by Jesus's reserved

---

10. Mk 10:35–38.

11. Chrysostomus [pseudo], *Opus Imperfectum in Matthaeum*, Sermo XXXV, ed. J.-P. Migne, PG, vol. 56 (Paris, 1862), 829.

12. Cf. Viviano, "The Gospel According to Matthew," 663.

13. 1Kg 1:16.

response to it: "To sit at my right hand and at my left, this is not mine to grant, but it is for those for whom it has been prepared by my Father."[14] Jesus declines to *promise* to give her sons seats in the Kingdom, even when the two sons pledge to do what it takes to inherit the Kingdom. Jesus's reaction is different from his response to the repentant thief, who asked to be remembered in Jesus's Kingdom: "Jesus, remember me when you come into your kingdom," to which Jesus replied, "Truly I tell you, today you will be with me in Paradise."[15] Jesus does not give any conditions to the repentant thief. The difference between the mother's and the thief's requests is that the latter does not ask for any special place in the Kingdom. It is enough for him to be in Jesus's Kingdom.

But what does the mother have in mind when she makes the petition to Jesus? Following the Ignatian approach,[16] can one give a positive interpretation to her request? For instance, one can interpret places at Jesus's right and left as a sign of closeness and solidarity with Jesus and a total embrace of the Kingdom preached and embodied by Jesus. The two disciples are so resolved to belong to Jesus's Kingdom that they are ready to do what it takes to become outstanding participants in the Kingdom of God. When Jesus asks them, "Are you able to drink the cup that I am about to drink?" they respond, "We are able."[17] The cup is a metaphor for suffering.[18]

Jesus says that the mother and her sons do not know what they

---

14. Mt 20:23.

15. Lk 23:42–43.

16. Before entering into the First Week of the *Spiritual Exercises*, Ignatius of Loyola presents the following presupposition: "In order that both he who is giving the Spiritual Exercises, and he who is receiving them, may more help and benefit themselves, let it be presupposed that every good Christian is to be more ready to save his neighbor's proposition than to condemn it. If he cannot save it, let him inquire how he means it; and if he means it badly, let him correct him with charity. If that is not enough, let him seek all the suitable means to bring him to mean it well, and save himself."

17. Mt 20:22–23.

18. Cf. David L. Turner and Darrel L. Bock, *Matthew and Mark*, Cornerstone Biblical Commentary, vol. 11 (Carol Stream, IL: Tyndale House Publishers, 2005), 260.

are asking for. Saint Jerome imagines that the mother's request is inspired by Jesus's declaration that he will rise on the third day. Thus, she thinks that Jesus will establish his Kingdom immediately after his resurrection rather than at the second coming. Jerome explains: "The woman thought that immediately after the Resurrection he would begin his reign, and what was promised for the second advent would be fulfilled at the first. And with a feminine eagerness she longs for the presence of what she has forgotten belongs to the future."[19] Jerome's view calls to mind the question a disciple put to Jesus after his resurrection: "Lord, is this the time when you will restore the kingdom to Israel?"[20] In his response to this question, Jesus, again, mentions the Father as the one who knows the time when the Kingdom will be established: "It is not for you to know the times or periods that the Father has set by his own authority."[21] Thus, just as it is the prerogative of the Father to give seats in the Kingdom, it is the Father's right to decide when to establish the Kingdom.

It is possible that the mother's request expresses a vague and inadequate longing for something deeper. Before the grand mystery of the Kingdom, one is awestruck and cannot but stutter one's desire to be part of it. The mother of the two disciples is like Peter, who, upon seeing the glory of the transfigured Jesus, asked to build three tents, and the narrator says that Peter did not know what he was saying.[22] Jerome puts this parallel well: "The mother of the sons of Zebedee asks this by a womanish error springing from a feeling of piety. She did not know what she was asking. It is not surprising that she is convicted of ignorance. For it was said of Peter, when he wanted to make the three tabernacles: 'not knowing what he was saying.'"[23] Like Peter who sees the glory of the transfigured Lord

---

19. Jerome, *Commentary on Matthew* III, trans. Thomas P. Scheck, The Fathers of the Church, vol. 117 (Washington, DC: Catholic University of America Press, 2008), 226.

20. Acts 1:6.

21. Acts 1:7.

22. Lk 9:28–36.

23. Jerome, *Commentary on Matthew* III, 226.

and wants to savor it a little longer, the mother of the sons of Zebedee has probably intuited that the Kingdom preached and embodied by Christ is the ultimate goal of human life; she therefore wants her children to secure places in it.

The mother of the sons of Zebedee is like that woman who, upon hearing the word of Jesus, exclaimed, "Blessed the womb that bore you and the breasts that fed you,"[24] or the person who, upon listening to Jesus's teaching regarding banquets, said, "Blessed is anyone who will eat bread in the kingdom of God!"[25] These people are moved by Jesus's teaching about the Kingdom and intuit its beauty and sublimity. However, their vision is not entirely accurate, and Jesus takes time to correct their statements. In this case, Jesus makes it clear to her that what matters is to enter the Kingdom of God and not the particular seats one is allotted.

By declining to grant the mother's request, Jesus, as it were, challenges her and her sons to search deeper in their hearts and to put a finger on their true desire, namely, to sit "at your right hand happiness forever."[26] Jesus's teaching about the Kingdom stimulates in his listeners the desire to be part of this reality. In fact, her petition comes in the context of Jesus's teaching on the Kingdom of God. Matthew 20 opens with the controversial parable about workers in the vineyard: "For the kingdom of heaven is like a landowner who went out early in the morning to hire laborers for his vineyard."[27] It is not unlikely that the mother of James and John would have been with the other disciples as Jesus told this parable. Hilary of Poitiers, in fact, imagines that she would have heard Jesus's teaching that the first shall be last and the last shall be first, which marks the conclusion to the aforementioned parable. Therefore, she makes this petition to ensure that her sons do not miss out on the Kingdom of God.[28]

---

24. Lk 11:28.

25. Lk 14:15.

26. Ps 16:11.

27. Mt 20:1.

28. Hilary of Poitiers, *Sur Matthieu* XX, 9, ed. Jean Doignon, SCh, vol. 258 (Paris: Cerf, 1979), 112.

While in this pericope the wife of Zebedee seems to come from her home to meet Jesus with the request, it is clear from the passion narrative that she actually is one of the women who accompany Jesus from Galilee up to his death:

> Many women were also there, looking on from a distance; they had followed Jesus from Galilee and had provided for him. Among them were Mary Magdalene, and Mary the mother of James and Joseph, and the mother of the sons of Zebedee.[29]

Her contact with Jesus is not a one-off event. She walks with Jesus, listens to his word, and provides for him, just like the other women. She does not abandon the *king of the Jews* even as he is rejected and condemned as a religious outlaw. She too, and not only her sons, is a disciple of Jesus. She is a believer in and belongs to Jesus's Kingdom. She, like the other women, watches Jesus's suffering and death from a distance. But it is not the distance that matters, but the presence: the perseverance to stay with Jesus even as the dark clouds of death descend upon him and the gusty winds of desolation hit him hard. One cannot overemphasize the consolation and strength the suffering Jesus draws from these women disciples, who are there even as things look hopeless.

On their part, the two sons prove themselves worthy of the Kingdom of God. John, popularly identified with the beloved disciple of Jesus, does not opt out of the most trying moment of Jesus's life. In the Gospel According to John, this disciple stands near Jesus's cross together with Jesus's mother, Jesus's aunt, Mary the wife of Clopas, and Mary of Magdala. Jesus hands over the disciple to Mary his mother, saying, "Woman, here is your son," and then to the disciple, "Here is your mother."[30] To entrust his own mother to the disciple is a great sign of Jesus's confidence in the disciple and an indication that the disciple belongs together with Jesus. This disciple is a citizen of Jesus's Kingdom. Jerome also reports

---

29. Mt 27:55–56.
30. Jn 19:25–26.

that, according to legend, John was put into a cauldron of boiling oil on account of his faith. Thus, though his life was spared and died in his old age at Patmos, John drank the cup of suffering. Jerome compares him to the three Hebrews in the fiery furnace who were tested in the fire though their lives were spared.[31]

James proved himself no less worthy of the Kingdom, for he sacrificed his life for the Kingdom of God during the persecution of Herod Agrippa I: "About that time King Herod laid violent hands upon some who belonged to the church. He had James, the brother of John, killed with the sword."[32] James drank the cup that Jesus himself drank. He died for his adherence to the Kingdom of Jesus.

One cannot but conjecture that the mother of James and John inculcated in her sons the love of the Kingdom and taught them to remain committed to it. Maybe she was one of those who "looked forward to the restoration of Israel."[33] Granted, their desire for places at the right and at the left of Jesus in the Kingdom needed to be purified before it could reflect their true longing. They saw "in a mirror, dimly,"[34] but with the passage of time, their vision of things became more consonant with the true meaning of the Kingdom.

Reflection

The request of the mother of James and John often attracts negative evaluation, being dismissed as nothing but self-serving ambition on the part of the mother and her sons. However, a deeper reflection on the request might suggest a genuine, albeit inchoate, longing for the Kingdom preached and embodied by Jesus Christ. By remaining faithful to Jesus, the two disciples and their mother truly *drank of the cup* of suffering and received places in the Kingdom of God, together with the other disciples. All our desires, even trivial ones, point us to a higher desire; all our thirsts, even little

---

31. Cf. Jerome, *Commentary on Matthew* III, 227.
32. Acts 12:1–2.
33. Cf. Lk 2:25.
34. 1Cor 13:12.

ones, are a manifestation of the ultimate thirst for the Kingdom of God; all our petitions, even petty ones, are an expression of our deepest yearning, namely, a place in the Kingdom of God.

When the disciples asked Jesus to teach them how to pray, Jesus taught them the prayer of the Our Father, in which the one praying asks that the Kingdom of God come. The desire for the Kingdom of God is expressed before the petition for daily bread, forgiveness of trespasses, or deliverance from evil. In other words, Jesus wants his disciples to seek first the Kingdom of God and all else shall be given unto them.[35] In a sense, the mother of the sons of Zebedee seeks just that: the Kingdom of God. She does not ask for wealth or renown or long life for her children. Like Solomon who chose wisdom over against long life or victory over his enemies, she knows the *mother* of all blessings: the Kingdom of God.

Conclusion

The prostrated figure of the mother of James and John calls to mind the stories of so many women who bend their knee at the feet of powerful people to intercede for their children. It beckons memories of mothers sitting along the streets and byways of our cities, holding out their hands for a coin or two to feed their children at home. It evokes the memory of many women who suffer scorn and humiliation on account of their insistent calls and visits to educational institutions or public offices that provide bursaries so their children can go to school. Consider the mother who kneels and pleads for a place closer to the doctor in a hospital queue snaking its way out into the main road, because her child is in danger of death. All these mothers want the best for their children, and behind their temporal requests is the desire for the ultimate happiness for their children, namely, the Kingdom of God. Like Mrs. Zebedee, they are mothers in search of places for their sons and daughters in the beatific vision.

---

35. Mt 6:33.

Prayer

Lord God, you know what lies in the depth of every person; you test our thoughts and purify our intentions so that we may search for higher things and be freed from vainglory. Help us to fix our eyes on your Kingdom, trusting in your promise that all else shall be added unto us. Through Christ our Lord. Amen.

Chapter 12

The Syro-Phoenician Woman: Mother of Cultural Bridges

Introduction

In the face of pressing needs, some taboos and sociocultural boundaries lose their grip on people's comportment. The quest for solutions leads people beyond cultural divides and leads to encounters with those on the other side of the divide. For instance, when two nations are threatened by a common enemy, they may spontaneously forge an alliance and put in parentheses whatever separates them. These days, especially in Africa, members of one religious affiliation easily cross over to another tradition in search of healing and liberation from various life-diminishing circumstances. Protestants may approach a Catholic priest and ask for holy water, just as Catholics sometimes jump the denominational chasm and ask for healing prayers from Pentecostal pastors. In the face of life-threatening situations, cultural, political, or religious differences often become superfluous. Such is the story of the Syro-Phoenician woman, who, faced with her daughter's demonic possession, does not hesitate to ask for help from a member of a community that does not share warm relations with her own people. But the woman builds bridges that overcome the sociocultural gulf between Jesus and her.

The Story

There are two accounts of the encounter between Jesus and the Syro-Phoenician woman: Mark 7:24–30 and Matthew 15:21–28. To appreciate the continuities and discontinuities between the two accounts, a synoptic table is in order.

Mark 7:24–30	Matthew 15:21–28
From there he set out and went away to the region of Tyre. He entered a house and did not want anyone to know he was there. Yet he could not escape notice, but a woman whose little daughter had an unclean spirit immediately heard about him, and she came and bowed down at his feet. Now the woman was a Gentile, of Syro-Phoenician origin. She begged him to cast the demon out of her daughter. He said to her, "Let the children be fed first, for it is not fair to take the children's food and throw it to the dogs." But she answered him, "Sir, even the dogs under the table eat the children's crumbs." Then he said to her, "For saying that, you may go—the demon has left your daughter." So she went home, found the child lying on the bed, and the demon was gone.	Jesus left that place and went away to the district of Tyre and Sidon. Just then a Canaanite woman from that region came out and started shouting, "Have mercy on me, Lord, Son of David; my daughter is tormented by a demon." But he did not answer her at all. And his disciples came and urged him, saying, "Send her away, for she keeps shouting after us." He answered, "I was sent only to the lost sheep of the house of Israel." But she came and knelt before him, saying, "Lord, help me." He answered, "It is not fair to take the children's food and throw it to the dogs." She said, "Yes, Lord, yet even the dogs eat the crumbs that fall from their masters' table." Then Jesus answered her, "Woman, great is your faith! Let it be done for you as you wish." And her daughter was healed instantly.

The two accounts present, with significant parallels and differences, the encounter between Jesus and the woman. What is common to both versions is the presentation of the woman as a gentile; Jesus is in gentile territory. In addition, in both accounts, the woman approaches Jesus and makes her request regarding her little daughter. As for her gesture before Jesus, Mark says she falls down at his feet (*prosepesen pros tous podas autou*). In this context the Greek verb *prospiptein* means to fall down. Matthew, instead, says she worships him or renders homage to him (*prosekynei autou*). The verb *proskynein* means to worship, to go down on one's knees, or to do obeisance. Both gestures, in Mark and in Matthew, speak of obeisance and supplication.[1]

The difference, however, is that in Mark the woman seems to be already in the presence of Jesus when she makes her petition, and the entire dialogue between Jesus and her takes place while she is already in the presence of Jesus. In Matthew, on the contrary, the initial request is made at a distance. When Jesus apparently ignores her, she walks toward him and kneels before him. In Matthew, the woman is shown to be in motion toward Jesus—in spite of his initial coldness—while Mark paints a rather static picture of the encounter between Jesus and the woman.

Another difference is that in the Markan account, Jesus is in the house.[2] This detail is quite striking, given that Jesus is in gentile territory, for Tyre was located to the northwest of Galilee.[3] Is he in the house of a Jew living in the diaspora? Is he in the house of a gentile convert to Judaism (proselyte)? Collins and Attridge remark that,

---

1. Cf. Daniel J. Harrington, "The Gospel According to Mark," in *The New Jerome Biblical Commentary*, ed. Raymond E. Brown et al. (London: Geoffrey Chapman, 1990), 612.

2. This story would have parallels with the account of the sinful woman who cleans and anoints Jesus's feet in the house of Simon the Pharisee. Cf. Luke 7:36–50, except that this woman, though a sinner, was a fellow Jew.

3. While in Mk 3:8 the people from the region of Tyre come to Jesus, in this passage it is Jesus who goes to them.

Since Bethsaida is near Capernaum, it makes more narrative sense for Jesus to enter a house there and attempt
to remain hidden. It makes less sense for him to do so
in the region of Tyre. The description of the woman as a
Syro-Phoenician may have prompted the relocation of the
incident.[4]

The emphasis on the woman's identity as a *gentile* rather than a
Jew would also make little sense in pagan territory but would not
be superfluous in Jewish territory.[5] In any case, the fact that the
house is accessible to a gentile woman, who comes and kneels
before him to ask for his favor, already hints at the dissolution of
the Jew–gentile boundaries.

The Old Testament provides a precedent of the interaction
between Israel and Tyre. Hiram, king of Tyre, is said to have
provided Solomon with the cedar wood, juniper wood, and gold
needed for the building of the temple and the royal palace. In
return, Solomon gave his Phoenician ally some towns in Galilee,
including the plain among the mountains of Naphtali, which he
renamed Cabul land.[6] In Isaiah, Galilee is called "the territory of
the nations"[7]—a likely reference to the foreigners who came to
settle in this region. In this case, the boundaries between Jew and
non-Jew would not have been watertight. In fact, Judaism in Galilee "for centuries had had to live side by side with strong pagan
influence."[8]

While it is common for Jesus to be a guest in the house of sinners,
these hosts are usually Jews (Zacchaeus, for instance). Nonetheless, the fact that Jesus once sends his disciples to ask the Samari-

---

4. Adela Y. Collins and Harold W. Attridge, *Mark: A Commentary* (Minneapolis: Fortress Press, 2007), 364.

5. Cf. ibid.

6. 1 Kg 9:10–14.

7. Isa 9:1; Mt 4:15.

8. John P. Meier, *A Marginal Jew: Rethinking the Historical Jesus*, vol. 1: *The
Roots of the Problem and the Person* (New York: Doubleday, 1991), 207.

tans to welcome him while he is on his way to Jerusalem[9] suggests that Jesus is open to being a guest in a non-Jewish house.

Whatever may be the case, the woman overcomes the distance between Jesus and herself by entering the house where Jesus is (Markan account). It is noted that "the woman is doubly marginal: a woman alone in a man's world; a Gentile and hence unclean."[10] It takes a lot of courage to surmount such a challenge and to present herself before a man of such great renown.

In Matthew, instead, Jesus seems to be outside. The woman is said to shout her request to him, an indication of the distance between Jesus and herself. The woman is also presented as moving toward him until she kneels before him. This scenario is reminiscent of the incident at Jericho, where Jesus is passing by and a blind man cries out to him, until the blind man is brought near Jesus and then makes his request known. In fact, the initial cry of both the man at Jericho and the Syro-Phoenician woman addresses Jesus as son of David and asks for mercy.

Lord, Son of David

In the Markan version, the woman addresses Jesus simply as Sir. The Greek word used here is *Kyrie*, often translated as "lord." The Matthean text uses more explicit Christological titles: Lord, Son of David.[11] If one goes by the Matthean version, it can be argued that

---

9. Lk 9:52–53.

10. Benedict T. Viviano, "The Gospel According to Matthew," in *The New Jerome Biblical Commentary*, ed. Raymond E. Brown et al. (London: Geoffrey Chapman, 1990), 658. On the basis of the historical information regarding her region of provenance, some have tried to conjecture on the social status or economic condition of the woman. It is imagined that she was a widow (or a single mother) and a poor woman, with no one to represent her interests in the public sphere. Cf. Jane E. Hicks, "Moral Agency at the Borders: Rereading the Story of the Syrophoenician Woman," *Word & World* 23 (2003): 81. However, it is difficult to establish her status on the basis of the information furnished in the gospel accounts.

11. It is not clear why the Jerusalem Bible translates the Markan *Kyrie* as "sir," while the same word in Matthew is translated as "Lord."

the woman shares the faith of the people of Israel, for she acknowledges Jesus as the son of David, which title is applied to Jesus by
the blind man at Jericho[12] and during Jesus's triumphant entry into
Jerusalem: "Hosanna to the Son of David! Blessed is the one who
comes in the name of the Lord! Hosanna in the highest heaven!"[13]
This Christological title has deep roots in Israel's Messianic tradition.[14] By using these titles, she clearly shows that she assents to the
faith of the people of Israel, in spite of her gentile background. This
is the second bridge that highlights a relationship between Jesus
and herself. As Isaiah says, "Do not let the foreigner joined to the
LORD say, 'The LORD will surely separate me from his people.'"[15]
Since she has bound herself to the Jewish expectation, she is entitled to an audience with the one who embodies the Messianic hope.

Little Daughter, Little Dogs

Jesus's initial response to the woman's supplication is a subject of
difficult interpretation: "Let the children be fed first, for it is not
fair to take the children's food and throw it to the dogs" (Mark);
"It is not fair to take the children's food and throw it to the dogs"
(Matthew). At first glance, Jesus's response appears to be offensive,
if not xenophobic. How can he call gentiles "little dogs"?

But when one considers that Jesus is probably using a proverb,
the offensiveness of the answer is toned down: "Jesus's response
takes the form of a proverb. [. . .] In the proverb the children represent the Jews and the dogs represent the Gentiles. But this is not
the same as using the term 'dogs' as a racial slur. The form of his
statement is proverbial."[16] As a proverb, the use of *little dogs* can-

---

12. Lk 18:38. In this story, when the blind man asks who is passing by, the
crowd tells him it is Jesus the Nazarene; but when he calls out to Jesus, he calls
him "Son of David," a clear sign of the blind man's faith in Jesus as the Messiah.

13. Mt 21:9.

14. Cf. 2Sam 7:12–14; Isa 9:1–7.

15. Isa 56:3.

16. Allen Black, *Mark*, The College Press NIV Commentary (Joplin, MO:
College Press, 1995), 137.

not be taken literally and therefore it is not necessarily an insult. The woman understands the import of the proverb and, having a good command of proverbs, she is able to respond with a counter aphorism[17]: "Sir, even the dogs under the table eat the children's crumbs" (Mark); "Yes, Lord, yet even the dogs eat the crumbs that fall from their masters' table" (Matthew). As in the initial request, in Mark the woman addresses Jesus as "sir," while in Matthew she calls him "Lord," suggesting that the latter account has a more deliberately christological intent.

Further, there is an apparent play on words between little girl and little dogs. In Greek, the word for little dog (puppy) is *kynarion*, while a little daughter is *thygatrion*. The use of diminutives changes the tone of the conversation. While dogs, especially stray ones, were regarded as unclean, hence the association between gentiles and dogs, little dogs (puppies) were "not stray or watch dogs but well cared for pets that [shared] the life of the family. The suggested image is that of a well-to-do family, as is confirmed by the circumstance that meals are not served on a floor mat but on a real table, under which the little dogs can find a spot for themselves."[18] She transforms the metaphor of scavenging dogs into domestic dogs, thereby making her daughter and herself members of Jesus's household.[19] Thus, though she and her daughter are not daughters of Abraham by descent, they are nonetheless little puppies that belong to Abraham's household and are therefore entitled to some share of the household food.

---

17. In many languages, one finds proverbs that seem to contradict one another. For instance, in Chewa the saying *Ukayendera zyengo usati asakhwi afumbula* (literally, when you go into the forest looking for fruits do not get distracted by the footprints of elephant shrews) is contradicted by the proverb *Wayenda m'tchire wayendera zonse* (he who goes into the forest goes for everything) or *Okaona nyanja adakaona ndi mvuu yomwe* (those who went to see the lake also saw the hippopotamus).

18. Bas M. F. van Iersel, *Mark: A Reader-Response Commentary* (London: T&T Clark, 2004), 250.

19. Collins and Attridge, *Mark*, 367.

Expanding the Horizon of the Mission of the Servant of Yahweh

To rebuff the woman's petition, Jesus says that he has been sent only to the lost sheep of the House of Israel. That clearly excludes her. Jesus's response is an allusion to Isaiah 49, the second Servant Song: "And now the LORD says, who formed me in the womb to be his servant, to bring Jacob back to him, and that Israel might be gathered to him."[20] This mission statement clearly circumscribes the work of Jesus within Jewish territory. Matthew uses the adverb "only," thereby leaving little possibility for Jesus to overstep his mission territory. Elsewhere, when Jesus sent his disciples on a mission, he told them to "go nowhere among the Gentiles, and enter no town of the Samaritans, but go rather to the lost sheep of the house of Israel."[21] On the basis of this apostolic regulation, Jerome argues that Jesus initially does not respond to the woman's request, not out of pride or disdain for her but in order not to go against the regulation that he himself had imposed on his disciples.[22]

Though Mark does not include this saying, his use of the adverb "first" when talking about the feeding of children would seem to leave some scope for gentile inclusion, albeit secondary, in Jesus's mission:[23] "Let the children be fed first, for it is not fair to take the children's food and throw it to the dogs."

Thanks to her insistence, the woman pushes further the boundaries of Jesus's mission. She brings, as it were, more inclusive biblical traditions to bear on her request. For instance, the same Servant Song that appears to have inspired Jesus's description of his mission later extends the mission of the Servant of Yahweh to other nations: "It is too light a thing that you should be my servant to raise up the tribes of Jacob and to restore the survivors of Israel; I will give you

---

20. Isa 49:5.

21. Mt 10:5–6.

22. Jerome, *Commentaire sur saint Matthieu* II, 15, 22, ed. Emile Bonnard, SCh, vol. 242 (Paris: Cerf, 1977), 330.

23. Cf. Henry B. Swete, *The Gospel According to St. Mark: The Greek Text with Introduction, Notes and Indices* (London: Macmillan, 1898), 157.

as a light to the nations, that my salvation may reach to the end of the earth."[24] In addition, the infancy narrative presents the mission of Jesus as embracing gentiles as well. In his *Nunc Dimittis*, Simeon praises God because his eyes have "seen your salvation, which you have prepared in the presence of all peoples, a light for revelation to the Gentiles and for glory to your people Israel."[25] And, finally, before his ascension, Jesus sends his disciples to go and make disciples of all nations.[26] In other words, according to God's plan of salvation, the woman is not a total outsider. There are already many bridges that connect her with the Messiah. That is why she refuses to budge when Jesus shows reluctance to help her. She, like the centurion,[27] anticipates the participation of gentiles in the Kingdom of God.

Great Faith

After the dialogue with the woman, Jesus eventually grants her request. According to Matthew, Jesus says to her, "Woman, great is your faith! Let it be done for you as you wish." In the whole Gospel of Matthew, she is the only one said to have "great faith."[28] In the Gospel of Luke, Jesus says something similar to another gentile: a centurion who approaches Jesus and asks him to cure his servant. Jesus says of him, "I tell you, not even in Israel have I found such faith."[29] It is "presumably the woman's demonstration of faith that attracted Mark to this story."[30]

John Chrysostom comments on this episode in the context of Abraham's patience in bearing with his condition of childlessness for many years before Hagar was given to him. The delay, Chrysostom surmises, was meant to make the faith of Abram shine

---

24. Isa 49:6.
25. Lk 2:30–32.
26. Mt 28:19.
27. Lk 7:1–10.
28. Viviano, "The Gospel According to Matthew," 659.
29. Lk 7:10.
30. Black, *Mark*, at 7:29.

forth with greater splendor. By the same token, Jesus deliberately appears to ignore the Syro-Phoenician woman's request so that her faith and spiritual fortitude may be more conspicuous. Her faith is so deep that not "only did the severity of his words to her not deter the poor creature, but it even prompted her to greater earnestness."[31] She accepts to be called a puppy "so as to be acquitted of the ferocity of dogs and be admitted at once into the ranks of sons."[32] The Lord's initial reluctance to grant her wish was, as it were, meant to prod her to a greater expression of her faith in the Lord, much to the edification of the disciples. That is why Jesus eventually not only grants her desire but also praises her great faith.

The encounter between Jesus and the woman becomes an opportunity for her to demonstrate her faith. And she does that in a threefold manner: first, she calls out to him using Messianic or Christological titles; second, she kneels or bows before him; third, she includes herself and her daughter in God's plan of salvation. With these three poles, she builds a solid bridge of faith that gives her access to Jesus's saving power, and her daughter is freed from the power of the devil. The Syro-Phoenician woman is a mother imbued with a deep faith that surpasses cultural and religious boundaries. She anticipates the church's mission *ad gentes* to be embarked on after Pentecost. Mark says the woman heard about Jesus and went to meet him. Her faith comes from hearing,[33] and she believes what she hears even before she sees Jesus. Indeed, blessed are those who believe even without seeing.[34]

Reflection

The story of the Syro-Phoenician woman challenges humanity to "spread the tent wider"[35] in our quest for solutions to life's problems.

---

31. John Chrysostom, *Homilies on Genesis* XXXVIII, 9, trans. Robert C. Hill, The Fathers of the Church, vol. 82 (Washington, DC: Catholic University of America Press, 1990), 362.

32. Chrysostom, *Homilies on Genesis* XXXVIII, 9.

33. Cf. Rm 10:17.

34. Jn 20:29.

35. Cf. Isa 54:2.

Of old, Naaman the Syrian went beyond the borders of his nation to seek healing in Israel, after which he confessed the God of Israel as the true God.[36] A popular African proverb says that he or she who has tasted the *ugali* (food) prepared by one's mother thinks she is the best cook. Another proverb says that the child of a crocodile does not grow up in one pool. To grow in humanity, it is necessary to go beyond one's sociocultural boundaries. To appreciate the oneness of the human race, it is important to build bridges with those who are different from us, for, more often than not, the solutions to life's problems are to be found across the confines of one's sociocultural environment. In Origen's view, the woman actually comes *out of* (not simply *from*) the territories of Tyre and Sidon to meet Jesus. She goes beyond the confines of her nation. Origen adds that she would not have been able to address her cry of faith to Jesus had she not come out of the pagan territory. He then reads the idea of *coming out of* in an allegorical key, affirming that every time one sins, one is in pagan territory, and every time one returns to virtue, one comes out of pagan territory and returns to the territory of God. He reports that the word "Canaanite" meant disposed to vilification because of one's inclination to wickedness. By leaving the territories of Tyre and Sidon, the woman thus turned her back on this disposition to vilification and entered the territory of virtue.[37]

To some, the woman's confession of Jesus as Lord and son of David would have come across as a betrayal of one's religious tradition. Great bridge-builders are often subjected to the criticism of playing fast and loose with their cultural inheritance.

At the same time, it is important to remember that the woman approaches Jesus because *she has faith in him*. She does not treat him as a magician who can simply manipulate the forces of nature and heal her daughter even without the necessity of faith. These days, especially in Africa, there is a growing tendency to treat faith healers as magicians. It seems to matter no longer whether one subscribes to the faith represented by the healer. What seems to

---

36. 2Kg 5:1–19.

37. Origen, *Commentaire sur l'Evangile selon Matthieu* XI, 16, ed. Robert Girod, SCh, vol. 162 (Paris: Cerf, 1970), 356–58.

count is the efficacy of the cure. Thus, sacramentals degenerate into magic potions that no longer help us to name the world as a visible manifestation of the loving presence of God. They become objects to be manipulated in function of a desired result. Prayers, similarly, lose their meaning as words that name our relationship with God; instead, they become incantations hoped to bring about a desired result.

The long-winded "therapeutic itineraries"[38] that lead to modern hospitals, Christian ministers of various traditions, and African traditional healers—depending on the complexity or intractability of the problem—are sometimes motivated solely by the quest for efficacy and are devoid of any faith whatsoever. As Lado finds, "here efficacy seems to take priority over cognitive consonance."[39] The Syro-Phoenician woman is motivated by faith in Jesus, the source of life, rather than mere therapeutic efficacy. According to Jerome, the woman's confession of faith in Jesus means that she had already renounced the (erroneous) faith of her country and embraced the faith of the people of Israel.[40] She was not a religious syncretist. Understandably, sometimes people come to adopt a new belief system after experiencing its greatness. However, this does not justify adopting a new religion for every problem that crops up in one's life.

Conclusion

When the disciples asked Jesus to teach them how to pray, he taught them the prayer of the Our Father. He then told them parables of the friend at midnight[41] and the persistent widow,[42] both of which underscore the importance of persistence in prayer. The Christian is not simply a person who prays but one who prays persistently.

---

38. Ludovic Lado, *Catholic Pentecostalism and the Paradoxes of Africanization: Processes of Localization in a Catholic Charismatic Movement in Cameroon* (Leiden, the Netherlands: Brill, 2009), 61.

39. Ibid., 64.

40. Cf. Jerome, *Commentaire sur saint Matthieu* II, 330.

41. Lk 11:5–8.

42. Lk 18:1–8.

This persistence is not meant to twist God's arm, as it were, but to show in an unequivocal manner one's faith in God who alone has the power to save. The Syro-Phoenician woman is a shining example of faith that endures and does not falter in the face of obstacles or discouragements. Sometimes the greatest test of faith comes from God rather than Satan. While Job's test was administered by Satan—of course, with God's consent—the Syro-Phoenician woman's test of faith came from Jesus himself, and she passed with flying colors!

Prayer

Lord God, you sent your son to labor in the vineyard of your chosen people and to be a light to the nations so that your salvation may reach to the ends of the earth. Mercifully grant that all who search for you with a sincere heart may find a home in your Son's fold and see the glory of your saving presence in their lives. Through Christ our Lord. Amen.

Chapter 13

Mary: Mother of Meditation

Introduction

"Blessed are you among women." No woman in the history of humanity has been the subject of so many monographs, poetry, musical compositions, apparitions, devotions, and doctrinal controversy as Mary, mother of Jesus. Already in 431, the Council of Ephesus had to deal with the theological quarrel regarding the place of Mary in the economy of salvation. Against the Arianist tendency to limit her motherhood to the humanity of Jesus, the Council declared Mary *Theotokos*, Mother of God. Who is she whose statues are carried in procession in many a city during Holy Week? Who is she whom mothers call upon to intercede for their suffering children? Who is she over whom popes have risen to define dogmas such as the Immaculate Conception and the Assumption? Who is she around whom the church has developed many a solemnity and a feast in the liturgical year?

Her Origin

Luke introduces Mary as a young woman who lives in a town in Galilee called Nazareth.[1] The New Testament Galilee was a well-connected city, for the greatest roads of the ancient world passed through this region. Therefore, people from different cul-

---

1. Lk 1:26.

tural and ethnic backgrounds could be found there. It was commonly said that Galilee was on the way to everywhere, thanks to the *via maris* (way of the sea) connecting such continents as Africa, Asia, and Europe. On the contrary, Judaea was not open to the outside world, so much that it was common to say that Judaea led to nowhere. This may explain why the south was seen as the center of Jewish orthodoxy, while Galilee was looked down upon as the haven for heterodoxy.[2] In the Gospel of John, Nathanael is reported to have wondered whether anything good could come from Nazareth.[3]

However, God has a penchant for turning small things into great ones, as Mary will later sing in her *Magnificat*. Today one cannot speak of the Christian history of salvation without mentioning Nazareth. Today Nazareth boasts the sumptuously decorated Basilica of the Annunciation—designed by Giovanni Muzio—believed to be located at the spot where the angel Gabriel announced to Mary the good news that she would conceive and bear a child who would be named Jesus. The Greek Orthodox Church of the Archangel Gabriel is also to be found less than a quarter of a mile away from the Basilica of the Annunciation.[4] All in all, after the Jesus event, Nazareth is no longer that contemptible place looked down upon by the peoples, for something *good*, the good news, came from there.

Story of Her Birth

The childhood of Mary is not recorded in the canonical gospels. However, the apocryphal Gospel of James, also known as the Protoevangelium of James[5] (probably written in the first half of the

2. Cf. David Padfield, *Capernaum: The City of Jesus*, http://www.padfield.com/acrobat/history/Capernaum.pdf.

3. Jn 1:46.

4. Cf. Peter F. Vasko, *Our Visit to the Holy Land* (Jerusalem: Mount Olives Press, 2000), 5–15.

5. The term *"Protoevangelium"* was first applied to this "gospel" by Guillaume Postel in 1552 in his Latin translation of the text. Cf. Johannes Quasten,

second century), furnishes an account of the story of Mary's birth. The story, modeled on the infancy narratives of Jesus and inspired by an array of Old Testament motifs (birth of Isaac and Samuel, for instance), was meant to quench the thirst of early Christians who wanted to know as much as possible about the origins of Jesus and his mother. The Gospel of James is, by and large, a paraphrase and expansion of the canonical infancy narratives. According to Johannes Quasten, "the principal aim of the whole writing is to prove the perpetual and inviolate virginity of Mary before, in, and after the birth of Christ."[6] Though the perpetual virginity of Mary is not explicitly mentioned in the canonical gospels, Clement of Alexandria refers to the episode where a midwife (Salome) verifies the virginity of Mary after the latter has given birth.[7] This shows that the Gospel of James was known and, perhaps, regarded as a valid Christian text in the early centuries. Since not many are familiar with the story of Mary's infancy as reported by the Protoevangelium of James, it shall be reported here, albeit briefly.

The apocryphal Gospel of James reports that Mary's parents, Joachim and Anna, remained childless till an advanced age. Joachim was a very rich man. One day he went to offer a sin-offering to the Lord, but Reuben told him that it was not lawful for him to offer his gifts first, because he had begotten no offspring in Israel. Joachim looked in the register to see whether he was the only one who did not beget offspring in Israel. The records showed that all the righteous men in Israel (Abraham, for instance) had generated offspring. Overcome with sadness, Joachim decided to withdraw into the wilderness to pray and fast for forty days and forty nights, asking for God's favorable visit. Since he did not tell his wife about his decision to withdraw into the wilderness, Anna thought Joachim had died; so she mourned him and dressed in a widow's gar-

---

Patrology, vol. 3: *The Beginnings of Patristic Literature from the Apostles Creed to Irenaeus* (Allen, TX: Christian Classics, 1995), 118.

6. Ibid., 120–21.

7. Cf. Clement of Alexandria, *Stromata* VII, 93, 7, ed. Alain le Boulluec, SCh, vol. 428 (Paris: Cerf, 1997), 284.

ments. One day she walked into her garden, where she sat under a laurel tree and prayed to the Lord for the fruit of the womb: "O God of our fathers," she prayed, "bless me and heed my prayer, just as you blessed the womb of Sarah and gave her a son, Isaac."[8] After her prayer of lament, the angel of the Lord appeared to her and promised her that she would bear a child who would be "spoken of in the whole world."[9] Joachim also received the same message from the angel of the Lord. She conceived and gave birth to a girl, whereupon Anna exclaimed, "My soul is magnified this day."[10] She called the child Mary.

When Mary was a year old, her parents gave a big party to which were invited the chief priests, the priests, the scribes, and the elders of all the people in Israel. Joachim and Anna brought the child to the priests, and they blessed her, saying, "O God of our fathers, bless this child and give her a name eternally renowned among all generations."[11] When Mary was three years old, the parents took her up to the temple of the Lord in order to fulfill the promise they had made to the Lord. When they reached the temple, the priest took her and blessed her, saying, "The Lord has magnified your name among all generations; because of you the Lord at the end of the days will reveal his redemption to the sons of Israel."[12] Mary was then placed on the third step of the altar, where she danced with her feet. The parents left her in the temple and they returned home.

Mary remained in the temple till the age of twelve when the council of priests decided, after consulting the Lord in the Holy of holies, to give her in marriage to one of the widowers of the people of Israel. The priest who was assigned the task of consulting the Lord was Zacharias, who later became dumb and was replaced by

---

8. *The Protoevangelium of James* 2, 4, in *The Apocryphal New Testament: A Collection of Apocryphal Christian Literature in an English Translation*, ed. James K. Elliott (Oxford: Clarendon Press, 1993), 58.

9. Ibid., 4, 1.

10. Ibid., 5, 2.

11. Ibid., 6, 2.

12. Ibid., 7, 1.

Samuel. When the widowers gathered, the lot fell on Joseph. After some hesitation on account of his age, Joseph took Mary as his ward.[13]

Clearly, there are many parallels between the story of Mary's infancy and that of Jesus. For instance, their birth is announced by an angel. In addition, temple functionaries pronounce blessings upon Mary and foretell her greatness, just as they do with Jesus. Zacharias, John the Baptist's father in Luke's infancy narrative, appears in Mary's story as the one sent to consult with God in the Holy of holies. Just as in Luke, Zacharias later loses his speech. Though this gospel is not canonical, it still nourishes the church's vibrant flower of popular piety. For instance, the church keeps the memorial of Sts. Joachim and Anna on July 26. The feast of the presentation of the Blessed Virgin Mary occurs on July 21. The Gospel of James paints a portrait of Mary as one who dwells in the presence of the Lord, meditating on his law day and night, to borrow the words of Psalm 1.

Turning the Rails of Dreams

Long ago Rainer Maria Rilke wrote the following lines, which Georg Hans Gadamer uses as an epigraph to his book *Truth and Method*:

> Catch only what you've thrown yourself, all is mere skill and little gain; but when you're suddenly the catcher of a ball thrown by an eternal partner with accurate and measured swing towards you, to your center, in an arch from the great bridgebuilding of God: why, catching then becomes a power—not yours, a world's.

These words aptly describe the destiny of Mary. The canonical accounts start with the story of Mary's betrothal to Joseph, of

---

13. Ibid., 8–9.

the House of David.[14] One can imagine her grooming herself to become an ordinary wife taking care of an ordinary household, with its blessings and trials. Maybe she was dreaming of raising a family with many vibrant children who would grow up to become successful members of society. Like any other person, perhaps Mary was catching the dreams she herself had thrown.

However, the visit of the angel Gabriel changes the course of her life and the content of her dreams. Through the angel, Mary becomes aware of an even greater dream she has to catch, a dream thrown by her eternal partner, a dream thrown with "accurate and measured swing" toward her. It will touch the very center of her life. And if she catches it, the world will no longer be the same, for the dream has the power to transform darkness into light, death into life, chaos into order.

The angel Gabriel says to her, "Greetings, favored one! The Lord is with you."[15] When she looks disturbed by these words, the angel explains further:

> Do not be afraid, Mary, for you have found favor with God. And now, you will conceive in your womb and bear a son, and you will name him Jesus. He will be great, and will be called the Son of the Most High, and the Lord God will give to him the throne of his ancestor David. He will reign over the house of Jacob forever, and of his kingdom there will be no end.[16]

At that point, she realizes that her betrothal to Joseph is no mere coincidence but part of God's plan. Joseph belongs to the royal family of David, and Mary's son will thus be a member of David's lineage. Through her, the great prophecies of the Old Testament will come to pass. As it is written in the Book of Isaiah, "Look, the young woman is with child and shall bear a son, and shall name

---

14. Lk 1:27.
15. Lk 1:28.
16. Lk 1:31–33.

him Immanuel."[17] Like Eve, the *mother of humanity*, Mary will be the one to give a name to her son. Like Hagar, Mary is the recipient of the revelation regarding the identity and destiny of her son. Her womb will carry the Prince of Peace.

But Mary senses there will be an obstacle to the angel's prophecy: "How can this be, since I am a virgin?"[18] Given that she is promised in marriage to Joseph, it is difficult to understand Mary's problem. After all, the angel's prophecy clearly connects the son to Mary's future husband Joseph, namely, membership in the royal family. Nor does the angel specify when she will conceive the child. If she would conceive that very day, Mary's query would make sense, but if she would conceive after settling down with Joseph, then the anxiety would not hold much sway. Is the narrator, through Mary's question, simply creating a narrative cue to announce the virginal birth of Jesus, or does Mary intuit something in the angel's message that is not explicitly stated? In any case, the angel tells her that she will conceive by the power of the Holy Spirit, and because of that "the child to be born will be holy; he will be called Son of God."[19]

Does the angel's answer convince Mary? Will she accept? Within that moment the whole universe stands still. It awaits the all-important response of the virgin. Saint Bernard the abbot imaginatively prompts her to accept the mission, for the salvation of the whole world rests on the balance of her *fiat*:

> You have heard, O Virgin, that you will conceive and bear a son; you have heard that it will not be by man but by the Holy Spirit. The angel awaits an answer; it is time for him to return to God who sent him. We too are waiting, O Lady, for your word of compassion; the sentence of condemnation weighs heavily upon us.[20]

---

17. Isa 7:14.

18. Lk 1:34.

19. Lk 1:35.

20. Bernard the Abbot, *Homily* IV, 8–9, in *The Liturgy of the Hours, Approved by the Episcopal Conferences of the Antilles, Bangladesh, Burma, Canada, of the*

In that instant Mary hears the cry of Adam exiled from Paradise. She hears the petition of Abraham, David, and other holy patriarchs. She sees the whole world pleading with her to say yes. Bernard, the abbot, adds urgency to the occasion: "Answer quickly, O Virgin. Reply in haste to the angel, or rather through the angel to the Lord. Answer with a word, receive the Word of God. Speak your own word, conceive the divine Word. Breathe a passing word, embrace the eternal Word."[21]

This is an absolute novelty; never before in the history of Israel has it happened that a woman should conceive without the cooperation of a man. There are many accounts of barren women who, even in their old age, received the gift of fecundity and gave birth to sons and daughters. Mary will be the first (and the last) to conceive without the help of a male partner. This is God's *technology*, which surpasses all human understanding and invention. How does she explain it to her parents, relatives, and friends? Will she not be dismissed as a heretic? She simply does not have a precedent in the history of humanity.

It is also an absolute novelty that the Son of God should take a human form and be born of a woman. In the mythologies of the ancient world, gods were said to occasionally take human forms and mix with people. Homer's *Odyssey* is replete with divinities that walk in the company of people and even marry them. Miraculous events were thus attributed to the visit of the gods. In the history of Israel, angels were also known to come down and represent God. However, conceiving and giving birth to the Son of God does not have a precedent in the history of Israel. The very titles given to

---

Pacific CEPAC (Fiji Islands, Rarotanga, Samoa and Tokelau, Tonga), Ghana, India, New Zealand, Pakistan, Papua New Guinea and the Solomons, the Philippines, Rhodesia, South Africa, Sri Lanka, Tanzania, Uganda, and the United States of America for Use in Their Dioceses and Confirmed by the Apostolic See, vol. 1: *Advent & Christmas Seasons*, English translation prepared by the International Commission on English in the Liturgy (Bangalore, India: N.B.C.L.C., 2005), 345.

21. Ibid.

Mary's son are the titles of God himself, meaning that she will give birth to God.

Without an analogous situation, meaning becomes almost impossible to forge, for meaning is constructed on the basis of an already-existing reality. When the angel says to Mary, "for nothing is impossible to God,"[22] probably he is not simply addressing the difficulty of conceiving without a man, but also the difficulty of making sense of the situation without a precedent. Mary finds herself in front of novelty: "I am about to do a new thing; now it springs forth, do you not perceive it?"[23] It is an event that requires new interpretative categories. It is a historical *new wine* that needs to be stored in new conceptual *wineskins*. Only God is capable of forging meaning without precedents. Mary's is not only a biological task but also a hermeneutical responsibility: she has to mediate this absolutely new meaning.

Fortunately, she will not do this job alone; God will allow a few other people to access this mystery: Joseph, Elisabeth, the shepherds, the Magi, Simeon, and Anna. This is one of God's ways of making Mary's hermeneutical task *possible*. An apparently *mad* idea shared by a community is more acceptable than a common-sensical opinion held by a single person.

Mary discerns the urgency of the project. So she opens her arms and embraces the eternal Word with her *fiat*. She opens her hands and catches the dream from above: "Here am I, the servant of the Lord; let it be with me according to your word."[24] It is done! It is accomplished! She conceives before she marries Joseph. As Matthew recounts, Mary was found to be with child before they came to live together, thanks to the power of the Holy Spirit.[25] When Joseph gets the news of Mary's pregnancy, he is disturbed and wants to terminate the relationship, except that the angel of the Lord appears to him in a dream and tells him not to be afraid

---

22. Lk 1:37.
23. Isa 43:19.
24. Lk 1:38.
25. Mt 1:18.

to take Mary as his wife, because she has conceived by the Holy Spirit. Unlike in Luke's account where it is Mary who has to give a name to the son, in Matthew it is Joseph who will name the son Jesus, because he is the one to save his people from their sins.[26]

Mary's *fiat* is a sign of her submissiveness to the Lord; she acknowledges the fact that she is a servant of the Lord. But at the same time, Mary's subjectivity cannot be underestimated; she is a subject of history capable of weighing situations and making informed decisions. The fact that she commits herself to the cause may suggest that God's plan, though difficult to understand, is viable and worth adhering to. She owns the plan. She does not drag her feet into it simply because she is God's handmaid; rather she applies herself to it as she would execute her own idea. Her faith response is firmly grounded on the lodestone of God's salvific plan. It is something she is ready to suffer and die for. She has internalized God's plan and is fired up with enthusiasm to collaborate with God so God's dream may come true.

Dancing in the Rain

"Shower, O heavens, from above, and let the skies rain down righteousness; let the earth open, that salvation may spring up, and let it cause righteousness to sprout up also; I the LORD have created it";[27] so sings Isaiah, summoning the heavens to play their part in ushering in the messianic era. By the power of the Holy Spirit, Mary conceives the Righteous One, after which she sets out as quickly as she can for the hill country to a town in Judah. Her destination is Zechariah's house. She goes to meet her cousin Elisabeth.[28]

The text says she goes "with haste." One could interpret that as the fear of a young woman who runs away from her parents and relatives before people discover she is pregnant out of wedlock. Is Mary running quickly away from Nazareth to seek refuge in the

---

26. Mt 1:20–21.

27. Isa 45:8. In the liturgy of the Roman Catholic Church, this verse serves as the entrance antiphon for the fourth Sunday of Advent.

28. Lk 1:39–40.

house of her elderly cousin Elisabeth, hoping for the latter's under-standing and comfort? Is Mary escaping the judgmental eyes of her relatives and friends, hoping to live incognito in the hill country of Judah?

Her hasty departure would rather seem to be indicative of her enthusiasm about the good news she has just received. She cannot wait to compare notes with her cousin Elisabeth, who is also privy to God's salvation plan. She cannot wait to embrace the one who has embraced the same message of God. Mary's is a fiery haste, not a fearful one. The very encounter of the two women speaks of their enthusiasm about their missions. One cannot but picture the two women rushing at each other and embracing each other with immense energy and joy. Elisabeth speaks first:

> When Elizabeth heard Mary's greeting, the child leaped in her womb. And Elizabeth was filled with the Holy Spirit and exclaimed with a loud cry, "Blessed are you among women, and blessed is the fruit of your womb. And why has this happened to me, that the mother of my Lord comes to me? For as soon as I heard the sound of your greeting, the child in my womb leaped for joy. And blessed is she who believed that there would be a fulfillment of what was spo-ken to her by the Lord."[29]

Elisabeth is so moved by Mary's visit that she leaps with the energy of youth. In her joy, she gives a loud cry, just as some women are wont to do when they meet their loved ones at the airport. It is an encounter of two graced women; it is a graceful encounter. At Elis-abeth's place, Mary not only sees with her own eyes what the angel told her but also receives another Spirit-inspired prophecy about her own place in the history of salvation. Elisabeth is an *intertext* that helps Mary to deepen her understanding of the angel's *text*. At the same time, Mary's pregnancy widens the horizon of Elisabeth's own grace experience and shows that the birth of John is but part of

29. Lk 1:41–45.

God's wider plan of salvation. The two women confirm each other's faith experiences and mitigate the *abnormality* of their situations. A shared abnormality is more bearable than a normal condition borne alone.

Then Mary takes the word and her word takes the form of a song, the *Magnificat*. Mary's song of praise shows her enthusiasm and joy at what God is doing in the world through her: "My soul magnifies the Lord, and my spirit rejoices in God my Savior."[30] In her attempt to make sense of her situation, she borrows the hymn of her ancestor Hannah, who was also graced with the birth of a son against the odds of barrenness. Hannah's song is another *intertext* that helps Mary to relate her experience with the history of the people of Israel. Thus, though God is doing something totally new through her, this event is in continuity with, and a fulfillment of, the work God had begun of old. Mary's pregnancy is in accordance with "the promise he made to our ancestors, to Abraham and to his descendants forever."[31] While Hannah's son Samuel would anoint David as king, Mary's son will inherit the throne of his ancestor David and bring David's kingdom to its consummation in the Kingdom of God. Mary's hermeneutical task is becoming achievable through intertextuality.

Fruit of the Womb

The birth of Jesus is associated with Augustus Caesar's decree that a census should be made of the whole inhabited world,[32] the *oecumene*. The census is a *worldwide* event, pointing to the *ecumenical* scope of Jesus's birth. Already, Mary begins to appear as an actress on the global stage. She and Joseph travel from Nazareth in Galilee to Judaea, to David's town called Bethlehem, because Joseph is of David's lineage.[33] Jesus, heir to David's throne, has to be born in David's own town, in the house of bread, for that is what

---

30. Lk 1:46–47.
31. Lk 1:55.
32. Lk 2:1.
33. Lk 2:4.

Bethlehem means. By juxtaposing the worldwide census and the birth of Jesus in David's town, the narrator would seem to show that Jesus's Kingdom goes well beyond the confines of David's kingdom and embraces the whole inhabited world.

But not all is glorious. Though they are in Joseph's homeland, though they are in David's own town, Mary and Joseph are subjected to a difficult experience: she has to deliver her first-born son in a manger, because there is no room for them in the inn. Whatever pastoral or messianic symbolism may be attributed to this event, one cannot downplay the inconvenience of having to deliver one's first-born son in a squalid environment. Is Mary confused, given the apparent contradiction between the identity and status of the child, on the one hand, and, on the other, the material conditions in which he is born? Does the message of the angel turn into a good-sounding fable? Can she still fall back on Elisabeth's prophecy that Mary is the mother of my Lord? Things do not seem to add up. How can a lord be laid in a manger?

Shepherds and Magi: More Signs

As Mary is trying to reconcile the prophecies about the child and the circumstances in which he is born, God prepares another sign for Mary, perhaps to help her to make sense of what is apparently an impossible puzzle to resolve. An angel appears to shepherds and breaks to them the "good news of great joy for all the people: to you is born this day in the city of David a Savior, who is the Messiah, the Lord."[34] In the angel's message, the two recent events in Mary's life have explicitly been brought together: the universality of Jesus's reign ("great joy for all the people") and the town of David, a symbol of David's throne. Further, Elisabeth's prophecy that Jesus is Lord is also corroborated by the angel's message to the shepherds.

Then the angel gives them a sign: "You will find a child wrapped in bands of cloth and lying in a manger."[35] When the shepherds

---

34. Lk 2:10–11.
35. Lk 2:12.

go to the place of Jesus's birth, they find everything as the angel told them. They are deeply moved by the correspondence between what they see and what the angel told them. The shepherds are given a sign that helps them to find the Christ. Unbeknownst to them, they themselves are a sign to Mary. What they relate helps her to understand more about the child she has just given birth to. The shepherds receive a sign so they can become a sign.

The encounter between Mary and the shepherds is characterized by reciprocity: the shepherds' faith is strengthened by the congruence between the angel's indications and what they see on the ground. In turn, the account of the angels eliminates any shadow of doubt in Mary's heart regarding the truthfulness of what she has heard so far about her son. In her meditation, she perceives the internal consistency of things, in spite of a few apparent bugs.

Shepherds come to pay homage to a descendant of David, who was also a shepherd and was called to shepherd the people of Israel. Jesus himself is the "good shepherd" called to lead to the pasture the people of God.[36] He lies in a manger because he himself will become food for his sheep. He is the bread of life[37] to be broken for the life of the world. That is why he is born at Bethlehem, the house of bread. Mary has to put together all these pieces of the jigsaw puzzle of the mystery of salvation. She treasures "all these things" and ponders them in her heart.[38]

Instead of the visit of the shepherds, Matthew reports the visit of the wise men from the east. The sign by which they know that the "king of the Jews" is born is a star. Herod is perturbed by the news, and he engages the services of chief priests and scribes to determine the location of the birth of the Christ. They inform him that, according to the prophet Micah,[39] the Christ was to be born at Bethlehem in Judaea. The prophet describes the Christ as one who will shepherd the people of God. From the wise men, Herod

---

36. Jn 10:11–14; Ez 34:31.
37. Jn 6:35.
38. Lk 2:16–19.
39. Cf. Micah 5:1.

establishes the exact date on which the star appeared. Meanwhile, the wise men continue with their search, and the star halts over the place where the child is. They go into the house and find the child with his mother Mary. They fall to their knees, do him homage, and offer him gifts of gold, frankincense, and myrrh.[40]

The gesture of bending the knee[41] speaks of the majesty of Jesus. Both the star (cosmic element) and prophecy (verbal element) confirm the birth of the Messiah. Even pagans acknowledge the kingship of Jesus. The gifts offered to the newborn king are reminiscent of Isaiah 60:6: "A multitude of camels shall cover you, the young camels of Midian and Ephah; all those from Sheba shall come. They shall bring gold and frankincense, and shall proclaim the praise of the LORD." The gifts offered are costly and speak of the royal status of Jesus.

Mary has to process these signs and deepen her understanding of the import of her mission and the destiny of her son. The escape to Egypt that follows immediately after the visit of the wise men[42] points to the vulnerability of her son, in spite of all the signs of his greatness heralded by the Magi and the shepherds. Yet, the escape, for all the inconveniences it occasions, is, according to Matthew, a fulfillment of Hosea 11:1: "Out of Egypt I called my son," which prophecy creates a nexus between Jesus and Israel.

Signs in the Temple

When the time comes for Jesus to be presented to the Lord according to the Law of Moses,[43] Mary and Joseph go to the temple in Jerusalem. In that city there is a man named Simeon: "a righteous and devout man" who was "looking forward to the consolation of Israel, and the Holy Spirit rested on him. It had been revealed to

---

40. Mt 2:1–12.

41. The Greek verb here is *proskyneō*, which designates an attitude toward the Risen Lord. Cf. Ulrich Luz and Helmut Koester, *A Commentary on Matthew 1–7* (Minneapolis: Fortress Press, 2007), 114.

42. Mt 2:13–15.

43. Cf. Lev 12:2–4.

him by the Holy Spirit that he would not see death before he had seen the Lord's Messiah."[44] Moved by the Spirit, Simeon comes to the temple and meets Jesus and his parents. He takes the child in his arms and blesses God with the canticle *Nunc Dimittis*: "Master, now you are dismissing your servant in peace, according to your word; for my eyes have seen your salvation, which you have prepared in the presence of all peoples, a light for revelation to the Gentiles and for glory to your people Israel."[45]

Then Simeon makes a prophecy about the child and the mother, to the amazement of the child's parents: "This child," says Simeon, "is destined for the falling and the rising of many in Israel, and to be a sign that will be opposed so that the inner thoughts of many will be revealed—and a sword will pierce your own soul too."[46] At that moment, Anna (the name means mercy or favor), eighty-four-year-old and widowed prophetess, comes up and begins to praise God; she speaks of the child to all who looked forward to the salvation of Jerusalem. From the time her husband died, she has never left the temple, serving God night and day with fasting and prayer.[47]

As in the previous prophecies, the message Mary receives in the temple is ambivalent, marked by the usual *highs* and *lows* of Jesus's and her own destiny. While, on the one hand, Simeon and Anna speak of the child as the fulfillment of the hope of Israel, they also mention the sword that will pierce Mary, because her son is bound to be a sign of contradiction. It is Mary's task to decipher these seemingly contradictory signs in order to create out of this corpus a coherent text.

The encounter in the temple is a complex web of *signs* signaled by the very name of the old man who comes to meet them in the temple. In the Old Testament, Simeon was a name given to one of the sons of Jacob and Leah, and Leah chose this name in order to thank God who had seen that she was not loved by her husband.

---

44. Lk 2:25–26.
45. Lk 2:29–32.
46. Lk 2:33–35.
47. Lk 2:36–38.

In other words, Simeon, related to the root of the Hebrew word for "hearing,"[48] meant that the Lord had heard her prayer.[49] The incarnation of the word of God is a sign that God has heard the prayer of his people who have been waiting for the coming of God's salvation.

Simeon's hymn of praise underscores the joy of *seeing* God's salvation. This theme is redolent of the joy of Jacob, who, in his old age, is granted the opportunity to see his son Joseph again. As he embraces his son, Jacob is moved to tears and says, "I can die now, having seen for myself that you are still alive."[50] Similarly, Anna, Tobit's wife, rejoices upon seeing her son Tobias again. She runs forth and throws her arms round his neck and says, "Now that I have seen you, my child, I am ready to die."[51] Her long-awaited dream has been realized.

The pericope juxtaposes the law and the Spirit, the old (Simeon and Anna) and the new (the baby Jesus),[52] not in antagonism but in the spirit of complementarity. The requirement to observe the Law of Moses becomes an occasion for Mary to receive more signs that confirm what she has heard and seen so far. Indeed, "just as the Roman census [...] resulted in the journey to Bethlehem, so Jewish observance resulted in the journey to Jerusalem."[53] By putting side by side the old and the new, the narrator shows that Jesus is the fulfillment of the old hope, just as the life and ministry of Jesus draw their meaning from the old covenant. In this pericope, "the ancient faithfulness of God meets its new visible manifesta-

---

48. Cf. Dt 6:4.

49. Gen 29:33. Contrary to later hagiography, the Lucan text does not present Simeon as a priest. He is simply one of the devout Jews living in Jerusalem. Cf. François Bovon and Helmut Koester, *Luke 1: A Commentary on the Gospel of Luke 1:1–9:50* (Minneapolis: Fortress Press, 2002), 100.

50. Gen 46:30.

51. Tobit 11:9.

52. The passage balances three references to the law with three mentions of the Spirit. Cf. Bovon and Koester, *Luke 1*, 96.

53. Ibid.

tion, for the same God stands behind both Simeon and Jesus."[54]
It is possible that in writing this pericope Luke draws inspiration
from Malachi 3:1:[55] "See, I am sending my messenger to prepare
the way before me, and the Lord whom you seek will suddenly
come to his temple." Jesus, the awaited angel of great counsel, has
come to his temple.

But the signs offered to Mary are not without tension, even con-
tradictions. First, while the son is a source of joy and a light to the
nations, he is also a sign that will be opposed and is destined for the
"fall and for the rise" of many in Israel. The prophecy resembles the
description of Yahweh in Isaiah: "He will be . . . a stumbling-stone,
a rock to trip up the two Houses of Israel; a snare and a trap for
the inhabitants of Jerusalem, over which many will stumble, fall
and be broken, be ensnared and made captive."[56] Jesus is the sign
of the new covenant; those who follow him will rise, while those
who reject him will fall. For some, Jesus's teaching and actions will
be a scandal, a stumbling block; but for others, he is the power and
the wisdom of God.[57] The rejection of her son, culminating in his
crucifixion and death, will be a sword piercing Mary's heart.

The visit to the temple was an event full of portent signs that
confirm the divine destiny of Mary's son and unveil some of the
challenges Mary has to face in her mission as Mother of God. The
meeting, though triggered by the need to meet the requirements
of the law, is "directed by God"[58] and becomes an occasion for the
fleshing out of the significance of the events that have happened
thus far. As she walks out of the temple Mary has a lot to chew on
in prayer, and she is probably confirmed (strengthened) further
in her faith and vocation. Just as the shepherds received the sign
of the baby Jesus and ended up becoming a sign to Mary, Simeon

---

54. Ibid., 107.

55. Cf. Raymond Brown, *The Birth of the Messiah: A Commentary on the Infancy Narratives in Matthew and Luke* (New York: Doubleday, 1979), 445.

56. Isa 8:14–15; cf. Bovon and Koester, *Luke 1*, 104.

57. 1Cor 1:24.

58. Bovon and Koester, *Luke 1*, 97.

and Anna see in Jesus the sign of God's salvation, and in turn they become a sign of the consistency of all the prophecies she has received thus far.

Finding the Lost Son

In some parishes in Italy, there is a tradition whereby, in the early hours of Good Friday, Christians process with the statue of Our Lady, visiting seven churches in the city. The significance of the procession, it is said, is that Mary is looking for her son. The tradition stems from the events of Holy Thursday, when Jesus is handed over to the Jewish authorities.

This popular devotion is reminiscent of the account of the finding of Jesus in the temple. Jesus (twelve years old) and his parents go up to Jerusalem for the feast of the Passover. When the days of the feast are over, the parents start off home, but the boy Jesus stays behind in Jerusalem without his parents knowing it. After a day's journey, they look, to no avail, for him among their relations and acquaintances. So they return to Jerusalem, searching for him everywhere. Three days later, they find him in the temple, sitting among the teachers, listening to them, and asking them questions. Then the mother says to him, "Child, why have you treated us like this? Look, your father and I have been searching for you in great anxiety."[59] Then Jesus replies, "Why were you searching for me? Did you not know that I must be in my Father's house?"[60] The parents do not understand what he means.[61]

It is difficult to tell why Luke narrates this story. Some are of the opinion that he wants to present Jesus in the light of the heroes in Jewish and Greek biography, who, at the age of twelve, demonstrate superior intelligence. Such heroes include Samuel, Daniel, Cyrus, Cambyses, Alexander, and Epicurus.[62] The difficulty in harmonizing this episode with what comes before may point to the possi-

---

59. Lk 2:48.
60. Lk 2:49.
61. Lk 2:41–50.
62. Cf. Bovon and Koester, *Luke 1*, 111.

bility that this pericope comes from a different tradition dealing with a stage of Jesus's life different from both the infancy and his public ministry. The style of Greek in this passage is also said to be different from that of the rest of the infancy narratives. Originally, Luke's infancy narrative may have ended at verse 40: "The child grew and became strong, filled with wisdom; and the favor of God was upon him." Having inserted the temple episode, Luke would then have added verse 52 in imitation of verse 40. In fact, verse 52 reads, "And Jesus increased in wisdom and in years, and in divine and human favor."[63]

Some scholars see prophecies of the passion and the resurrection in this account. For instance, the *three days* after which the parents find Jesus in the temple would seem to parallel the three days between Jesus's death and resurrection. Jesus's pilgrimage to the temple is but a prefiguration of his pilgrimage to the heavenly temple. This, according to this school of thought, is what Mary does not understand.[64] However, other scholars point out that Jesus is said to have risen "on the third day" and not "after three days."[65]

According to Jean Galot, what Mary fails to understand is the meaning of Jesus's words, "I must be in my Father's house." He explains that the source of Mary's difficulty lies in that, while she speaks of "your father" to refer to Joseph, Jesus responds with "my Father" to designate God. Galot thus affirms that "the episode attests that Jesus' understanding of his sonship ... certainly went far beyond anything his mother knew of his origin."[66]

However, if one considers other details in the account, it becomes difficult to dismiss outright the view that sees passion and

63. Raymond E. Brown, Karl P. Donfried, Joseph A. Fitzmyer, and John Reumann, eds., *Mary in the New Testament: A Collaborative Assessment by Protestant and Roman Catholic Scholars* (Philadelphia: Fortress Press, 1978), 158.

64. Cf. James K. Elliot, "Does Luke 2:41–52 Anticipate the Resurrection?" *Expository Times* 83 (1971): 87–89; René Laurentin, *Jésus au Temple. Mystère de Pâques et foi de Marie en Luc 2. 48–50* (Paris: J. Gabalda, 1966), 159, 182.

65. Cf. Bovon and Koester, *Luke 1*, 111.

66. Jean Galot, *Who Is Christ? A Theology of the Incarnation*, trans. Angeline Bouchard (Rome: Gregorian University Press, 1980), 339.

resurrection motifs in the pericope. First, of all annual feasts, Luke chooses the Passover, the feast associated with Jesus's passion.[67] Second, after the messages and signs Mary has received thus far, it would be difficult to imagine that she would not understand that Jesus is not Joseph's biological son. From the annunciation, Mary knows that Jesus is the Son of the Most High. Probably what she does not understand is the meaning of Jesus's remaining behind in the temple, only to find him three days later. In the summary, Luke repeats the formula, "His mother treasured all these things in her heart."[68] She has to piece together all these signs in order to understand both her son's destiny and her role in the history of salvation.

Interceding for Humanity in Need

In his paschal homily, an ancient Christian writer calls Jesus a *choregos*, that is, a person who finances a party. In this case, the party in question is the paschal festivity, which the author designates "mystical *choregia*."[69] By offering himself as a paschal lamb, Jesus makes it possible for the people of God to celebrate their redemption from slavery.

The image of Jesus as someone who funds a feast is well captured by the story of the wedding at Cana, where Jesus provides wine for the festivity. The story goes that one day Jesus and his disciples attend a wedding at Cana. Jesus's mother, who in the fourth gospel is never mentioned by name,[70] is also present. At a certain point, wine runs out, and Jesus's mother approaches her son to inform him about the problem. Jesus responds with an enigmatic rhetor-

---

67. Cf. Mt 26:17–35; Lk 22:7–23; Jn 19:12–37.

68. Lk 2:51.

69. Cf. Pseudo-Hippolytus, *Homilia in sanctum Pascha* LXII, 1–4, in *La Pasqua nella Chiesa antica*, ed. Raniero Cantalamessa (Turin, Italy: Società Editrice Internazionale, 1978), 27–28.

70. Cf. Ernst Haenchen, *John 1: A Commentary on the Gospel of John Chapters 1–6*, trans. Robert W. Funk (Philadelphia: Fortress Press, 1984), 172.

ical question and a cryptic statement: "Woman, what concern is that to you and to me? My hour has not yet come."[71]

Without access to nonverbal language, it is difficult to determine the tone of the exchange between Jesus and his mother. Is it a playfully jovial conversation between mother and son? Is it a serious and pensive dialogue? The tone of voice would matter in the interpretation of Jesus's answer.[72]

Augustine reads Jesus's intriguing reply in the light of the distinction between the humanity and the divinity of Christ. While the North African father's intention is to refute the claim of heretics that Jesus did not have a human mother, he concedes that Jesus's statement ("Woman, what concern is that to you and to me?") is meant to show that the miracle he is about to perform does not proceed from the order of his humanity but rather from his divinity. The complexity of his argument merits an extensive quotation:

> Our Lord, Jesus Christ, was both God and man. In regard to the fact that he was God, he had no mother; in regard to the fact that he was man, he did. Therefore she was the mother of [his] flesh, the mother of [his] humanity, the mother of the weakness which he took for our sake. But the miracle he was about to do, he was going to do according to [his] divinity, not [his] weakness, in regard to the fact he was a God, not in regard to the fact that he was born weak. But the weakness of God is stronger than men. Therefore his mother demanded a miracle; but he does not, as it were, acknowledge the human womb, as he is about to perform divine deeds, as if saying, "That in me which does a miracle you did not give birth to, you did not give birth to my

71. Jn 2:4.

72. Cf. Rudolf Schnackenburg, *The Gospel According to St. John*, vol. 1: *Introduction and Commentary on Chapters 1–4*, trans. Kevin Smyth (New York: Herder and Herder, 1968), 328–29.

divinity; but because you bore my weakness, I shall recognize you then, when that weakness will hang on the cross."[73]

Augustine's argument is that Mary did not give birth to the divinity of Christ, for Jesus was God even before the incarnation. By the same token, it was the humanity of Jesus (taken from Mary)—not his eternal divinity—that died on the cross. As Augustine writes, "For that through which Mary had been made was not dying, but that which was made from Mary was dying. The eternity of [his] divinity was not dying, but the weakness of [his] flesh was dying."[74] Augustine continues that when Jesus says, "My hour has not yet come," he is referring to the hour of his death, when the flesh he received from Mary will be subjected to passion and death. But for the time being, when Jesus is about to act according to his divinity, he will, as it were, put in brackets Mary's role as his mother according to the flesh. And that is why he calls her "woman" instead of "mother."

It is important to recognize the theological milieu of Augustine's convoluted argumentation. While seeming to diminish Mary's status as the Mother of God (*Theotokos*), Augustine is actually fighting the heretics who did not even want to accept that the Son of God had a mother at all. Augustine, therefore, holds fast to the statement that Jesus's mother was at the wedding to show that the Evangelist acknowledges that Jesus had a mother.

Returning to the gospel narrative, it is fascinating that Mary does not seek further clarification, nor does she verbally persuade her son to do something; instead, she turns to the servants and tells them to "do whatever he tells you."[75] And surely Jesus instructs them to fill six huge jars with water. He then tells them to draw out some and to take it to the steward of the feast. When the steward

---

73. Augustine, *Tractates on the Gospel of John*, Tractate VIII, 9, 1, trans. John W. Rettig, The Fathers of the Church, vol. 78 (Washington, DC: Catholic University of America Press, 1988), 188.

74. Ibid., VIII, 9, 2.

75. Jn 2:5.

tastes it, he discovers it is good wine, better than what they have been drinking thus far. This is the first of Jesus's *signs* through which he manifests his glory.[76]

Mary seems to understand that her son has the power to provide wine to the nuptial community. Given that it is the first of Jesus's *signs* (miracles), Mary's perception of her son's power is mystical. Her faith in the son is the "assurance of things hoped for, the conviction of things unseen."[77] On the basis of what she has seen and heard so far, she is confident in her son's capacity to come to the aid of a people in need. So she facilitates the launching of her son's series of *signs* of the Kingdom. In other words, "Mary has sensed that Jesus will act, even though his answer remains mysterious to her. Unassumingly she does her best to facilitate her Son's intervention—hers is a delicate touch, which is in keeping with the biblical picture of Mary: hers is a faith from which the mysteries of the divine plans are ultimately concealed."[78]

John Chrysostom compares Mary to the Syro-Phoenician woman who, in spite of Jesus's apparent rejection to heed her request, perseveres in her request until Jesus grants her desire. When Jesus initially seemed to turn the Syro-Phoenician woman away by declaring that it is not right to give the children's food to dogs, the woman insisted. Similarly, when Jesus tells Mary that his hour has not yet come, Mary still goes ahead and mobilizes the servants so they can be at standby for Jesus's intervention. "From this," concludes Chrysostom, "we learn that even if we are unworthy of receiving our request, often we make ourselves worthy by our perseverance to do so. That is why His Mother both persevered and wisely brought the servants to Him, so that the request might come from more people."[79] Her knowledge of the vocation of her

---

76. Cf. Jn 2:1–11; Schnackenburg, *The Gospel According to St. John*, 334–37.

77. Heb 11:1.

78. Schnackenburg, *The Gospel According to St. John*, 331.

79. John Chrysostom, *Commentary on Saint John the Apostle and Evangelist*, *Homily* 21, trans. Thomas A. Goggin, Fathers of the Church, vol. 33 (New York: Fathers of the Church, 1957), 215.

son as the embodiment of the providence of God makes her persevere in her request.

Mary uses her closeness to the Son of God to intercede for the family hosting the event. The wedding at Cana is but the beginning of Mary's ministry of intercession for humanity. Since then, Christians have never ceased to approach her, asking her to petition her son to provide various kinds of *wine* to a humanity thirsting for God's love. It is on account of her faith in her son that she can approach him and tell him that humanity has no wine. Out of his abundance, Jesus finances the paschal banquet for the entire human race.

Jesus's mother invites all God's children to do what Jesus tells them to do, echoing, as it were, the Father's words at the transfiguration of Jesus: "This is my Son, my Chosen; listen to him!"[80] At the transfiguration, the disciples are asked to listen to Jesus, while at Cana, Mary gives an explicitly performative value to the "listening"; she tells the servants to "do" whatever Jesus tells them. It is by "hearing" and "doing" the word of Jesus that one becomes a mother, a brother, or a sister of Jesus: "My mother and my brothers are those who hear the word of God and do it,"[81] says Jesus. Rightly, when a certain woman once exclaimed from the crowd, "Blessed is the womb that bore you and the breasts that nursed you,"[82] Jesus's immediate rejoinder was, "Blessed rather are those who hear the word of God and obey it!"[83]

John Chrysostom explains thus Jesus's reply to the woman's exclamation: "The reply is not that of one rejecting his mother, but of one who shows that her motherhood would not have been of profit to her if she herself were not virtuous and obedient."[84] Augustine similarly argues that Mary is the mother of Jesus because she did the Father's will, not simply because she begot Jesus in the

---

80. Lk 9:35.
81. Lk 8:21.
82. Lk 11:27.
83. Lk 11:28.
84. Chrysostom, *Commentary on Saint John*, Homily 21.

flesh. Paraphrasing Jesus's reply to the woman in the crowd, Augustine writes, "My mother whom you have called happy is happy for the reason that she keeps the Word of God, not that the Word was made flesh in her and dwelt among us, but that she keeps the very Word of God through which she was made and which was made flesh in her."[85] Spiritual union with God is more valuable than temporal offspring, adds Augustine. At Cana, Mary teaches others to enter into the spirit of her performative *fiat*. She anticipates Jesus's teaching that whoever hears his word and does it is like a wise person who built his house on the rock.[86]

Mary, Mother of Jesus's Disciples

After the miracle at Cana, Mary maintains her silence up to the end of the gospel accounts. During Jesus's passion and death, she stands at the foot of the cross:

> Standing near the cross of Jesus were his mother, and his mother's sister, Mary the wife of Clopas, and Mary Magdalene. When Jesus saw his mother and the disciple whom he loved standing beside her, he said to his mother, "Woman, here is your son." Then he said to the disciple, "Here is your mother." And from that hour the disciple took her into his own home.[87]

The mother of Jesus, together with a few other disciples, does not abandon her son in the hour of his passion and death. Whereas in Mark the women who followed Jesus are placed at a distance,[88] John places them at the foot of the cross. Their standing at the foot of the cross is the highest expression of solidarity with the rejected and crucified Jesus. John Chrysostom marvels at the manner things

---

85. Augustine, *Tractates on the Gospel of John*, Tractate X, 3, 2.
86. Mt 7:24.
87. Jn 19:25–27.
88. Cf. Mk 15:40–41.

were turned upside-down in the sense that the "weaker sex at that time appeared the stronger."[89]

Mary is not left alone before the almost incomprehensible *sign* from God. Just as in the infancy narratives she was in the company of Elisabeth, Simeon, Anna, the shepherds, the Magi, and others, she now stands together with some women and one of the male disciples. Sorrow shared is more bearable than joy savored alone.

Mary is there, perhaps in tears, perhaps speechless. The death of her son is a difficult *sign* to decipher, except if she remembers what Jesus once said: "When I am lifted up from the earth, will draw all people to myself."[90] Earlier in the same gospel account, Jesus compared himself to the bronze serpent Moses raised on the standard in the desert, and all who gazed upon it received life: "Just as Moses lifted up the serpent in the wilderness, so must the Son of Man be lifted up, that whoever believes in him may have eternal life."[91] The crucified one is a sign and source of salvation for the world. In that lowliest moment, God raises up the sign of salvation.

Then Jesus performs a gesture of utmost importance: he hands over his disciple to Mary, addressing her as "woman." Prior to this event, Mary had heard him call her "woman" at the wedding at Cana. In the Marian piety of the twelfth century, Mary came to be related to the figure of Eve or the "messianic Zion[92] giving birth to her children."[93] Some contemporary Catholic exegetes, such as Raymond Brown, see in this gesture Mary becoming the mother of Jesus's disciples and therefore mother of the church. In this interpretation, Brown follows the reflection of Ambrose of Milan, who, in his commentary on the Gospel of Luke, presents Mary at the

---

89. John Chrysostom, *Commentary on Saint John*, Homily 85, trans. Thomas A. Goggin, Fathers of the Church, vol. 33 (New York: Fathers of the Church, 1957), 433.

90. Jn 12:32.

91. Jn 3:14–15.

92. Cf. Isa 66:7–11.

93. Pheme Perkins, "The Gospel According to John," in *The New Jerome Biblical Commentary*, ed. Raymond E. Brown et al. (London: Geoffrey Chapman, 1990), 982.

foot of the cross as a figure of the church to whom Christians are entrusted.[94] Brown also reads John 19:26 in the light of Genesis 2:4, where Adam gives birth to a son and names him Cain because "with the help of God I have begotten a man." By adopting the beloved disciple, Mary, as it were, begets a son, a disciple of Jesus.[95]

While these interpretations are plausible, one could also analyze the contexts in which Jesus uses the term *woman* in the Gospel According to John, in which he addresses someone as "woman" on three different occasions: at Cana, at the cross, and by the empty tomb. At Cana, the people are in need of wine, and Mary shares in their distress. She approaches her son with an implicit request for help. In his reply, Jesus calls her "woman." While on the cross, Jesus looks at his mother in sorrow. She is a woman in need of consolation. Jesus addresses her again as "woman" and gives her the disciple as her son. In fact, John Chrysostom presents the gesture as a sign of Jesus's solicitude for his grief-stricken mother: "Since he himself was now departing, he entrusted her to the disciple to take care of. Because as his mother she would naturally be grief-stricken and need a protector, with good reason he placed her in the keeping of his beloved disciple."[96]

Augustine, instead, creates a contrast between the Cana and Golgotha events; while at Cana, Jesus was acting out of his divine nature and therefore did not, as it were, recognize Mary as the mother of his divinity; at the cross it is the humanity of Christ that is thrown into the foreground, since it is according to the weakness of the flesh that Jesus drinks the chalice of his passion and death. Therefore, he acknowledges Mary as mother, that is, mother of the suffering flesh. Augustine writes, "[At Cana], as he was about to perform divine deeds, he rebuffed as though unknown the mother, not of his divinity, but of his weakness; but now, enduring human

---

94. Cf. Ambrose of Milan, *Traité sur l'Evangile de s. Luc* VII, 10, ed. Gabriel Tissot, SCh, vol. 52 (Paris: Cerf, 1958), 12.

95. Cf. Raymond E. Brown, *The Gospel According to John*, vol. 2 (Basingstoke, UK: Pickering & Inglis, 1983), 925–26.

96. Chrysostom, *Commentary on Saint John*, Homily 85.

sufferings, with human affection he commended her from whom he had been made man. For then [at Cana] he who had created Mary was making himself known by power, but now That to which Mary had given birth was hanging on the cross."[97] This contrast notwithstanding, it is clear that Augustine discerns a connection between the use of the word "woman" for Mary.

In the third instance, Mary of Magdala is weeping at the tomb and asking to know where the body of the Lord has been placed. Evidently, she is a woman in distress and in sorrow. Jesus addresses her as "woman" and then consoles her by revealing himself to her. Thus, it would appear that in John there is a specific way in which Jesus uses the term *woman*, and in all three instances, the addressee is in distress and in need of some form of consolation.

Beasley-Murray remarks that Jesus's "brief words to his mother and the disciple are not just a commendation or suggestion; they are more like a testamentary disposition, in language reminiscent of adoption."[98] Jesus makes use of his right, even as a crucified man, to make a testament, which he presents using the official formula of the old Jewish law.[99] The beloved disciple becomes the official custodian of Jesus's mother, while he is in turn given to Mary as son.

Believing without Seeing?

No gospel account relates an encounter between the Risen Lord and his mother. For Ignatius of Loyola, this is an anomaly, for how could Jesus not appear to his own mother after the resurrection! To fill in this lacuna, Ignatius inserts a contemplation in which the Risen Lord appears to his mother before appearing to the rest of the disciples. In his description of the Lord's first apparition, Ignatius writes,

---

97. Augustine, *Tractates on the Gospel of John*, Tractate 119, 1, trans. John W. Rettig, The Fathers of the Church, vol. 92 (Washington, DC: Catholic University of America Press, 1995), 45.

98. George R. Beasley-Murray, *John*, Word Biblical Commentary, vol. 36 (Dallas, TX: Word, 2002), 349.

99. Cf. Tobit 7:12.

He appeared to the Virgin Mary. Although this is not
stated in Scripture, still it is considered as understood by
the statement that he appeared to many others. For Scripture supposes that we have understanding, as it is written,
"Are you without understanding?" (Matt 15:16).[100]

Ignatius is convinced that it is only after the apparition to the
Virgin Mary that Jesus appears to Mary Magdalene, Mary the
mother of James, and Salome.[101] The third apparition, according to
Ignatius, is that recounted in Matthew 28:8–10. In the absence of
scriptural support, Ignatius falls back on the Lord's appearance to
"many others" to add the appearance to Mary. But a question can
be asked: Why do the evangelists not mention Mary the mother of
Jesus in the resurrection accounts? Why should Mary be lumped
together with an anonymous "many others"? Do the resurrection
apparitions serve a purpose that Mary may not need? Does Jesus
appear only to those who need to be confirmed in their faith, those
who have been so devastated by the passion and death of Jesus that
they risk losing the little faith they have? To answer this question,
it is important to review the resurrection accounts and determine
the state of mind in which the recipients of the apparitions are.

In Mark 16:1–8, Mary Magdalene, Mary the mother of James,
and Salome bring spices to anoint Jesus. On the way to Jesus's
tomb, they wonder who will roll back the stone for them from the
entrance of the tomb. But when they look up, they see the stone
already rolled back. They enter the tomb and find a young man sitting on the right side, clothed in white garments. They are utterly
amazed, but the young man tells them not to be amazed, for Jesus
whom they seek is not here, he is risen. The women are seized
with fear and go out bewildered, saying nothing to anyone. In this
account, it is not clear whether the women understand the *signs* of
the resurrection at the tomb and the message of the young man.

---

100. Ignatius of Loyola, *The Spiritual Exercises* [hereafter Exx], no. 299,
trans. George E. Ganss (Anand: Gujarat Sahitya Prakash, 1993), 116.
101. Cf. Mk 16:1–11.

One thing is clear: they are amazed and afraid. They need to be strengthened in their faith in the resurrection.

A slightly different version of the story is found in Matthew 28:1–10.[102] The women go to the tomb and there is a great earthquake, during which an angel descends from heaven, rolls back the stone, and sits on it. The angel tells them not to be afraid, for Jesus whom they seek is not here; he has been raised from the dead just as he said.[103] The women leave the tomb in haste, "fearful and over-joyed," but on the way Jesus meets them and tells them, "Do not be afraid; go and tell my brothers to go to Galilee; there they will see me."[104] In this story, before the encounter with the Risen Lord the women experience a mixture of fear and joy, and the Lord appears to them to remove the fear so that they may return home with pure joy.

In the story of the Emmaus disciples, their discussion about the "things that happened to Jesus the Nazarene" shows that they have not understood the meaning of Jesus's passion and death; nor is their faith in the resurrection firm. They seem to have lost hope: "But we had hoped that he was the one to redeem Israel. Yes, and besides all this, it is now the third day since these things took place."[105] The accounts of the women who came from the tomb may not have convinced them.[106]

From their description of the events, Jesus establishes that they are "slow of heart to believe all that the prophets have declared."[107] They need to be taken through the law and the Prophets to understand that Jesus was destined to suffer and die in order to enter into his glory. Yet, that lesson does not suffice; Jesus's words set their hearts on fire, but they cannot put their finger on what it all means

---

102. Cf. Lk 24:1–12.
103. Mt 28:5.
104. Mt 28:10.
105. Lk 24:21.
106. Lk 24:22–24.
107. Lk 24:25.

until he breaks the bread for them. The Emmaus disciples needed help to believe in the resurrection.

The Johannine resurrection account also underlines the lack of comprehension on the part of the disciples. Mary of Magdala goes to the tomb early in the morning, she finds the stone removed from the tomb and she runs back to Simon Peter to tell him that "they have taken the Lord out of the tomb, and we do not know where they have laid him."[108] When Peter and the beloved disciple go to inspect the tomb, they find Jesus's burial clothes rolled up, and the beloved disciple sees and believes, "for as yet they did not understand the scripture, that he must rise from the dead."[109]

Mary of Magdala stands outside the tomb weeping. As she weeps, she bends over into the tomb and sees two angels in white sitting where Jesus had been buried. They say to her, "Woman, why are you weeping?"[110] to which she replies, "They have taken away my Lord, and I do not know where they have laid him." When she turns, she sees a man, whom she mistakes for a gardener. The man asks her again, "Woman, why are you weeping? Whom are you looking for?"[111] Mary tells him that she wants to know where they have placed the body of the Lord, and then Jesus calls her by name: "Mary!" At that point she recognizes him and embraces him. Here, again, Mary's faith in the resurrection needed some help, for her eyes were so full of tears that she could not see beyond the tomb. The extended dialogue is Jesus's pedagogy for bringing Mary to the gradual awareness that he has risen. As it were, Jesus walks her through the signs of the resurrection before manifesting himself to her.

In the account of the Lord's appearance to the disciples, John emphasizes that the disciples stay behind locked doors for fear of the Jews.[112] Jesus appears to them and shows them his hands and

---

108. Jn 20:2.
109. Jn 20:9.
110. Jn 20:13.
111. Jn 20:15.
112. Jn 20:19.

his side. They rejoice when they see him. But Thomas is not present when the Lord appears to them. When Thomas returns, they relate to him what they have seen, but Thomas refuses to believe until he sees the mark of the nails in Jesus's hands and puts the finger into Jesus's nail marks and into his side. Thomas's doubt is categorical; so Jesus comes back almost a week later and lets Thomas put his finger into Jesus's side, at which point Thomas exclaims, "My Lord and my God!"[113] Thomas's faith in the resurrection needed the help of the Lord's apparition.

Now, what can one infer from the evangelists' silence on the apparition of the Risen Lord to his mother? Could it mean that her faith in the resurrection is so firm that she does not need the help of the Lord's appearance? "Have you believed because you have seen me? Blessed are those who have not seen and yet have come to believe,"[114] says Jesus to Thomas the Twin. Can Mary be said to be one of those "blessed" who believe in the resurrection of the Lord even without seeing him? In the Johannine resurrection accounts, the beloved disciple is said to have believed *after* seeing the *signs* in the empty tomb.[115] He "sees" the burial clothes in the tomb and then believes. Mary the mother of Jesus does not even go to the tomb. One cannot but recall Elisabeth's prophecy before Mary breaks out in the *Magnificat*: "Blessed is she who believed that there would be a fulfillment of what was spoken to her by the Lord."[116]

It would appear that, from all that she has heard and seen right from the annunciation up to the Lord's passion and death, Mary's faith in the resurrection is rendered solid and does not need further props. If she saw the Risen Lord, she did so because she was in the company of the other disciples, not because her faith needed to be purified, illumined, and reinforced.

However, there is something to be gained from the Ignatian

---

113. Jn 20:28.
114. Jn 20:29.
115. Jn 20:8.
116. Lk 1:45.

contemplation of the apparition of the Risen Lord to his mother. One of the reasons to justify this contemplation is linked with the Risen Lord's ministry of consolation. During the *Triduum mortis*, reasons Gaston Fessard, our Lady was afflicted with sorrow on account of her son's suffering, death, and descent to hell. Christ's apparition to her thus helps Mary to pass over from the negative state of sorrow to the positive state of celestial joy. Structurally, continues Fessard, opening the Fourth Week with the apparition to Mary creates continuity with the Third Week, which closes with the affliction and solitude of our Lady.[117]

In a similar vein, Adrien Demoustier discerns parallels between the incarnation and the resurrection. In the former, the Son of God assumed human flesh, and at the resurrection the soul of Christ, which had been separated from the body, is reunited to the risen body. Since it is through Mary that the Son of God assumed flesh, it is reasonable that Mary should be the first witness of the unity of the soul and body of the Risen Lord as well. Further, in the contemplation of the Incarnation, Ignatius presents Mary as the first human being to receive the good news of the Incarnation of the Son of God.[118] In the composition of place, Ignatius invites the retreatant to see the "place or house of our Lady. I will note its different parts, and also her room, her oratory, etc."[119] It is at the same place where, according to Ignatius's imagination, the annunciation took place. By locating the first apparition of the Risen Lord at the very place of the annunciation, Ignatius throws into high relief the fact that the resurrection is the completion of the work of redemption begun at the incarnation.[120]

One can also focus on Ignatius's mention of Mary's oratory as a pointer to Mary's spirit of prayer and recollection. The worst has

---

117. Cf. Exx 208; Gaston Fessard, *La dialectique des Exercices Spirituels de Saint Ignace de Loyola*, Études Publiées souls la Direction de la Faculté de Théologie S.J. de Lyon-Fourvière, vol. 53 (Paris: Editions Montaigne, 1956), 132–33.

118. Cf. Exx 102–108.

119. Exx 220.

120. Cf. Adrien Demoustier, *Les Exercices Spirituels de s. Ignace de Loyola. Lecture et pratique d'un texte* (Paris: Editions Facultés Jésuites, 2006), 389–96.

happened to her, but she remains solid in her faith and returns to her oratory to meditate in her heart all that has just happened. It is thanks to her prayerful spirit that she can see beyond the dark clouds of Calvary and the stifling narrowness of the tomb.

Conclusion

The story of Mary shows that she is a mother whose life is inseparably linked to her son's life, ministry, death, and resurrection. In her life and vocation, she is sustained by key messages and signs that help her to make sense of and to carry out her unique role in the history of salvation. She draws strength from a community of believers who, each in his or her own way, confirm the message she received from the angel Gabriel. Like the first parents, Mary walks in the *garden* of signs and becomes familiar with the works of God's hands. She meditates on every sign from God. It is this familiarity with God's words and actions that enables her to recognize in the cross the *tree of life* through which the whole world receives God's salvation. Her faith in the resurrection is firm and unshakable, even in the wake of the dark clouds that descend on Good Friday. She is truly the Mother of God and the mother of all believers. She is the mother of meditation.

Prayer

God our Father, to accomplish your plan of salvation you chose Mary to be the tabernacle of Jesus Christ your Son; you sustained her faith with signs and wonders; you opened her heart and mind to the secrets of your plan, and she rejoiced to be a humble instrument of the salvation prepared for your peoples. Through her intercession, strengthen the faith of your people, especially those being tested in various ways, so that we too may rejoice to bear fruits of your Kingdom. Through Christ your Son and our Lord. Amen.

Part III

Mothers of the Christian Tradition

Chapter 14

Felicitas and Perpetua: Mothers in Chains

Introduction

It is a given that many of us would rather compromise our convictions, creeds, or confessions than put in jeopardy the lives of our own children. Countless women are stuck in dysfunctional marriages just for the sake of their children. A mother's love can mollify the staunchest of her principles in order to ensure the well-being of her children. But this was not the case with Perpetua and Felicitas (also known as Felicity), two African Christian mothers of the early third century, who, for the sake of Christ, forewent the consolation of nursing their own infants. They loved Christ more than their children.

Vivia (or Vibia) Perpetua and Felicitas were catechumens and then Christians, from Carthage (modern-day Tunisia), in North Africa. They suffered martyrdom in the early third century. During the reign of Lucius Septimius Severus (AD 145–211), conversion to Christianity or to Judaism was prohibited, especially since Christians refused to be conscripted into the military. They also refused to participate in religious events of the Roman Empire, such as sacrificing to pagan gods for the health of emperors. Consequently, persecution against Christians ensued, and both Christianity and the catechumenate were banned. Perpetua and Felicitas were among the catechumens apprehended by the government and forced to renounce their Christian faith and to sacrifice to the gods.[1]

Perpetua: Suffering the Loss of All Things

"I remember three years ago looking into the entrance pool of Julia's stately domus and finding I was beautiful." So opens Amy Rachel Peterson's historical novel entitled *Perpetua: A Bride, a Martyr, a Passion*, which imaginatively reconstructs, on the basis of the historical nucleus provided in Perpetua's diary, the three years of Perpetua's life before her martyrdom in 203.[2] Peterson imagines Perpetua contemplating her own newly discovered beauty— for hitherto she never thought herself beautiful—reflected in the fountain waters. While the opening of the novel presents her as a woman absorbed in her own beauty, a narcissist of a sort, Perpetua was later to become aware that the baptismal bath would give her a beauty surpassing all beauty afforded by the accessories of human civilization. The waters of baptism would make her desirable in the eyes of the heavenly groom who saw the immense beauty of her soul. Perpetua's is thus a story of a passionate soul that abandons everything in order to attain the love of Christ, the heavenly groom.

The historical details of Perpetua's life before her conversion to Christianity are difficult to determine. Historical accounts report that Perpetua came from a noble family and had received a reasonably good education. Her father was probably a man of good standing in society and was determined to bring his children up in the best manner possible. Contrary to the popular belief in a Roman predilection for male children, Perpetua's father had a preference for his daughter.

In her penetrating imagination, Amy Peterson presents the

---

1. Cf. Alban Butler, *Butler's Lives of the Saints: March*, revised by Teresa Rodrigues (Collegeville, MN: Liturgical Press, 1999), 60.

2. Amy R. Peterson, *Perpetua: A Bride, a Martyr, a Passion* (Lake Mary, FL: Relevant Books, 2004).

young Perpetua picking her way along the rough road, paved with cobblestones and gravel, to give homage to "the maze of nebulous gods and goddesses,"[3] particularly Isis at whose temple Perpetua finds herself paradoxically drawn to and repelled by the intonation of the morning prayers. Most of the devotees of Isis are widows who, as Perpetua imagines, are probably simply trying to escape the obligation to remarry. She is aware that as a virgin her presence at Isis's shrine may come across as a little awkward and out of sync with popular religious usage. Nonetheless, she goes ahead and buys Spanish wine, which she pours before the stone statue of the goddess. Perpetua is conscious of her lukewarm religiosity in comparison with, for instance, the ardent devotion of a certain woman who says her prayers with a great sense of animation, waving her hands in the air. This devotee, later identified as Lady Julia (Aelius's wife,[4] who the previous night had indulged in a drunken dance with a certain Marius and therefore went to Isis to expiate her sins), concludes her prayers by kissing the base of the statue.[5] Isis is not the only deity Julia pays homage to: she prays to Venus at night and to Isis in the morning.

In her ensuing conversation with Julia, Perpetua exudes a critical attitude toward pagan religious tenets, which makes Julia gently reprimand her: "How can you speak against the gods like that? You act as if you know better than they."[6] Then Julia goes on to attribute to Christianity—which she calls an "illegal cult"—all the horrible things that ever happen. Julia's invective against Christians is unrelenting: "When truly horrible things are done, Perpetua, godless people do them. You know of that illegal cult, those Christ-followers. They deny all the gods of Rome. Those people commit the most unspeakable atrocities. It is terrible even to think of

---

3. Ibid., 6.

4. Aelius Hilarianus was senior procurator of Carthage at the time. Cf. Thomas Heffernan, review of *Perpetua's Passions: Multidisciplinary Approaches to the Passio Perpetuae et Felicitatis, Church History* 83 (2014): 723.

5. Peterson, *Perpetua*, 7.

6. Ibid., 13.

them."[7] Among the "atrocities" attributed to Christians are incest and cannibalism. Even the abandoned children Christians adopt and look after are dismissed as children from the *cesspools*. More seriously Julia claims that the Christians eat the flesh and drink the blood of these helpless children.

Though Perpetua is not yet a Christian, she responds to Julia's slander of the new religion with a dose of skepticism, maintaining that such accusations are mainly based on the ignorance of what Christians really do in their secret rites. In her heart, Perpetua finds it hypocritical to accuse Christians of cannibalism when the people of Carthage sacrifice their children to the gods, which practice Perpetua thinks evil, especially given that both the people and the gods do not seem to know that it is evil to sacrifice children.

From her brother Saturninus, Perpetua hears about a certain writer called Tertullian who writes what Saturninus calls apologetics, namely writings in defense of the Christian faith. Saturninus has read Tertullian's works, which their father, though not a sympathizer of Christianity, has acquired and keeps in his library. In fact, Perpetua's father calls Tertullian an idiot and Christians enemies of the state. Whether out of conviction or simply to placate her father, Perpetua agrees with her father's evaluation of Christians as atheists and cannibals. Saturninus, however, objects to such an accusation and entertains the idea that Christianity might as well be the best thing that ever happened to Rome.[8]

Perpetua later discovers that Nana, the deceased aunt of Perpetua's personal servant Selina, used to pray to Jesus. Perpetua initially mistakes Jesus for a goddess and Selina corrects her that Jesus is not a she, he is the Messiah! Selina adds that Nana believed that Jesus was the only God.[9]

One day, Perpetua pulls Tertullian's book and starts to read it. She finds his words sweet and pure; unfortunately, she has to put the book away when she hears her father's voice and noncha-

---

7. Ibid., 14.
8. Ibid., 22–23.
9. Ibid., 25.

lantly picks up Plato's book instead.[10] When Saturninus finds her overwhelmed with sadness, he confides in her that he believes in Tertullian's God, adding that this God is the only reality big enough to console and answer Perpetua's questions. In fact, Saturninus, Perpetua's younger brother, is a Christian! This sudden, unexpected confession fills Perpetua with fear and anxiety that her only brother could be killed. But Saturninus assures her with an equally terrifying declaration: "God has told me one thing, Perpetua. I will not die before you do."[11] Saturninus then gives her a little catechism class modeled on Tertullian's apologetic approach that appeals to people's tacit knowledge and acknowledgment of the one true God.

Subsequently, Perpetua learns from her father that even Claudia (Perpetua's mother) and her uncle have *fallen prey* to Christianity. A little earlier, in fact, her mother had mentioned to her that she no longer sacrificed to Isis. Her father, an avowed objectivist, informs her that the mother, who has far less education than Perpetua, has to undergo three years of *indoctrination* before she is baptized into the *disgusting cult*. When the festival of Tanit comes around, Claudia does not throw the banquet as she used to do before her conversion to the new religion. On that particular day, Perpetua's mother confesses to believing that "Jesus Christ is the only God."[12]

The festival of Tanit marks Perpetua's turning point. On that very day, Tumnus, Lespia's son (Lespia being Selina's sister), a child very dear to Perpetua, is sacrificed to Ba'al. Perpetua gets a hint about the impending sacrifice from her mother, and the former hastens to save the little boy. Unfortunately, she arrives a little too late at the scene of the sacrifice, for the priest has already put his hand on the little child lying on a low table. The gory sight of the toddler's torso dripping with blood being cast into the red-hot embers intoxicates Perpetua with rage and sends her shouting to

---

10. Ibid., 32.
11. Ibid., 36.
12. Ibid., 43.

Ba'al and Tanit, "You are not good. You are not God."[13] When she survives the chase of defenders of the gods, she ends up in an unfamiliar place called a basilica, the worshipping place of Christians. Saturninus is there with other Christians. There Saturninus and a bearded elder—none other than Tertullian himself—give her Christian instruction. They narrate to her the story of Jesus—his preexistence, public ministry, death, and resurrection. At the end of the long session, Perpetua embraces the new deity. Jesus is no longer Tertullian's God but also hers.[14]

Amy Peterson's creative reconstruction of the life of Perpetua shows, among other things, the hostility that Christians suffered in the early centuries before Christianity became legal in the Roman Empire. In such an environment, conversion to Christianity was a risky affair. Peterson shows how Perpetua's conversion to, and perseverance in, the Christian faith was partly aided by members of her own family (her mother, her brother, and Selina her personal servant) who had already embraced the faith. The evils of pagan religion, especially child sacrifice, also contributed to her repudiation of the gods. The favorable conditions notwithstanding, Perpetua's faith journey was full of trials, leading to the ultimate sacrifice of her own life.

Carrying the Cross

It is possible that Perpetua later married, though it is not clear who the husband was. One of the hypotheses is that he abandoned her when she converted to Christianity, perhaps to shield himself from the unsavory consequences of his wife's conversion.

Having refused to comply with the government order to renounce her Christian faith, Perpetua was arrested together with other catechumens: Felicitas, Revocatus, Saturninus, and Secundulus. While awaiting judgment, they received baptism, which step aggravated their crime. As Perpetua recounts, "Precisely within

---

13. Ibid., 57.
14. Ibid., 70.

the space of these days we received baptism; and the Spirit told me to ask of the water [of baptism] nothing but the power to endure the suffering of the flesh."[15]

They were subsequently brought to the municipal prison and locked up in a very dark dungeon. The horrible darkness of Roman prisons was one of the worst punishments of Christian martyrs, who saw in this darkness the abode of the devil. Perpetua was twenty-two years old and had a little child whom she was still nursing. Fortunately, she was allowed moments of respite in a sort of interior courtyard. She would take advantage of the few moments of her *relaxation* in the courtyard to suckle her baby.

For the Sake of the Child

For Perpetua, the pressure to renounce her Christian faith and to return to the pagan religion came directly from her father, who saw in her conversion not only foolhardiness but also a source of shame for the family, which was of noble standing. Christianity was then considered to be a religion for lowly people and slaves.[16] Her conversion was therefore a public scandal and an embarrassment to the family. The father was thus determined not only to save his daughter's life but also to salvage the reputation of the family.

The father visited Perpetua several times and tearfully pleaded with her to change her mind and to renounce her newly embraced faith. He implored her, "Have pity, my daughter, on my grey hair; have pity on your father. If I merit to receive from you the name of

---

15. *Passion of Perpetua and Felicity* III, 5, in *Passion de Perpétue et de Félicité suivi des Actes*, ed. Jacqueline Amat, SCh, vol. 417 (Paris: Cerf, 1996), 108. Translation mine.

16. Recent studies, however, show that by the third century, Christianity was already attracting men and women from the upper echelons of Roman society. This was probably in reaction to the inadequacies of traditional pagan religions, the complexities of mystery cults, and the inflexibility of ascetic philosophical traditions. Christianity was especially attractive to women because of its emphasis on equality of all in Christ. Cf. William Farina, *Perpetua of Carthage: Portrait of a Third-Century Martyr* (Jefferson, NC: McFarland Publishers, 2009), 3.

father . . . , if it is true that I have preferred you to all your brothers, do not make of me an object of shame before people."[17] Perpetua felt pity for her father; however, she refused to budge. She argued that just as a pitcher could not be called by any other name, she too could not change her name of Christian.

Sympathetic to Perpetua's father, Roman magistrates weighed in to dissuade Perpetua from adhering to her Christian faith so that she could save her life and the good name of her family. The gesture they asked her to perform was, in their opinion, so little that any Roman in his or her right mind would not refuse to do it in order to save one's life: they were *only* asking her to sacrifice to the gods for the health of emperors.

But the greatest pressure by far came from the fact that she had a little child who needed her care, love, and protection. She writes,

> Now, coming out of the prison, each one of us was free to attend to his or her occupations: for me, I suckled my child already half dead from hunger. Anxious for him, I would speak to my mother about it and I would comfort my brother and I would entrust them with my son . . . Later, I obtained the permission to keep the child with me in prison; and soon I felt better, I was relieved of the pain and the anxiety which I suffered on account of my son.[18]

In his attempt to dissuade his daughter from embracing martyrdom, Perpetua's father often reminded her about her child: "Think of your son who after [your death] will not be able to live,"[19] he would say. On the day of interrogation (leading to her condemnation), the father came again carrying in his arms Perpetua's son. The father said, "Sacrifice [to the gods] and have pity on your little child," to which Hilarianus the senior procurator added, "Save the

---

17. *Passion* V, 2.
18. *Passion* III, 8–9.
19. *Passion* V, 3.

grey hair of your father, save your little child. Offer the sacrifice for the health of the emperors!"[20]

Perpetua was so attached to her son that, even after receiving the death sentence, she asked the deacon Pomponius to go and ask her father to fetch her the child, since the baby had remained with her in prison and was used to being breast-fed. But the father refused to give her the baby. With the grace of God, the baby no longer had the desire to receive his mother's milk, nor did she suffer any inflammation on her breasts. She was thus free from her anxiety for her son and from breast pains.[21]

Visions of Rupture

While in prison, Perpetua's faith was sustained by visions of things heavenly. In one of the visions, she saw a brass ladder of an extraordinary height, which went up to heaven; it was so narrow that only one person at a time could climb it. At the foot of the ladder was a huge snake, which lay in wait for those who would attempt to climb the ladder. On the edges of the ladder were iron spikes. Saturus, who had instructed them in the faith, climbed first. He arrived at the summit of the ladder and said to Perpetua, "Perpetua, I am waiting for you; but take care not to be bitten by the snake," to which Perpetua responded, "It will do me no harm, in the name of Jesus Christ." Perpetua put her foot on the head of the serpent and climbed up the ladder. From above, she saw a huge garden and, sitting in it, a grey-haired man dressed like a pastor. The old man was milking the sheep. Around him was a multitude of people dressed in white. The man raised his head, saw Perpetua, and said to her, "You are welcome, my child." He called her and gave her some cheese; she received it with both hands and ate it. All those present said, "Amen."[22] At that point, she awoke from her dream.[23] For her, this vision was a confirmation of their impending martyrdom.

---

20. *Passion* VI, 2–3.
21. Cf. ibid., 7–8.
22. Cf. Rev 7:9–14.
23. Cf. *Passion* IV, 3–10.

Commenting on this vision, Augustine interprets the serpent in the light of the serpent that tempted Eve.[24] He writes, "The dragon was trampled on by the blessed Perpetua's chaste foot and victorious tread, when the ladder by which she would go to God was set up and revealed. Thus the head of the ancient serpent, which had been the ruin of woman as she fell, was made into a step for woman as she ascended."[25] Reading the same vision in a tropological key, Augustine relates Perpetua's ascent to a life of virtue: "These virtues climb up to heaven by trampling on the head of the serpent, as it hisses and whispers its various suggestions. In fact, you have triumphed over all lusts, once you have crushed the tyrannous power over you of love of this life, which all lusts serve as its accomplices."[26]

In another vision, Perpetua saw her brother Dinocrates, who had died at the age of seven. It would appear that she was very affected by his death and used to think about him a lot. One day, when the Christian prisoners were praying, her voice rose and she suddenly pronounced the name of Dinocrates. At that point, she offered a long prayer of intercession for him, asking that God might be merciful to him. On that night, Perpetua had a dream in which she saw Dinocrates come out of darkness, where he was dying from heat and thirst. He carried on his face a wound that he had at the moment of his death, for he had died of an ulcer. Then she saw a pool full of water, but its edge was too high for a child. Dinocrates attempted to drink from it but could not touch the water. When she woke up, she was sad because she understood that her brother was in great pain, but she was sure her prayers could relieve his torments. She therefore prayed for him day and night until the day she (together with the other believers) was transferred to the military prison in readiness for their martyrdom.

Another day, while she slept, she had a dream that comforted

---

24. Cf. Gen 3:15.

25. Augustine, *Sermon* 280, 1, in *The Works of Saint Augustine: A Translation for the 21st Century*, vol. III/8: *Sermons 273–305A*, trans. Edmund Hill (New York: New City Press, 1994).

26. Ibid., 4.

her: she saw the brother again, and where there had been a wound there was only a scar. The edge of the pool was lowered up to the navel of a child; thus Dinocrates could drink from it, after which he played with the water, as children are wont to do. When she woke up, she understood that her prayers had obtained relief for her brother.[27]

These visions have an eschatological character, for they speak of the consummation of the Christian calling in the Kingdom of God. Perpetua's share in Christ's victory over evil is symbolized by her stepping on the head of the serpent that guards the steps to heaven, while her vision of people dressed in white is a common motif in the apocalypse. In other words, Perpetua, "at least spiritually, [has already] moved on to heaven, even while [she is] fighting the crafty enemy in the trials of prison and execution."[28]

Felicitas

The historical details of Felicitas's life are even scantier than those of Perpetua. It is believed that Felicitas was a young woman and was in her eighth month of pregnancy when she was arrested. It is popularly believed that she was Perpetua's slave,[29] but there is no credible documentary evidence to substantiate such a claim. Amy Rachel Peterson presents her as a young and not very beautiful woman with an aura of kindness about her. Felicitas "wore the extremely simple tunic of the serving class" whose roughness she smoothed with her hand as they talked.[30] Peterson's description corroborates the view that Felicitas came from a humble

---

27. Cf. *Passion* VII, 4–VIII, 4.

28. Dorothy Elm von der Osten, "Perpetual Felicity: Sermons of Augustine on Female Martyrdom (s. 280–282 auct. [Erfurt 1])," *Studia Patristica* 49 (2010): 209.

29. Johannes Quasten, *Patrology*, vol. 3: *The Beginnings of Patristic Literature from the Apostles Creed to Irenaeus* (Allen, TX: Christian Classics, 1995), 181; Eugene Hoade, "Perpetua and Felicity, SS," in *New Catholic Encyclopedia*, vol. 11 (Washington, DC: Catholic University of America, 2003), 130.

30. Peterson, *Perpetua*, 79.

background, belonging to the plebeians (common folk) rather than to the patricians (nobility).

Groaning in Travail

When Felicitas was apprehended by the government on account of her faith in Jesus, she was in her eighth month of pregnancy. Her greatest worry, therefore, was that her pregnancy would prevent her from receiving the gift of martyrdom, for the law prohibited the execution of expectant women, so as not to mix innocent blood with the blood of criminals. Her Christian companions shared her anxiety at the prospects of having to abandon the path of martyrdom on account of the child in her womb. In unison they addressed their prayer to the Lord two days before the day of their martyrdom.

Immediately after the prayer, labor pains seized her. Since she was only eight months pregnant, her travail was so great she suffered immensely. One of the jailers said to her, "If you suffer so much now, how much more will you suffer when you are thrown to the beasts, because of your refusal to sacrifice [to the gods]?"[31] But she replied, "Now it is me suffering what I suffer; but up there, someone else in me will suffer for me, because I too am going to suffer for him."[32]

Augustine makes Felicitas's bold statement clearer: It is Christ living in the martyrs that conquers in them so that, since they lived not for themselves but for him, they might remain alive even when they were dead.[33] Christ who made himself weak for them was undefeated in them.[34] Augustine adds that while Felicitas suffered the pain of childbearing, the grace of Mary, that is, the glory of heaven, awaited her. As it were, "the debt owed by the woman was exacted, but the one whom the virgin bore was there to give relief."[35]

---

31. *Passion* XV, 5.
32. Ibid., 6.
33. Cf. Augustine, *Sermon* 280, 4.
34. Augustine, *Sermon* 281, 1.
35. Cf. Ibid., 3.

She then gave birth to a daughter. Felicitas's sister took the daughter and raised her as her own child.

The Garland of Martyrdom

On the appointed day, Perpetua and Felicitas, in the company of the other confessors, left the prison in order to appear in the amphitheater, where games had been prepared for the amusement of the spectators. And one of the activities would be the combat between the Christian confessors and ferocious beasts. Perpetua marched to the amphitheater with a bright face and with the confidence of a matron that she was, knowing that she was a beloved daughter of God. Felicitas also walked to her place of martyrdom rejoicing that she had given birth before the day of her death. She was passing from one bloodbath to another, from the midwife to the sword. Her second baptism would cleanse her of the blood of her delivery.[36]

On their way out to the amphitheater, the confessors were told to wear costumes for the event; men were to dress as priests of the god Saturn, while women were to put on the vestments of the priestesses of Ceres. But Perpetua and others firmly declined to wear these pagan vestments. So they were allowed to keep their prison gowns. Perpetua sang a hymn, while Revocatus, Saturninus, and Saturus shouted threats to the spectators. The crowds were disgusted to see milk dropping from Felicitas's breasts, for she had just delivered. The scant dressing of Perpetua was equally repugnant to the spectators, so they asked that both women be given more decent gowns. The two women held each other's hands as they gallantly walked to their destiny.[37] Before dying, the martyrs embraced one another in order to conclude their martyrdom with the rite of peace.[38] They were martyred in AD 203.

For Augustine, the martyrdom of these brides of Christ was their glorification. The blood of these martyrs watered the seed of

---

36. *Passion* XVIII, 1–4.
37. Cf. ibid., 1–7.
38. Cf. *Passion* XXI, 7.

faith, so much that the descendants of those who roared with plea-sure at the death of the martyrs in the amphitheater now raise their voices in praise of the virtues of Perpetua and Felicity; at that time the theater was filled with unbelievers who went to gratify their impious senses with the sight of martyrs being killed by beasts, but now the churches are filled with believers who honor the martyrs; the shouts of mockery of the ungodly have become Christians' shouts of joy and admiration.[39]

The significance of their faith and martyrdom is attested by the fact that they are among the saints mentioned in the Roman canon, also known as the First Eucharistic Prayer, which is one of the old-est Eucharistic prayers in Christian tradition:

> To us, also, your servants, who, though sinners, hope in your abundant mercies, graciously grant some share and fellowship with your holy Apostles and Martyrs: with John the Baptist, Stephen, Matthias, Barnabas, Ignatius, Alexander, Marcellinus, Peter, Felicity, Perpetua, Agatha, Lucy, Agnes, Cecilia, Anastasia and all your Saints: admit us, we beseech you, into their company, not weighing our merits but granting us your pardon.[40]

Their feast day falls on March 7.

Reflection

The faith of Perpetua and Felicitas was so great that they overcame the natural attachment of a mother to her child and embraced martyrdom. The two women "are not only *mulieres* [women], but also *matres* [mothers]."[41] Perpetua's father sought to use her little

---

39. Augustine, *Sermon 280*, 2.

40. *The Roman Missal Renewed by Decree of the Most Holy Second Ecumenical Council of the Vatican, Promulgated by Authority of Pope Paul VI and Revised at the Direction of Pope John Paul II: English Translation According to the Third Typical Edition* (Nairobi: Paulines Publications Africa, 2011), 570.

41. Elm von der Osten, "Perpetual Felicity," 208.

baby as bait to hook Perpetua back into paganism. But Perpetua gallantly sought a good that surpasses biological maternity. That is why Tertullian calls Perpetua "the most heroic martyr."[42] For Felicitas, the fragility of her newborn daughter did not stand in the way of her determination to offer her life for her faith in Christ. The blood of childbirth had not yet dried when she marched into the amphitheater to shed the blood of martyrdom.

Perpetua and Felicitas loved the Kingdom more than father, mother, brothers, sisters, or children.[43] Significantly, the readings assigned to their feast day are Romans 8:31–39 and Matthew 10:34–39. In the first reading, Paul affirms that nothing can come between Christians and the love of Christ, even if they are subjected to hardship, distress, persecution, famine, nakedness, peril, or the sword.[44] Indeed, "neither death, nor life, nor angels, nor rulers, nor things present, nor things to come, nor powers, nor height, nor depth, nor anything else in all creation, will be able to separate us from the love of God in Christ Jesus our Lord."[45] In the gospel reading, Jesus warns his disciples that "whoever loves father or mother more than me is not worthy of me; and whoever loves son or daughter more than me is not worthy of me."[46] Perpetua and Felicitas loved the Lord more than their son and daughter, respectively. And now they enjoy "perpetual felicity," to borrow Augustine's expression.[47]

The influence of the lives of these saints cannot be overemphasized. As William Farina observes, "Over 1,800 years later, [Perpetua's] diary still serves as inspiration for Christians and non-Christians alike. Perpetua and Felicity belong to a surprisingly

---

42. Tertullian, *A Treatise on the Soul* LV, trans. Peter Holmes, ANF, vol. 3 (Grand Rapids, MI: Wm. B. Eerdmans, 1978), 231.

43. Cf. Mt 10:37; Lk 14:26.

44. Rm 8:35.

45. Rm 8:38–39.

46. Mt 10:37.

47. Augustine, *Sermon* 280, 1; *Sermon* 281, 3; *Sermon* 282, 1.

small group of saints uniformly honored by all denominations of the Christian faith."[48] They are iconic women and mothers of faith.

Conclusion

A life given in love is a life worth remembering. There are many mothers who today give their lives in countless forms of *bloodless martyrdom* because of their fidelity to God. Christians encounter competing allegiances in their lives. Sometimes the choice is not simply between good and evil but between good and a greater good. Perpetua and Felicitas were confronted with the choice between the good of the love of their children and the greater good of the love of Christ. Like Mary, they chose the better part,[49] preferring love of Christ to any human love.

Prayer

God, in your mercy you granted courage to your servants Perpetua and Felicitas to overcome the torment of death; they loved you more than their little children. Grant, we pray, that we too may be detached from the goods of this world and choose to love you above all else, knowing that you are the source of all goodness. Through Christ our Lord. Amen.

---

48. Farina, *Perpetua of Carthage*, 2.
49. Cf. Lk 10:42.

Chapter 15

Helena: Mother of the Holy Cross

Introduction

Just as Mary is associated with her son Jesus, St. Helena's story is intertwined with that of her son Constantine the Great. In the Eastern tradition, she is called the equal of the apostles. In Byzantine iconography, she is depicted in the company of her son, and there is a crown between them.

Her Story

Helena was born around 248 or 249 in Drepanum (modern-day Herkes) in Bithynia (Asia Minor). Her birthplace was later named Helenopolis after her, though it is likely that Justinian, not Constantine, made Helenopolis into an important and prosperous city.[1] She is believed to have come from a humble family background. She probably served as an innkeeper (*stabularia*), an occupation esteemed as lowly in Roman society, for "the life of a *stabularia* was one spent in servitude, very probably including sexual servitude."[2] This may explain why those writing about her often specify that

---

1. Cf. Jan W. Drijvers, *Helena Augusta: The Mother of Constantine the Great and the Legend of Her Finding of the True Cross* (Leiden, the Netherlands: Brill, 1992), 9.
2. Ibid., 15.

she was a "good" *stabularia*, in order to show that she was a morally upright woman in spite of her occupation.[3]

Helena was married to Constantius Chlorus, who was then a private officer in the army. It is speculated that, since Constantius and Helena belonged to two different social classes, they simply cohabited and could not be formally wed, because the law would not permit a marriage between an aristocrat and a member of a humble social class.[4] She bore him a son, Constantine. Constantius was a virtuous man. He was "a prince never charged with any vice, a good soldier, and nobly born, being descended from the emperor Claudius II and from Vespasian."[5] However, when Constantius was offered the opportunity to become Caesar (coregent) by Emperor Maximianus Herculius in Diocletian's newly introduced tetrarchy, Constantius was obliged to divorce Helena in order to marry Theodora, Maximianus's stepdaughter.

Maximianus was known for his brutality and vanity, and for the exorbitant taxes he imposed on his subjects. Though a decree was issued to extirpate Christians in the Empire, it would appear that Constantius never implemented it.[6] It is even said that Constantius had Christians among his officers. Constantius once gave his Christian officers the choice between offering sacrifices to pagan gods, so to win his favor, or remaining faithful to their God and lose his beneficence. Those who chose to sacrifice to pagan gods he eliminated from his service, arguing that if they were ready to betray their God for personal interest, they could as well betray a

---

3. Ambrose, for instance, describes her as *bona stabularia*. Cf. Ambrose, *On [the Death of] Emperor Theodosius* 42, trans. Roy J. Deferrari, in *Funeral Orations by Saint Gregory Nazianzen and Saint Ambrose*, The Fathers of the Church, vol. 22 (New York: Fathers of the Church, 1953), 325–26.

4. Cf. Drijvers, *Helena Augusta*, 18.

5. Alban Butler, *The Lives of the Fathers, Martyrs, and Other Principal Saints*, vol. 7 (New York: P. J. Kenedy & Sons, 1886), 387.

6. Cf. Jean Daniélou and Henri Marrou, *The Christian Centuries*, vol. 1: *The First Six Hundred Years*, trans. Vincent Cronin (London: Darton, Longman, and Todd, 1964), 233.

mortal like him. Constantius is reported to have been "remarkably indulgent to the poor Christians."[7]

Helena's Son Constantine

As the political arrangement required, Constantine, Constantius's son, was sent to the court of Diocletian (in Nicomedia) as a guarantee of his father's fidelity to his superiors. Diocletian was known as Augustus of the East, while Maximianus was Augustus of the West. Constantine received training in the imperial court in which he stayed from around 293 to 305.[8] Butler, on the authority of Eusebius, wistfully remarks: "Thus was that prince, like another Moses, brought up amidst the enemies of truth, whom he was one day to extirpate."[9]

Constantine had a reputation for being a prince of good morals, well-formed both in mind and body, and with an impressive genius for war. On his deathbed, Constantius appointed Constantine his successor. In 306, the troops in York proclaimed him the successor of his father.[10] Eusebius attributes Constantine's accession to power to a divine intervention. "He is the only one to whose elevation no mortal may boast of having contributed,"[11] declares Eusebius.

Maximianus recognized Constantine as emperor on condition that the latter divorce his first wife Minervina and marry Maximianus's daughter Fausta.[12] Constantine immediately summoned

---

7. Butler, *The Lives of the Fathers*, 387.

8. Cf. Drijvers, *Helena Augusta*, 11.

9. Butler, *The Lives of the Fathers*, 387; cf. Eusebius, *The Life of Constantine* I, 12, in *Eusebius Pamphilius: Church History, Life of Constantine, Oration in Praise of Constantine*, ed. Philip Schaff, trans. Arthur C. McGiffert (Grand Rapids, MI: Christian Classics Ethereal Library, 1890), 485.

10. Cf. Drijvers, *Helena Augusta*, 21.

11. Eusebius, *The Life of Constantine* I, 24.

12. Constantine later had Fausta killed, together with his eldest son Crispus, apparently on account of an alleged adulterous liaison between Crispus and his stepmother. Cf. Hans Lietzmann, *A History of the Early Church*, vol. 3: *From Constantine to Julian*, trans. Bertram L. Woolf (London: Lutterworth Press, 1961), 138.

his mother to the imperial court and conferred on her the title of Augusta.

Maximianus was succeeded by his son Maxentius, who set out to fight Constantine. The latter's army was inferior in number. In a society riddled with many gods, Constantine had a wide variety of gods and goddesses to address himself to. However, having considered the unhappy lot of those who entrusted themselves to the protection of the gods, he decided to implore the one God worshipped by Christians. Eusebius's report is worth quoting at length:

> Being convinced ... that he needed some more powerful aid than his military forces could afford him, on account of the wicked and magical enchantments which were so diligently practiced by the tyrant, he sought Divine assistance, deeming the possession of arms and a numerous soldiery of secondary importance, but believing the cooperating power of Deity invincible and not to be shaken. He considered, therefore, on what God he might rely for protection and assistance. While engaged in this enquiry, the thought occurred to him, that, of the many emperors who had preceded him, those who had rested their hopes in a multitude of gods, and served them with sacrifices and offerings, had in the first place been deceived by flattering predictions, and oracles which promised them all prosperity, and at last had met with an unhappy end, while not one of their gods had stood by to warn them of the impending wrath of heaven; while one alone who had pursued an entirely opposite course, who had condemned their error, and honored the one Supreme God during his whole life, had found him to be the Savior and Protector of his empire, and the Giver of every good thing.[13]

Thus, Constantine implored God for help against Maxentius. While he was praying, Constantine saw a sign from heaven. A lit-

---

13. Cf. Eusebius, *The Life of Constantine* I, 27.

tle after noon, as the sun was beginning to decline, he saw a "trophy of a cross of light in the heavens, above the sun, and bearing the inscription, 'Conquer by this [sign].'"[14] The following night, Christ ordered him to make a representation of the cross he had seen and to use it for an ensign in battle. This ensign came to be called the *labarum*, the imperial military banner consisting of the Greek letters *chi* (X) and *rho* (P), the first two letters of the Greek for Christ.[15] There were no fewer than fifty men of great valor and strength entrusted with the carrying and care of the banner.[16]

Maxentius, known for terrorizing even his subjects (going as far as violating the wives of his own senators) was defeated at the battle of the Milvian Bridge and drowned in a river on his escape.[17] The defeat and death of Maxentius brought relief to the people of Rome, who had suffered many atrocities at the hands of the tyrant. Thus, the senate decided that a triumphal arch be built in Rome in honor of Constantine. Statues of Constantine were also erected in various public places. In these statues, Constantine is seen holding in his hand a long cross instead of a lance. On the pedestal was the following inscription: "By virtue of this salutary sign, which is the true test of valor, I have preserved and liberated your city from the yoke of tyranny. I have also set at liberty the Roman senate and people, and restored them to their ancient distinction and splendor."[18]

Constantine gave his soldiers a form of prayer to be recited on Sunday. The prayer reads as follows:

---

14. Ibid., 28.

15. Cf. ibid., 29–31. It is doubtful whether Constantine's victory over Maxentius marked the former's conversion to Christianity. The historical fact is that Constantine, perhaps in keeping with the practice of the time, delayed his baptism until the deathbed. However, after the victory over Maxentius, Constantine exercised greater sympathy toward Christianity. Daniélou and Marrou, *The Christian Centuries*, 235–36.

16. Cf. Eusebius, *The Life of Constantine* II, 8.

17. Eusebius reads this event in the light of Exodus 14, whereby Pharaoh's army perished in the sea while pursuing the people of Israel. Cf. ibid., I, 38.

18. Ibid., 40.

> We acknowledge thee the only God: we own thee, as our
> King and implore thy succor. By thy favor have we gotten
> the victory: through thee are we mightier than our ene-
> mies. We render thanks for thy past benefits, and trust
> thee for future blessings. Together we pray to thee, and
> beseech thee long to preserve to us, safe and triumphant,
> our emperor Constantine and his pious sons.[19]

Constantine also consulted those steeped in Scripture and
enquired of them about the Christian God and about the sign he
had seen. His instructors in the faith affirmed that what he had
seen was a sign of immortality, Christ's victory over death won on
the cross. Henceforth, Constantine devoted himself to the reading
of the Scriptures and appointed priests as his counselors.[20]

Constantine proclaimed Christ to the Romans and legalized
the Christian religion, which faith later became the state religion
of the empire, exposing, in his letter to the provinces, the error
of idolatry,[21] all the while avoiding coercing anyone to become
a Christian.[22] He admitted bishops to his table, in spite of their
wretched dress and appearance. He also built sacred edifices
and gave the Lateran Palace to the bishop of Rome. In 313, Pope
Melchiades held a synod in this palace, in the apartment of Fausta,
Constantine's wife. Constantine also issued numerous edicts in
favor of Christianity. Eusebius lyrically compares Constantine to
the sun:

> As the sun, when he rises upon the earth, liberally imparts
> his rays of light to all, so did Constantine, proceeding at
> early dawn from the imperial palace, and rising as it were

---

19. Ibid., IV, 20.

20. Cf. ibid., I, 32.

21. Cf. ibid., II, 47–48. Constantine's letter is redolent of Nebuchadnezzar's
decree to all peoples, nations, and languages, legalizing the worship of the God
of Shadrach, Meshach and Abed-Nego. Cf. Dan 3:95–97.

22. Cf. Eusebius, *The Life of Constantine* II, 56.

with the heavenly luminary, impart the rays of his own beneficence to all who came into his presence. It was scarcely possible to be near him without receiving some benefit, nor did it ever happen that any who had expected to obtain his assistance were disappointed in their hope.[23]

During Constantine's era, Christianity made inroads into the Roman society. The first Christian symbols appeared on the coins in 315, which was no mean gain, considering that coins were a powerful instrument of propaganda. Places of Christian cult also multiplied, and the architectural form of the basilica was adopted by Christians. The legalization of Christianity was accompanied by the restriction of pagan practices. In 318, for instance, private sacrifices and sorcery were banned. Constantine educated his children as Christians and considered himself the first Christian emperor.[24]

Helena's Conversion

What was the role of Helena in Constantine's Christian faith and subsequent exploits? To answer this question, one has to ascertain the time of Helena's conversion to the Christian faith. Some historians believe that Helena had great sympathy for the Christian faith right from her childhood. Others, however, are of the view that her interest in Christianity would have begun after marrying Constantius Chlorus, who is said to have been well disposed to Christians during the Diocletian persecution. Still others think that her faith journey began after hearing the preaching of a priest called Lucian, who was later martyred. Drijvers opines that it is rather safe to date her conversion to after 312.[25]

It is possible that Helena's conversion was due to her son Constantine's missionary zeal, and the conversion of his mother would

---

23. Ibid., I, 43.

24. Cf. Daniélou and Marrou, *The Christian Centuries*, 236–37.

25. Cf. Drijvers, *Helena Augusta*, 35.

have been the greatest reward of his missionary zeal.[26] Butler writes, "It appears from Eusebius that St. Helen was not converted to the faith with her son, till after his miraculous victory; but so perfect was her conversion, that she embraced all the heroic practices of Christian perfection."[27] He adds, "She was advanced in years before she knew Christ; but her fervor and zeal were such as to make her retrieve the time lost in ignorance."[28] In his account of the death and burial of the empress, Eusebius heaps praises on her in the following words: "He [Constantine] rendered her through his influence so devout a worshiper of God (though she had not previously been such) that she seemed to have been instructed from the first by the Savior of mankind."[29] She embraced the Christian faith with the magnanimity of a mother and the conviction of an elder.

Helena the Pilgrim

In 326, probably at the age of eighty, Helena undertook a pilgrimage to the Holy Land, where she prayed in thanksgiving on behalf of her son and her grandchildren.[30] She also caused churches to be erected in places associated with the life and death of Jesus such as Bethlehem, Golgotha, and the Mount of the Ascension.[31] Reflecting on her works in the Holy Land, Ambrose writes:

> Good hostess, who so diligently searched for the manger of the Lord. Good hostess, who did not ignore that host who cared for the wounds of the man wounded by robbers. Good hostess, who preferred to be considered dung, to gain Christ! For that reason Christ raised her from dung

---

26. Ibid., 36.
27. Butler, *The Lives of the Fathers*, 388.
28. Ibid., 389.
29. Eusebius, *The Life of Constantine* III, 47.
30. Cf. ibid., 42.
31. Cf. ibid., 43.

to a kingdom, for it is written that "He raised up the needy from the earth, and lifted up the poor out of the dunghill."[32]

Augusta Helena was also known for her charitable works to the poor. In church, she did not seek to distinguish herself from the ordinary people gathered to pray, but rather conducted herself with great simplicity and dressed modestly.[33]

Searching for the Cross

Helena is associated with the finding of the cross on which Jesus died. In 326, Constantine wrote to Macarius, bishop of Jerusalem, asking that a magnificent church be built on Mount Calvary where Christ was crucified. Helena took upon herself the responsibility to ensure the execution of this work. At the same time, she desired to discover the cross upon which Jesus died. Ambrose writes:

> The Spirit inspired her to search for the wood of the Cross. She drew near to Golgotha and said: "Behold the place of combat: where is thy victory? I seek the banner of salvation and I do not find it. "Shall I," she said, "be among kings, and the cross of the Lord lie in the dust? Shall I be covered by golden ornaments, and the triumph of Christ by ruins?[34] Is this still hidden, and is the palm of eternal life hidden? How can I believe that I have been redeemed if the redemption itself is not seen?"[35]

In her view, the discovery of the cross would deal a second blow to the devil, who suffered the first defeat through the death of Christ,

---

32. Ambrose, *On [the Death of] Emperor Theodosius*, 42. Ambrose here quotes Psalm 113:7: "He raises the poor from the dust, he lifts the needy from the dunghill, to give them a place among princes, among princes of his people."

33. Eusebius, *The Life of Constantine* III, 45.

34. This discourse is reminiscent of David's motivation for building the Temple. Cf. 2 Sam 7:1–16.

35. Ambrose, *On [the Death of] Emperor Theodosius*, 43.

born of a woman. In a similar manner, she, also a woman, would put an end to the devil's ploy to obscure the sign of redemption: "You were vanquished by Mary, who gave the Conqueror birth ... Today, also, you shall be vanquished when a woman discovers your snares. That holy woman bore the Lord; I shall search for his cross. She gave proof that he was born; I shall give proof that he rose from the dead. She caused God to be seen among men; I shall raise from ruins the divine banner which shall be a remedy for our sins."[36]

As the legend goes, during the excavation of the site believed to be Golgotha, three crosses were found together. They also found the nails with which the soldiers crucified him. To identify the true cross of Christ, at the suggestion of Bishop Macarius, the three crosses were taken to a sick woman. After Helena's prayer, the bishop applied the crosses to the sick person, who was immediately restored to health at the touch of the cross of Christ.[37]

Ambrose's account, however, is simpler: during the excavation, three crosses were found; to ascertain which one belonged to Christ, Helena simply went back to the gospel account where she found that Christ was crucified between two thieves and that an inscription was placed over his head.[38] The cross with an inscription was then considered to be that of Jesus. Ambrose adds that when she discovered the true cross, Helena adored not the wood but the King who died upon it, for adoring the wood would be idolatry, as pagans are wont to do.[39]

Part of the relic of the cross remained in Jerusalem, under the custody of Bishop Macarius, while another part was sent to Constantinople, where it was exposed for the solemn veneration of the people. One of the nails, placed in diadem, was sent to Rome and is kept in the Basilica of the Holy Cross in Jerusalem, built in Helena's palace, where it is exhibited to the faithful to this day.

---

36. Ibid., 44.
37. Cf. Butler, *The Lives of the Fathers*, 390.
38. Cf. Ambrose, *On [the Death of] Emperor Theodosius*, 45.
39. Cf. ibid., 46.

The liturgical feast of the Exaltation of the Cross traces its origins from the veneration of the relic of the cross in Jerusalem after the dedication of the church of the Holy Sepulcher on September 13, 335. The relic was exposed for people's veneration the following day, September 14, the date for the feast of the Exaltation of the Cross to this day.[40]

Helena died about 330. Her feast falls on August 18, though it has disappeared from the calendar of the Roman Catholic Church. In liturgical art, the Christian empress is depicted holding a cross. A *kontakion* (a hymn in the Orthodox Church) dedicated to the Christian emperor and his mother goes thus: "With his mother Helen, Constantine today brings to light the precious Cross: the shame of unbelievers, the weapon of Orthodox Christians against their enemies, for it is manifest for us as a great and fearful sign in struggle!"[41] The hymn puts in the foreground Helena's role in the promotion of the Christian faith in the Roman Empire.

Reflection

Helena came to the faith late in her life; yet, when she converted, her zeal for Christ was fiery. Having lost her husband to another woman of a nobler social standing, Helena found, through her son, the noblest bridegroom: Christ. And she fell in love with him so much that she braved a taxing journey to the homeland of her beloved groom. She wanted to see and to touch the very wood of the cross on which Christ wrought the salvation of the world. Henceforth, she would proclaim to the world "what was from the beginning, what we have heard, what we have seen with our eyes, what we have looked at and touched with our hands, concerning the word of life."[42]

---

40. Cf. Massey H. Shepherd, "Cross," in *Encyclopaedia Britannica*, vol. 6 (Chicago: Encyclopaedia Britannica, 1970), 813.

41. Troparia and Kontakia for May 21: Equal of the Apostles and Emperor Constantine with his Mother Helen: https://oca.org/saints/troparia/2012/05/21.

42. 1Jn 1:1.

Having discovered the love of Christ, she could say with Paul: "I count everything as loss because of the surpassing value of knowing Christ Jesus my Lord. For his sake I have suffered the loss of all things, and I regard them as rubbish, in order that I may gain Christ."[43] Thus, she did not hestitate to lavish her wealth and energy on the poor and on holy places.

Helena is the patron saint of archaeologists, difficult marriages, divorced people, converts, and empresses.

In the early centuries Christianity was largely regarded as the religion of the poor and the lowly. But the conversion and zeal of Helena provides a resounding counterinstance. With the support of her son, she built the Christian Empire and revealed the splendor of the Christian faith. Till today, there are women of noble social standing who support the church's work of evangelization and charity. Faith has the power to open people's hearts to the cry of the poor. May such mothers find consolation and support in the life of Saint Helena.

Prayer

O God, ruler of all nations, who moved Helena to embrace and to preach through her works the mystery of the cross, grant that those in authority may profess faith in the crucified, to whom all authority in heaven and on earth has been given, so that their lives may shine forth in charity, generosity, and humility. Through Christ our Lord. Amen.

---

43. Phil 3:8.

Chapter 16

Monica: Mother of Tears

Introduction

In his *Confessions*, Augustine prays that God may "inspire those of them who read this book to remember Monica, your servant, at your altar and with her Patricius, her husband, who died before her, by whose bodies you brought me into this life, though how it was I do not know."[1] St. Monica, Augustine's mother, is worth remembering for her remarkable faith, especially her solicitude for the spiritual well-being of her son. While Helena embraced the Christian faith thanks to the zeal of her son Constantine, Augustine's conversion to Christianity can largely be attributed to the prayers and tears of his mother, Monica.

Information about the life, works, and death of Monica is found in Augustine's own writings, especially the *Confessions*, written between 397 and 400, a few years after he had become bishop in Africa. He was about forty-three when he wrote the *Confessions*.[2] Monica is such a dominant figure in the book that "the relationship between mother and son that weaves in and out of the *Confessions* forms the thread for which the book is justly famous."[3] Augustine

---

1. Augustine, *Confessions* IX, 13, trans. Richard S. Pine-Coffin (Middlesex, UK: Penguin, 1961), 204–5.
2. Cf. Peter Brown, *Augustine of Hippo: A Biography* (London: Faber and Faber, 1967), 28, 161.
3. Ibid., 29.

is so passionate about his mother that he is determined to omit not a word that his mind can bring to birth concerning his mother.[4]

Her Story

Monica was born around 331, in the city of Thagaste, in present-day Algeria. She was born into a fairly wealthy family, for her parents could afford the services of domestic servants. Her parents, being Christians, were determined to bring her up on Christian principles. An aged household servant was charged with the care of Monica, the same old woman who had carried Augustine's grandfather on her back when he was a baby. The old woman enjoyed a special honor in the family not only because of her advanced age but also on account of her outstanding character, especially her skill in bringing children up. The old woman inculcated in Monica and in the other children a wise and sober life. Augustine recalls that, "except at the times when they ate their frugal meals at their parents' table she would not allow them to drink even water, however great their thirst, for fear that they might develop bad habits."[5] The old nanny wanted to curb any propensity to excessive drinking on the part of the young girls. She was sure that if the appetite for wine were checked while they were young, they would not fall into the trap of alcoholism when they became adults.

However, in spite of the old woman's disciplinary measures, Monica used to take wine in secret. Augustine narrates:

> Yet in spite of this, as your servant my mother used to tell me herself, she developed a secret liking for wine. Her parents, believing her to be a good and obedient child, used to send her to draw wine from the cask, as was the custom. She used to dip the cup through the opening at the top of the barrel, and before pouring the wine into the flagon she would sip a few drops, barely touching it with her lips, but

4. Augustine, *Confessions* IX, 8.
5. Ibid.

not more than this, because she found the taste disagree-
able . . . Each day she added a few more drops to her daily
sip of wine . . . It soon became a habit, and she would drink
her wine at a draught, almost by the cupful.[6]

For Augustine, Monica's fall into alcoholism was a sign that good
character was a gift from God and not a product of mere human
discipline. Such a habit could only be cured by God's healing power.[7] Fortunately, God used a servant-girl to cure Monica's sickness.
One day, when Monica was with the maid, a quarrel broke out
between them, whereupon the servant called Monica a drunkard.
Monica was deeply hurt by this name and resolved to break with
her wine-drinking habit. Henceforth, she lived a sober life. From
this incident, Augustine learned that God can use the reproach
of one's enemies, even unbeknownst to them, to correct one's
behavior.[8]

Married Life

Monica was married to Patricius, a man known for a hot temper,
though, at the same time, remarkably kind. At the time she married him, he was not a Christian. Monica drew inspiration from
the instructions regarding marriage outlined in 1 Peter 3: "Wives,
in the same way, accept the authority of your husbands, so that,
even if some of them do not obey the word, they may be won over
without a word by their wives' conduct, when they see the purity
and reverence of your lives."[9]

Monica exercised great patience and tact in her relationship with
Patricius. When her husband's temper was hot, she would keep
quiet and wait for him to calm down before explaining the matter
to him. She came to the conclusion that many women suffered
domestic violence because they lacked the patience not to respond

6. Ibid.
7. Ibid.
8. Ibid.
9. 1Pt 3:1–2.

to their husbands when the latter's temper was still hot (in a culture where women were expected to be subservient to their husbands). Augustine recalls how "many women, whose faces were disfigured by blows from husbands far sweeter-tempered than her own, used to gossip together and complain of the behavior of their men-folk."[10] Because of her diplomacy in the face of his cruelty, Monica never suffered any physical blows from Patricius, to the surprise of many women who knew her husband's irascibility. Though Patricius was unfaithful to her, she endured his betrayal with great patience, relying on God's help, who alone could give both chastity and faith.[11]

The women who followed Monica's example enjoyed peace in their families. Monica applied herself to the edification of her husband and, thanks to her prayers, won him over to Christ. They lived together in peace so much that, when she died at Ostia, Augustine expected that she would have wished to be buried beside him back in Africa, so that "after her journeyings across the sea . . . the earthly remains of husband and wife should be joined as one and covered by the same earth."[12]

Another challenge in Monica's married life was her relationship with her mother-in-law. Some servants in the household were in the habit of telling tales about Monica to Patricius's mother in order to besmirch Monica's reputation. These gossips rendered the relationship between the two women tense. However, Monica responded to her mother-in-law's prejudice with gentleness and patience, until the latter discovered that Monica was a woman of virtue. Henceforth, Patricius's mother ordered her son to punish every servant who would speak evil of Monica. Thus, "Patricius, who was anxious to satisfy his mother as well as to preserve the good order of his home and the peace of his family, took the names of the offenders from his mother and had them whipped as she desired . . . After this none of them dared to tell tales and the two women lived together

10. Augustine, *Confessions* IX, 8.

11. Ibid., 9.

12. Ibid., 11.

in wonderful harmony and mutual goodwill."[13] Monica had won another delicate battle.

Monica the Peacemaker

Augustine's mother had another gift: mediation. She knew how to lend a listening ear to aggrieved persons, allowing them to vent their anger about an absent person, but she would never report the matter to the person concerned, except that which was likely to bring about reconciliation between the estranged parties. Augustine notes that many conflicts are often fueled by people who traffic gossip between persons or parties at loggerheads. His remarks are instructive: "I know from bitter experience that a great many people . . . not only report to one disputant what the other has said, but even add words that were never spoken."[14] This tendency, observes Augustine, aggravates the enmity of warring factions. His mother, on the contrary, had the skill to sweeten sour relationships not only by refraining from trafficking in gossip but also by putting in a good word or two likely to improve relations between enemies. Monica lived out the Beatitude, "Blessed are the peacemakers, for they will be called children of God."[15]

Pious Widow

Patricius died and left Monica a widow. She never remarried but chose to devote the rest of her life to prayer and pious works. Augustine recalls that she used to give alms to the poor and had great devotion for the saints. Monica also used to go to church twice a day, in the morning and at night, without fail, where she listened to sermons and offered her prayers to God.[16]

In Milan, when Justina, the mother of the young emperor Valentinian, persecuted Ambrose because of his refutation of

---

13. Ibid., 8.
14. Ibid., 9.
15. Mt 5:9.
16. Cf. Augustine, *Confessions* V, 9.

Arianism (for Justina took the side of the Arianists), the church at Milan sought comfort and strength in the singing of hymns. This practice was borrowed from the Eastern churches. The faithful would keep watch in the church, ready to die with their bishop Ambrose. Monica used to attend these vigils, sometimes taking a leading part in them.[17]

She also used to hold holy conversations with spiritual men, such as Ambrose of Milan, whom she greatly revered. Augustine recalls that, following the custom in Africa, Monica would take meal cakes, bread, and wine to the shrines of saints on their memorial days. However, one day, the doorkeeper of the shrine told her that the bishop (Ambrose) had forbidden it because of the abuses such a practice often gave rise to and because of its resemblance to pagan rituals in honor of the dead. Monica "accepted his ruling with such pious submission that I was surprised to see how willingly she condemned her own practice rather than dispute his command."[18] Instead of bread and wine, she "learned to bring to the shrines of the martyrs a heart full of prayers far purer than any of these gifts."[19] Augustine imagines that his mother would not have given up the practice of carrying gifts to the shrines of saints had the prohibition come from another ecclesiastical authority she loved and revered less dearly than Ambrose. The bishop of Milan knew her well, and whenever Augustine went to see him, Ambrose would congratulate Augustine on having such a saintly mother.[20]

Sacrifice of Tears

St. Monica is famous for her tears offered to God for the conversion of her son Augustine who, for a long time, despised the Christian faith and wallowed in heretical doctrines such as Manichaeism. Monica had introduced Augustine to the faith as a child, though he remained unbaptized. Augustine recalls,

---

17. Cf. ibid., IX, 7.
18. Ibid., VI, 2.
19. Ibid.
20. Cf. ibid.

> For by your mercy, Lord, from the time when my mother
> fed me at the breast my infant heart had been suckled duti-
> fully on his name, the name of your Son, my Savior. Deep
> inside my heart his name remained, and nothing could
> entirely captivate me, however learned, however neatly
> expressed, however true it might be, unless his name were
> in it.[21]

As a child, Augustine had even begged his mother to let him be
baptized. However, as he grew up, he turned his back on the Christian faith and fell prey to heretical doctrines making the rounds in
town.[22] Monica spared no efforts in letting her son see the light of
the Gospel. She asked a certain learned bishop to talk to Augustine
so as to refute the latter's errors and to instill in him sound doctrine.
Surprisingly, the bishop refused to help Augustine, explaining to
Monica that her son was not yet ready for instruction, because he
was still captivated by the new heresy in town. The bishop then
advised Monica to leave the boy alone: "Just pray to God for him.
From his own reading he will discover his mistakes and the depth of
his profanity,"[23] the bishop advised. Monica could not believe her
ears and broke down in tears before the bishop, entreating him to
reconsider his position and to help her son. But the bishop insisted
that she should go. Then the bishop made a prophetic utterance: "It
cannot be that the son of these tears should be lost."[24]

Monica went home and continued to pray for her son, shedding
copious tears before God and asking God to look with pity upon
her and to move her son to conversion. Augustine recounts, "Night
and day my mother poured out her tears to you and offered her
heart-blood in sacrifice for me, and in the most wonderful way you
guided me."[25] With the flood of her tears, Monica "daily watered

---

21. Ibid., III, 4; VI, 4.
22. Cf. ibid., V, 9.
23. Ibid., III, 12.
24. Ibid.
25. Ibid., V, 7.

the ground as she bowed her head, praying to you for me."[26] The pain Monica suffered on account of her son's waywardness was far greater than the pain she had endured at childbirth. She had to go through this pain in order to give Augustine a spiritual birth.[27]

Her Faith

Faith "is the assurance of things hoped for, the conviction of things not seen."[28] Even before the conversion of her son, Monica was sure that God would one day answer her prayer. Just as Jesus had raised the son of the widow of Nain, so would God touch Augustine's spiritual bier, restore him to life, and give him back to his widowed mother. Augustine recalls that his mother believed that before her death she would see him a faithful Catholic.[29] In a language that comes across to us today as male chauvinism, Augustine remarks that Monica had the "weak body of a woman but the strong faith of a man."[30]

Her conviction regarding eternal life allowed her not to fear bodily death. She even considered death a blessing, for it signaled passage to eternal beatitude. Those who listened to her thus speak were astonished at "such courage in a woman."[31] Nor did she fear being buried far away from home, for she believed that nothing was far from God; the Lord would know where to find her on the day of the resurrection of the dead.[32] At the same time, she did not take God's mercy for granted. Before her death, she asked her son to remember her at the altar of the Lord after her departure from this life, so that her sins would be remitted.[33]

---

26. Ibid., 8.
27. Ibid., V, 9.
28. Heb 11:1.
29. Cf. Augustine, *Confessions* VI, 1.
30. Ibid., IX, 4.
31. Ibid., 11.
32. Ibid.
33. Cf. ibid., 10.13.

The Lord Answers Her Tears

"It cannot be that the son of those tears should be lost," said the bishop whom Monica had asked to help her son. True enough, God looked upon his lowly servant and answered her prayer. Augustine saw the light of the gospel and converted to the Christian faith. The process of Augustine's conversion started when he discovered the loopholes in the arguments proffered in defense of Manichaeism. While he had previously dismissed Christianity because he thought some articles of faith were without proof or evidence, he noticed that many affirmations held by the Manichaeans were equally without proof. Not even Faustus, a Manichaean bishop renowned for his prowess in rhetoric, could answer Augustine's questions about this philosophical system. According to Augustine's estimation, Faustus possessed more rhetoric than content.[34]

At Milan, Augustine listened, at first without interest, to the sermons of Ambrose, bishop of the city.

> At that time his [Ambrose's] gifted tongue never tired of dispensing the richness of your corn, the joy of your oil, and the sober intoxication of your wine . . . I listened attentively when he preached to the people, though not with the proper intention; for my purpose was to judge for myself whether the reports of his powers as a speaker were accurate, or whether eloquence flowed from him more, or less, readily than I had been told. So while I paid the closest attention to the words he used, I was quite uninterested in the subject-matter and was even contemptuous of it.[35]

Though the bishop of Milan could not match Faustus's rhetorical prowess, in Augustine's estimation, Ambrose made more sense than Faustus. In his sermons, Ambrose provided spiritual (figurative) explanations of scriptural passages Augustine had hitherto

---

34. Cf. ibid., V, 3.6–7.
35. Ibid., 13.

considered absurd. Gradually, Augustine began to consider the defensibility of the Catholic doctrine that the Manichaeans used to disparage. He fell in love with Catholic doctrine.[36] He also drew inspiration from his conversation with Simplicianus, Ambrose's spiritual father, who taught him to find the voice of the gospel in the books of the Platonists. The story of the conversion of Victorinus, an old man of great learning, was equally encouraging and edifying to Augustine.[37]

Slowly, Augustine began to reconsider his life. He was moved to tears of sorrow for his sins. It was his turn to offer the sacrifice of tears: "I flung myself down beneath a fig tree and gave way to the tears which now streamed from my eyes, the sacrifice that is acceptable to you . . . For I felt that I was still the captive of my sins."[38] As he wept, he heard the voice of a child in a nearby house. The child repeated the invitation, "Take it and read, take it and read." At the behest of that voice, Augustine took the Bible and decided to read the first passage on which his eyes should fall. The passage he opened was Romans 13:13–14: "Let us live honorably as in the day, not in reveling and drunkenness, not in debauchery and licentiousness, not in quarreling and jealousy. Instead, put on the Lord Jesus Christ, and make no provision for the flesh, to gratify its desires." No passage could speak to him more eloquently.[39] Thinking upon his life, Augustine asked for baptism. He was baptized by Ambrose at Easter in 387.[40]

Augustine's conversion brought joy to his mother, who saw in his acceptance of the faith God's answer to her prayers.[41] When Augustine related to her the story about the voice of the child and how he had read Romans 13, his mother was filled with joy. She "was jubilant with triumph and glorified you . . . For she saw

---

36. Cf. ibid., 14; VI, 4–5.
37. Cf. ibid., VIII, 2.
38. Ibid., 12.
39. Cf. ibid.
40. Cf. ibid., IX, 6.
41. Cf. ibid., VI, 13.

that you had granted her more than she used to ask in her tearful prayers and plaintive lamentations."[42] Such is the power of the prayer of intercession.

Her *Nunc Dimittis*

The conversion of her son filled Monica with so much joy that she felt she had received everything she had hoped for in life and was ready to depart from this life. A few days before her death, she said to her son,

> My son, for my part I find no further pleasure in this life. What I am still to do or why I am here in the world, I do not know, for I have no more to hope for on this earth. There was one reason, and one alone, why I wished to remain a little longer in this life, and that was to see you a Catholic Christian before I died. God has granted my wish and more besides, for I now see you as his servant, spurning such happiness as the world can give. What is left for me to do in this world?[43]

Monica was so concerned about the spiritual well-being of her son that she regarded his conversion as her project in this world. Once that project was accomplished, she felt she was ready to move on from this life. Like Simeon, she had seen the salvation that God had prepared for his people.[44]

Her Death

Monica died at Ostia, while they were waiting for transport to return to Africa. She was fifty-six when the Lord took her to himself. Accordingly, after her demise, Augustine offered the sacrifice

---

42. Ibid., 12.
43. Ibid., IX, 10.
44. Cf. Lk 2:29–31.

of redemption for her.[45] He also offered a "sacrifice of tears" for her, so that God would have mercy on her and grant her eternal rest. Augustine writes, "It was a comfort to me to weep for her and for myself and to offer my tears to you for her sake and for mine."[46] In his prayers of intercession for the soul of his mother, Augustine would pray thus:

> I offer to you, my God, [tears] for your handmaid. They flow from a spirit which trembles at the thought of the dangers which await every soul that has died with Adam. For although she was alive in Christ even before her soul was parted from the body, and her faith and the good life she led resounded to the glory of your name, yet I cannot presume to say that from the time when she was reborn in baptism no word contrary to your commandments ever fell from her lips.[47]

While Augustine prayed in thanksgiving for all the good works of his mother, he also prayed to God for her sins, uniting his prayer with the prayer of Christ, who is seated at the right hand of the Father and pleads for people. He says, "I know that my mother acted with mercy and that she forgave others with all her heart when they trespassed against her. Forgive her too, O Lord, if ever she trespassed against you in all the long years of her life after baptism."[48] Clearly, praying for his mother was the highest expression of gratitude to her.

Monica is the patron saint of alcoholics, married women, and mothers. Her feast falls on August 27, a day before the feast of her son Augustine.

---

45. Cf. Augustine, *Confessions* IX, 12.
46. Ibid.
47. Ibid., 13.
48. Ibid.

Conclusion

When Ambrose congratulated Augustine on having such a mother, the bishop of Milan was not simply flattering Monica. She was a woman of faith and of great virtue, who left no stone unturned to procure her own spiritual progress and the conversion of her son. She handled marital problems with wisdom and helped other women to cope with difficult husbands. She also knew how to reconcile those who were estranged, aware that Christians have received a ministry of reconciliation, as St. Paul says.[49] Monica mothered Augustine twice: in the flesh and in spirit, for it was thanks to her persistent prayers for him that God granted Augustine the grace of conversion.

There are many mothers, especially in the West, who suffer greatly to see their own sons and daughters abandon the faith and pander to modern social dogmas that reduce the meaning of human existence to sports, showbiz, and shopping. The unbelief of their children is a sword that pierces the hearts of such mothers. Monica's example is an invitation to all these mothers to raise their prayers to God with "loud cry and tears"[50] for the conversion not only of their sons and daughters but also of the whole world.

Prayer

O God, who received the sacrifice of tears of your handmaid Monica for the conversion of her dear son, hear the prayers of the many mothers who cry to you on account of their wayward children, so that they may rejoice at the spiritual rebirth of their sons and daughters. Through Christ our Lord. Amen.

---

49. Cf. 2Cor 5:18.
50. Heb 5:7.

Chapter 17

Dorothy Day:
Mother of Sacramentality

Introduction

One common view of mothers is that they are better peacemakers than fathers, more likely to seek a peaceful settlement of a conflict in order to protect their children from the turmoil that often characterizes the struggle for social transformation. Not too many mothers who fit that image would willingly allow their sons and daughters to take to the frontlines of a political protest likely to turn violent. But for Dorothy Day, being a mother did not deter her from standing on picket lines in pursuit of her dream to contribute to sociopolitical transformation for the benefit of the poor.

Dorothy, Tamar Teresa's mother, is well known for her social activism and works of charity. She founded the *Catholic Worker* newspaper and opened many houses of hospitality in various places in the United States of America. It is reported that there were 120 such houses when Dorothy was alive.[1] She engaged in intellectual work and at the same time applied herself to the care of the poor and the destitute, now distributing bread, now cleaning houses. She read with profit the *Imitation of Christ* and Karl Marx's *The Communist Manifesto*. Believing in the efficacy of ret-

---

1. Cf. Helen LaKelly Hunt, *Faith and Feminism: A Holy Alliance* (New York: Atria Books, 2004), 98.

roactive prayers, she once prayed for Karl Marx, whom children on the street fondly called Papa Marx, so that God would grant him eternal rest.[2] In sum, she was capable of a rare synthesis of schools of thought ordinarily considered opposed to each other. Someone once dismissively quipped that Dorothy would demonstrate with anyone, whether from the left or from the right, which remark she took as a compliment. In fact, she subscribed to Thomas Aquinas's dictum that "the truth is the truth" and proceeds from the Holy Spirit regardless of the lips whence it comes.[3] However, she knew how to sift truth from error in each philosophical system.

Her writings were sometimes dismissed as incoherent and lacking logic.[4] While those who belonged to the left criticized her for engaging in palliative social measures, such as feeding the hungry, those of a conservative political persuasion encouraged her not to soil her wonderful work of charity with socialist ideology. She criticized capitalism and upheld the "sacramental quality of property."[5] What is the secret of her capacity to reconcile these apparently contradictory thought patterns? I would argue that it is her sacramental worldview, her capacity "to find that which is of God in everyone,"[6] "to see only the good, the Christ, in others,"[7] that helped her to find the face and voice of God in people and things around her. Her writings embody a "style reflecting her belief in the sacramentality, the holy sublimity, of the everyday."[8]

Her Spiritual Journey

Dorothy Day was born in Brooklyn, on November 8, 1897, being the third of five children. Her family belonged to the lower middle

---

2. Cf. Dorothy Day, *Selected Writings*, ed. Robert Ellsberg (Maryknoll, NY: Orbis Books, 1992), 214.

3. Cf. ibid., 236.

4. Cf. Robert Ellsberg, preface to ibid., xii.

5. Ibid., 250.

6. Ibid., 306.

7. Ibid., 214.

8. Ellsberg, preface to ibid., xii.

class. The profession of her father (sportswriter) required the family to move from one place to another. First they moved to Oakland. Then, due to the San Francisco earthquake, they left for Chicago.

There was no religion in this family. Nonetheless, Dorothy developed a sense of God while she was still a child, thanks to neighbors who belonged to the Episcopal Church. She writes, "How much did I hear of religion as a child? Very little, and yet my heart leaped when I heard the name of God. I do believe every soul has a tendency toward God."[9] As children, Dorothy and her siblings did not look for God; they took God for granted.[10] She was later baptized in the Episcopal Church.

As she grew up, however, her piety waned and she adopted a new gospel that promised social and political transformation. She became a radical social activist. While in her first year at the University of Illinois in Urbana, she joined the Socialist Party. Her enthusiasm for social change made her abandon formal education and leave for New York to begin her career as a writer. She worked with such publications as *The Call* and *The Masses*, both of which propagated leftist ideology. Her university lecturers had taught her to dismiss religion as the "opiate of the people," which slogan she repeated to herself to silence any voice that drew her to religion. One of her professors sarcastically invited his students not to despise religion, because it had, down the centuries, brought solace to the weak. In other words, religion was for the weak and the enslaved, those incapable of shedding the "mind-forged manacles" of oppression—to borrow William Blake's expression. She recalls one particular lecture:

> It seems to me that I was already shedding it when a professor whom I much admired made a statement in class—I shall always remember it—that religion was something which had brought great comfort to people throughout the

---

9. Dorothy Day, *The Long Loneliness: The Autobiography* (New York: HarperOne, 1952), 12.

10. Cf. ibid., 17.

ages, so that we ought not to criticize it. I do not remember his exact words, but from the way he spoke of religion the class could infer that the strong did not need such props. In my youthful arrogance, in my feeling that I was one of the strong, I felt then for the first time that religion was something that I must ruthlessly cut out of my life.[11]

She was determined to get rid of any residue of religious sentimentality in order to advance her career as a political journalist:

I felt at the time that religion would only impede my work. I wanted to have nothing to do with the religion of those whom I saw all about me. I felt that I must turn from it as from a drug. I felt it indeed to be an opiate of the people and not a very attractive one, so I hardened my heart. It was a conscious and deliberate process.[12]

Her experience of poverty, loneliness, and oppression convinced her that Christ was a figure confined to the past, no longer walking the streets of her time. New prophets—the socialists—had taken Christ's place. The poor and the oppressed were the collective new Messiah poised to liberate captives of socioeconomic subjugation.[13] She lived with the poor and experienced first-hand the effects of the political and economic system that thrived on the exploitation of the weak. Her political activism landed her in prison on several occasions, giving her an opportunity to taste the squalid living conditions and the humiliation of prisoners. Such an experience further toughened her and made her resolve never to give up the fight against social injustice, as long as she knew that "behind bars all over the world there were women and men, young girls and

---

11. Ibid., 43.
12. Ibid.
13. Cf. ibid., 46.

boys, suffering constraint, punishment, isolation and hardship for crimes of which all of us were guilty."[14]

During an outbreak of influenza in World War I, she had a short stint working as a nurse in a hospital, a profession she respected but did not consider her calling. When she found it unbearable to deal with difficult patients, the assistant superintendent spoke to her of the dignity of the nursing profession and alluded to the "sacrament of duty"—a phrase Dorothy borrowed from Father McSorley.[15] When the epidemic was over, she returned to the profession of her dream—writing!

What Brought Her to God

Dorothy Day states that it had never been her intention to write an autobiography. Instead, she wanted to "tell of things that brought me to God and that reminded me of God."[16] She writes about her own life in order to "give an account of myself, a reason for the faith that is in me."[17] When one reads her autobiography and other writings, one cannot but conclude that these "things" that brought her to God were people, events, sounds, sights, and thoughts. In fact, for her, everything in some way mediated the presence and love of God. That is why she dedicates many pages to drawing up profiles of people she knew and worked with, events that left a mark in her life, books or articles that nourished her spiritual life, places she visited, the beauty of creation, and many other things.

Psalms and Canticles

Psalms played an important role in bringing her to a lively sense of the mystery of God. When she was a child, she loved to read and pray with the Psalms. She singles out for special mention the canticle *Benedicite* and the hymn *Te Deum*. She quotes parts of the

---

14. Ibid., 78.
15. Ibid., 91; Day, *Selected Writings*, 208.
16. Day, *The Long Loneliness*, 94.
17. Ibid., 11.

Te Deum and the *Benedicite* (often known as Canticle of Daniel),[18] adding that the latter "thrilled in my heart, and though I was only ten years old, through these Psalms and canticles I called on all creation to join with me in blessing the Lord. I thanked Him for creating me, saving me from all evils, filling me with all good things."[19] The canticle of creation made her aware of the fundamental unity or solidarity not only of humanity but of the entire creation.[20] Dorothy was so attached to the *Benedicite* that when she had grandchildren, she would sing this hymn to them.[21] As she confesses, the words of these biblical texts remained with her ever since.

At fifteen, she was convinced that God created human beings so they could be happy and enjoy the fullness of life.[22] However, Dorothy soon discovered that in real life, such solidarity was not always visible. Contrary to the biblical vision of humanity as the image of God, she saw human beings robbed of their dignity and reduced to unspeakable destitution and misery. The evangelical value of sharing one's coat was not often practiced in real life. She recalls what she saw as a child:

> Children look at things very directly and simply. I did not see anyone taking off his coat and giving it to the poor. I didn't see anyone having a banquet and calling in the lame, the halt and the blind ... I wanted life and I wanted the abundant life. I wanted it for others too. I did not want just the few, the missionary-minded people like the Salvation Army, to be kind to the poor, as the poor. I wanted everyone to be kind. I wanted every home to be open to the lame, the halt and the blind, the way it had been after the San Francisco earthquake. Only then did people really

---

18. The present author worked on this canticle for his doctoral dissertation. Considering the narrative context in which the hymn is inserted, it is preferable to call this song "The Canticle of the Three Servants in the Fiery Furnace."

19. Day, *The Long Loneliness*, 29.

20. Cf. ibid.

21. Cf. ibid., 223.

22. Cf. ibid., 38.

live, really love their brothers. In such love was the abundant life and I did not have the slightest idea how to find it.[23]

Praying with Others

A second path to God for Dorothy was praying and going to church in the company of others. At different stages in her life, Dorothy encountered people with a deep sense of religion, who helped her to discover her own spiritual life. When she was eight and still living in Oakland, for instance, she used to sing religious songs with a neighboring family that attended the Methodist church. A certain Birdie would take her to Sunday school and to church.

Later, when she was working at the hospital, Dorothy used to go to church, albeit reluctantly, with one Miss Adams. While at prayer, she would hear two voices, one from Psalm 8 ("What is man, that Thou art mindful of him, O Lord?"), reflecting a real desire to recognize her condition of creature before the Creator. The other voice questioned the meaning of existence: "What were we here for, what were we doing, what was the meaning of our lives?"[24] Gradually, the judgmental voice calling religion the opiate of the people gave way to a humble acknowledgment of the respectability of worship. She realized that her fellow workers and herself "were performing an act of worship," and she felt that "it was necessary for man to worship, that he was most truly himself when engaged in that act."[25]

Sacramentality of Creation and Human Relationships

Years later, Dorothy Day was living on Staten Island. It was there that she entered into what she called a "common-law marriage" with a man named Forster Batterham. The encounter with Forster, an anarchist of English descent with a passion for biology, awakened her to the sacramentality of creation and human relationships. Dorothy fell in love with Forster. On Staten Island, they fished

---

23. Ibid., 39.
24. Ibid., 93.
25. Ibid.

together, took walks together, and studied together. Through this relationship, "an entire new world opened up to me little by little."[26] Her contemplation of growing things instilled in her a "sacramental view of life. All things are [God's] and all are holy."[27]

During that time Dorothy went back to reading the Bible and the *Imitation of Christ*. Forster's passion for nature stirred in Dorothy a new fascination for the natural world. These experiences deepened her spiritual life, and she began to "think, to weigh things," and to "pray more."[28] When the bell for the *Angelus* rang at the nearby St. Joseph's Parish, Dorothy found herself praying, expressing her sentiments of thanksgiving for the beauty of creation. The sight of the workers praying on the beach warmed her soul, too.[29]

Nonetheless, the wasp of doubt would from time to time sting her soul and cast a long shadow of doubt on her piety. For instance, every time she knelt while praying she would question the sincerity of her religion: Was she praying because she was lonely? To whom was she praying? Then the accusing voice would repeat the Marxist dictum: "Religion is the opiate of the people." Gradually she learned to counter that voice by assuring herself that she was praying not because she was unhappy or lonely but because she was happy.[30] Then she would say the *Te Deum* along the beach. She also began to attend Sunday morning Masses regularly.

Paradoxically, the creation that drew Dorothy closer to God was a wall that prevented Forster from penetrating the realm of religious experience. Espousing a form of biological determinism, he did not see a reflection of God in the face of the natural world. All seemed to be reduced to the principle of material causality. She regrets, "His ardent love of creation brought me to the Creator of all things. But when I cried out to him, 'How can there be no

---

26. Ibid., 114.
27. Day, *Selected Writings*, 211.
28. Day, *The Long Loneliness*, 116.
29. Cf. ibid., 117.
30. Cf. ibid., 132–33.

God, when there are all these beautiful things,' he turned from me uneasily and complained that I was never satisfied."[31]

Dorothy also saw the love between her and Forster as a reflection (sacrament) of God's love, while Forster saw their relationship purely in human terms. She writes,

> I could not see that love between man and woman was incompatible with love of God. God is the Creator, and the very fact that we were begetting a child made me have a sense that we were made in the image and likeness of God, co-creators with him ... Because I was grateful for love, I was grateful for life, and living with Forster made me appreciate it and even reverence it still more. He had introduced me to so much that was beautiful and good that I felt I owed to him too this renewed interest in the things of the spirit.[32]

Dorothy was aware that even on the canvass of Scripture the marital act was painted as a symbol of the beatific vision: "The very sexual act itself was used again and again in Scripture as a figure of the beatific vision. It was not because I was tired of sex, satiated, disillusioned, that I turned to God. Radical friends used to insinuate this. It was because through a whole love, both physical and spiritual, I came to know God."[33]

Forster's love for outdoor life helped Dorothy to begin to breathe again after going through so many trials in her young adult life: "If breath is life, then I was beginning to be full of it because of him. I was filling my lungs with it, walking on the beach, resting on the pier beside him while he fished, rowing with him in the calm bay, walking through fields and woods—a new experience entirely for me, one which brought me to life, and filled me with joy."[34] Hers

---

31. Ibid., 134.
32. Ibid., 135.
33. Ibid., 140.
34. Ibid., 135.

was indeed a glimpse of the "joy of love," to borrow the title of Pope Francis's postsynodal apostolic exhortation.

Fruit of the Womb

Another important milestone in her faith journey was the experience of conceiving and giving birth to a child. Earlier in life she had fallen in love with an older man while she was working at the hospital. Robert Ellsberg describes the man as one "of a rather menacing charm."[35] Dorothy became pregnant by him but, given the inclement circumstances, she chose to terminate her pregnancy. Ellsberg comments that "it was a futile gesture, and the memory of this waste of life would remain with her always."[36] The painful mark left by this decision probably explains why she does not mention this episode in her autobiography; nor does the event appear in her selected writings.

But God gave her another chance. Her relationship with Forster led to another pregnancy, in the summer of 1925. She was twenty-seven by then. Dorothy was overjoyed at the prospect of having a child. She probably saw it as a compensation for the child she had lost to abortion.[37] Dorothy felt incomplete without a child:

> For a long time I had thought I could not bear a child, and the longing in my heart for a baby had been growing. My home, I felt, was not a home without one. The simple joys of the kitchen and garden and beach brought sadness with them because I felt myself unfruitful, barren. No matter how much one was loved or one loved, that love was lonely without a child. It was incomplete.[38]

She gave birth to a girl whom she named Tamar Teresa, after both Teresa of Avila and of Lisieux, fondly called the Little Flower. The

---

35. Ellsberg, introduction to Day, *Selected Writings*, xxi.
36. Ibid.
37. Ibid., xxii.
38. Day, *The Long Loneliness*, 135–36.

birth of Tamar brought so much joy to Dorothy that she wrote an article about it and published it in *The Masses*. Indeed, she wanted to proclaim the wonders of the Lord to the end of the earth.

Dorothy recalls the immense joy she felt when the medical personnel placed her child in her arms:

> If I had written the greatest book, composed the greatest symphony, painted the most beautiful painting, or carved the most exquisite figure, I could not have felt more the exalted creator than I did when they placed my child in my arms. To think that this thing of beauty, sighing gently in my arms, reaching her little mouth for my breast, clutching at me with her tiny beautiful hands, had come from my flesh, was my own child![39]

For her, the birth of her daughter was not reducible to biological processes. Rather, it was a tangible manifestation of God's love: "It was all very well to love God in His works, in the beauty of His creation which was crowned for me by the birth of my child."[40] Her deep love for the daughter is clear from her confession that Tamar "was . . . everything to me. I have not even to this day ceased to look upon her with wonder. When I looked at her tiny, perfect hands and my own, already worn though I was only twenty-seven, I marveled at her newness. Tamar crowing on the beach, learning to walk on the sands."[41] Such was the mother's love for her daughter.

Choosing Something Greater

Living through the prism of sacramentality means not only seeing God in all things but also seeing God through and beyond things. God's creation is transparent. When created realties become opaque and block the eye from seeing God through them, then they

---

39. Day, *Selected Writings*, 187.
40. Day, *The Long Loneliness*, 139.
41. Ibid., 236.

lose their sacramentality. Dorothy was able not only to find God in creation, relationships, and work but also to see in them something greater, namely, God—the source of all things. She always sought to find the infinite through the finite and never allowed the latter to prevent her from attaining to the former. Her search for God over against finite things brought her face-to-face with some hard choices.

The first difficult choice was to present Tamar for Christian baptism. Though Dorothy had not yet been baptized in the Catholic Church, she decided to have Tamar Teresa baptized, though she was aware that such a step would drive a wedge between her and Forster. She had to choose between God and human love. It was not a simple choice to make given that she treasured Forster's love, which was at its most tender stage. Deep within, she knew she did not want to be alone again. However, she was also aware that human love was but a sign of a more expansive and enduring love, namely, the love of God. In her autobiography she discusses the meaning of the Latin word *diligo* as signifying preference. To love something is to prefer it to something else. To love God is to prefer God to other things, even those very dear to us.[42] In the evangelical sense, to love God means to prefer God to father and mother, brothers and sisters: "Whoever loves father or mother more than me is not worthy of me; and whoever loves son or daughter more than me is not worthy of me."[43] God was a jealous God, and "in the eyes of God, any turning toward creatures to the exclusion of Him is adultery and so it is termed over and over again in Scripture."[44] To prefer the creature to the Creator is idolatry. Dorothy was not facing a choice between good and bad—for human love is also a good; rather, it was a choice between good and better. She was convinced that "we must give up over and over again even the good things of this world, to choose God."[45]

---

42. Ibid., 139.
43. Mt 10:37.
44. Day, *The Long Loneliness*, 149–50.
45. Day, *Selected Writings*, 216.

So Dorothy chose Tamar's baptism. She knew that faith was the greatest gift a mother could give to her child. She recalls, "I knew that I was not going to have her floundering through many years as I had done, doubting and hesitating, undisciplined and amoral. I felt it was the greatest thing I could do for my child."[46]

After Tamar's baptism, Dorothy and Forster brought their relationship to an end.[47] The religious sister who had made arrangements for Tamar's baptism encouraged Dorothy to become Catholic, too. Though she initially hesitated on account of her political convictions, she eventually received conditional baptism (because she had already been baptized in the Episcopal Church) and was later confirmed (on Pentecost Sunday), taking the name of Maria Teresa.

Choosing something greater also meant relativizing her love for her own daughter. Though she loved her daughter, Dorothy never lost sight of a greater love, the source of everything that is good. She did not become so attached to the daughter as to forget God. Inasmuch as she was full of joy at the birth of Tamar, Dorothy was able to see beyond the gift to the giver: "Such a great feeling of happiness and joy filled me that I was hungry for Someone to thank, to love, even to worship, for so great a good that had been bestowed upon me. That tiny child was not enough to contain my love, nor could the father, though my heart was warm with love for both."[48] Sacramentality means seeing God in creation but also seeing beyond creation to God.

She often asked God to enlarge her heart so that God may enter in.[49] She wanted her heart to contain more than her daughter. Apart from Tamar, Dorothy had to open her heart to the poor, the marginalized, the oppressed. Sometimes her sociopolitical activism left her little time for her daughter. She traveled much, visiting

---

46. Day, *The Long Loneliness*, 136.
47. Ibid., 142–44.
48. Day, *Selected Writings*, 187–88.
49. Cf. Day, *The Long Loneliness*, 24.

the houses of hospitality and attending conferences. Such absences sometimes made her feel that she was not a good mother. She would imagine her daughter complaining, "You are always away."

The fact that Tamar preferred to call her "Dorothy" instead of "Mother" roused some gnawing anxiety in Dorothy's heart, wondering whether she was being a good mother to the daughter. Dorothy tried to correct Tamar, encouraging the latter to call her "Mother" so people would know Tamar was her biological daughter rather than an adopted child. Dorothy was assaulted by a sense of failure as a mother so much that she decided to entrust Tamar to Mother Mary, saying to the latter, "You . . . will have to be her mother. Under the best circumstances I'm a failure as a homemaker. I'm untidy, inconsistent, undisciplined, temperamental, and I have to pray every day for final perseverance."[50]

By entrusting Tamar to Mother Mary, Dorothy was not turning Mary into a babysitter, just as some working-class women delegate to nannies the demanding responsibility of nurturing children. Nor was she reneging on her responsibility as a mother. Still less was it a sign that she did not love Tamar. Rather, her love for God drove her beyond the confines of her solicitude for her daughter. She had to reach out to those whose likeness to God had been obscured by degrading living conditions. In many pages of her writings, she describes cases of men, women, and children who were so defaced by poverty and disease that it was no longer easy to see God in them.[51] In an industrial society, some people were treated as chattels rather than as human beings and the temple of the Holy Spirit.[52] Unfortunately, difficult living conditions sometimes made the poor forget that they were temples of the Holy Spirit and comported themselves like animals.[53]

---

50. Day, *Selected Writings*, 161.
51. Cf. ibid., 224.
52. Cf. ibid., 241.
53. Cf. ibid., 248, 281.

The "Little Way"

Dorothy Day's name is now well known. However, her greatness emanates from the fact that she adopted Thérèse of Lisieux's "the little way," the spirituality of "little things." Her sacramental view of life meant that even little things are important and do manifest the love of God. Thérèse believed in the "significance of our smallest acts" and "of the things we leave undone. The protests we do not make, the stands we do not take, we who are living in the world!"[54] In the words of Helen LaKelly Hunt, Dorothy believed that "if we are of God, then everything we do matters. We have a responsibility to manifest the divine—in matters great and small ... To wash the dishes can be a sacrament if we do it in the spirit of attention and love."[55] In fact, between the "great" Teresa of Avila and the "little" Thérèse of Lisieux, she preferred the latter because of her emphasis on the significance of little gestures, not to speak of her sense of the fragility of the human person,[56] hence the name Little Flower. About the Little Flower, Dorothy writes, "She practiced the presence of God and she did all things—all the little things that make up our daily life and contact with others—for His honor and glory."[57] Like the Little Flower, Dorothy was not content to sit in her study and compose great world-changing discourses, but rather applied herself to small things that, however, contain the dynamite of love.

The "little way" also meant choosing to live with the poor. Dorothy, inspired by Peter Maurin, was a big advocate of voluntary poverty. She invited all to "rejoice in poverty, because Christ was poor. Let us love to live with the poor, because they are specially loved by Christ. Even the lowest, most depraved, we must see Christ in them, and love them to folly. When we suffer from dirt, lack of privacy, heat and cold, coarse food, let us rejoice."[58] She was convinced that

---

54. Ibid., 274.
55. LaKelly Hunt, *Faith and Feminism*, 96.
56. Cf. Day, *Selected Writings*, 194.
57. Ibid., 202.
58. Ibid., 231.

humanity's preoccupation with the accumulation of resources had brought about gross socioeconomic inequalities. She also believed in the potential of *little people*, common folk, to transform society. Day drew strength from Mao Zedong's saying: "Three common men will make a genius."[59] The common people, the poor, were not to be treated as mere objects of charity or commiseration. They were agents of change. Dorothy believed that there were thousands and thousands of geniuses in every city and in every village. What these people needed was the space to develop their potential for growth and development. Unfortunately, *big systems* suffocated the meaningful contribution of these *little* geniuses.

Conclusion

Dorothy Day died on November 29, 1980, in the very month she was born. While on earth, she blessed God for the wonders of creation and for the marvels of communion. *Benedicite omnia opera Domini Domino* was her song. Only a mystic can bless the Lord in the midst of the suffering she witnessed in this *vale of tears*. Only a person attuned to the mysterious workings of God can call upon the entire creation to praise God for God's goodness. Dorothy was one such mystic. She was able to acknowledge the dysfunctional character of society without falling prey to pessimism; she engaged in high-profile social activism without losing sight of the little demands of the Beatitudes, knowing that Jesus is manifested in such small gestures as the breaking of bread.

There are many mothers who find themselves torn between the duty to raise their children and the call to respond to the plight of the poor and the oppressed. On the one hand, they do not want to neglect their maternal responsibility, and, on the other, they desire to expand the tent of their love beyond the homestead. Such mothers find themselves in a moral quandary when the needs of their children compete with those of the greater humanity. Dorothy Day can inspire such women to choose that which manifests God in a

---

59. Ibid., 240.

greater manner. With the eyes of God, such mothers will discover that all the destitute children of the world are in fact their own sons and daughters. Therefore, it is never enough to provide maternal care to one's own biological children. As Isaiah says, "It is too light a thing that you should be my servant to raise up the tribes of Jacob and to restore the survivors of Israel; I will give you as a light to the nations, that my salvation may reach to the end of the earth."[60]

Prayer

O God, you reveal yourself to us through the wonder of creation and through human relationships. You inspired your servant Dorothy Day to proclaim in word and deed your compassion for the poor, the homeless, the sick, and the marginalized. Grant, we pray, that even in our day men and women will learn to find you in things small and great, so that your name may be praised in all things and in all places. Amen.

---

60. Isa 49:6.

Chapter 18

Mother Teresa: Mother of None, Mother of Many

Introduction

The mothers presented thus far have all been mothers also in the biological sense of the word. However, not all mothers of faith literally give birth to children. Some are spiritual mothers whose faith moves them to give to thousands of people the love of a mother without having given birth to them. Such is the motherhood of Mother Teresa, who touched many poor and abandoned people, helping them to recover their dignity as sons and daughters of God. The title "Mother," which accompanied her throughout her life, was not merely a residue of the tradition of the Loreto Sisters, who assumed this title upon committing themselves to perpetual vows of poverty, chastity, and obedience.[1] It was rather descriptive of what and who she was to the multitudes of men, women, and children to whom she reached out with love and joy.

Her Background

Mother Teresa was born Agnes Gonxha Bojaxhiu on August 26, 1910, in Skopje, Serbia. She was the youngest of the three children

---

1. Cf. Kathryn Spink, *Mother Teresa: A Complete Authorized Biography* (San Francisco: HarperSanFrancisco, 1997), 17.

born to Nikola and Dranafile Bojaxhiu. The father was a prosperous entrepreneur, being a supplier of medicines, oil, sugar, cloth, and leather. Because of his financial success, he was one of the leading figures in Skopje. Nikola was strict with his children and set high academic standards for them. Unfortunately, Agnes's father died in mysterious circumstances in 1919; some suspected he was poisoned for his involvement in politics. Agnes was only eight when her father died. After Nikola's death, the family lost its financial security, his business partner having claimed and appropriated the assets of the business. Dranafile assumed the role of breadwinner for the children through, among other things, sewing, embroidery, and selling cloth.

Lessons from the Mother

To understand the convictions and works of Mother Teresa, one has to go back to the convictions and works of her mother. Dranafile had a strong sense of solidarity with the needy, so much so that she used some of her hard-earned income to provide for the poor. Dranafile would say to her daughter Agnes, "My child, never eat a single mouthful unless you are sharing it with others."[2] The family knew how to "widen the tent"[3] of the family table to accommodate many poor people, both relatives and strangers, whom Dranafile welcomed with warmth and gentleness. One of the people Mother Teresa's mother used to look after was an alcoholic woman called File. The old woman had been abandoned by her family. Dranafile would visit File to bring her food, clean her house, wash her, and feed her. A certain poor widow died and left behind six children. Dranafile took them in and made them part of the family. Sometimes, Agnes would accompany her mother on charitable errands. In fact, Dranafile was intent on inculcating in her children the spirit of charity and self-giving.

Dranafile is also famous for her saying, "The family that prays

2. Ibid., 6.
3. Cf. Isa 54:2.

together stays together," an axiom very dear to the adult Mother Teresa. The Bojaxhiu family was very religious, and prayer enjoyed pride of place in their life. They prayed every evening, regularly attended church, and cherished the devotion to the Sacred Heart. Every year the family undertook a pilgrimage to the chapel of the Madonna of Letnice on the slopes of Skopje's Black Mountain.

Later, when Agnes had become a nun with the Loreto Sisters, she wrote a letter to her mother, telling her about her teaching work in India, adding that she headed the whole school. The mother wrote back and said to her, "Do not forget that you went to India for the sake of the poor."[4] The mother reminded her about the old woman she used to visit and look after:

> Do you remember our File? She was covered in sores, but what caused her far more suffering was the knowledge that she was all alone in the world. We did what we could for her but the worst thing was not the sores but the fact that her family had forgotten her.[5]

It was thanks to her mother's reminder about the importance of attending to poor people that Mother Teresa decided to embrace her *vocation within a vocation*, a life of total dedication to the poor of India.

Finding God's Will

Thanks to her devotion to Our Lady of the Black Mountain, Agnes became aware of her call to religious life by the age of twelve. One of the Jesuits introduced her to the Spiritual Exercises of St. Ignatius, and she was particularly struck by the threefold question: "What have I done for Christ? What am I doing for Christ? What will I do for Christ?"[6] Through her home parish, Agnes would hear news of

---

4. Cited in ibid., 19.

5. Cited in ibid., 20.

6. Cf. Ignatius of Loyola, *The Spiritual Exercises*, no. 53, tr. George E. Ganss (Anand, India: Gujarat Sahitya Prakash, 1993).

the missionary work of the Society of Jesus and of other missionaries in mission lands such as India. Agnes found the missionaries' accounts of their work with the poor and the sick particularly inspiring. As a child, she dreamed of working for the poor in Africa, but the news from India turned her heart to the Asian continent.

At the age of eighteen, Agnes applied to join the Loreto Sisters, some of whom were working in Bengal, India. She left for Ireland, where she spent six weeks learning English. As a postulant, Agnes chose the name of Sister Mary Teresa of the Child Jesus, for she wanted to follow Thérèse of Lisieux's path to holiness, which path consisted in fidelity in small things. In December 1928, she set sail for India.

What she saw in Sri Lanka shocked her profoundly. On the streets, she saw half-naked people and men who "like human horses pulled their little carts through the congested streets."[7] At Madras, she saw "indescribable" poverty. She wrote,

> Many families live in the streets, along the city walls, even in places thronged with people. Day and night they live out in the open on mats they have made from large palm leaves—or frequently on the bare ground. They are all virtually naked, wearing at best a ragged loincloth.[8]

Having arrived in India, she began her novitiate with the Loreto Sisters in May 1929. She made her temporary vows two years later, after which she was assigned to teach in the Loreto convent school in Darjeeling. Her work brought her in contact with India's poor. She contributed articles to the *Catholic Missions*—the very journal that nourished her zeal to work with the poor while she was still in her country—describing the poverty of the people she saw and interacted with. In her words, "It is not possible to find worse poverty."[9] Her observation of the suffering of the people was, in Igna-

---

7. Spink, *Mother Teresa*, 13.
8. Cited in ibid.
9. Cited in ibid., 17.

tian language, her "contemplation to attain divine love," for what she saw moved her to make a more radical option for the poor.

Call within a Call

Sister Teresa pronounced her final vows on May 24, 1937, and became Mother Teresa, according to the tradition of the Loreto nuns. Before her final commitment, news spread in the slums where she was working that she was going to become "Mother." The children in the slums were worried that their "Ma" (which means mother) was going to become "Mother," so one of them plucked up courage and asked her not to become "Mother" but to remain their "Ma." Mother Teresa writes,

> [The child] asked whether I would be coming back to them, because he had heard that I was going to become "Mother." He began to cry, and through his tears he said, "Oh, don't become Mother!" I held him to me and asked him, "What is the matter? Do not worry. I will be back. I will always be your Ma."[10]

India's involvement in World War II brought immense suffering to the people of India, particularly in Calcutta where Mother Teresa was working. Many "war babies" would be left at the doorsteps of Loreto, and one day she was presented with twenty-four babies to bottle feed.[11]

In the face of all these needs, "Mother Teresa began progressively to feel that something more was being asked of her."[12] Instead of waiting for the poor to come to the convent, she wanted to go out to the streets and bring them home. She received this insight on what she came to call Inspiration Day, an episode that took place while she was on a train to Darjeeling, on September 10, 1946. With the

10. Cited in ibid.
11. Cf. ibid., 19.
12. Ibid., 20.

help of the Belgian Jesuit Father Celeste Van Exem, she arrived at a decision to leave the Loreto Sisters so as to dedicate her life more fully to the poor. This was Father Van Exem's reading of the movement of the spirits in his spiritual daughter: "She was to leave Loreto but she was to keep her vows. She was to start a new congregation. That congregation would work for the poorest of the poor in the slums in a spirit of poverty and cheerfulness. There would be a special vow of charity for the poor."[13]

At the heart of the spirituality of the new congregation was to be Christ's cry of anguish on the cross, "I thirst,"[14] and his request to the Samaritan woman, "Give me to drink."[15] The new congregation, Missionaries of Charity, would dedicate itself to quenching "the infinite thirst of Jesus Christ on the Cross for love of souls."[16] In fact, the words *I thirst* were to be inscribed in every chapel of the Missionaries of Charity. Mother Teresa was deeply touched by humanity's thirst for love, care, and recognition, and this thirst was most evident among the poor. To the above verses she added Matthew 25:35: "I was thirsty and you gave me to drink."

Becoming Mother of Thousands

In her moments of desolation, Mother Teresa was acutely aware of the cost of her call, especially the fact that she did not have any children of her own. In her prayer, she once sighed, "Today, my God, what tortures of loneliness." Then turning to Mother Mary, she said, "I have no children as once you told your beloved Son, 'They have no wine.'"[17] To become a mother of thousands, she had to become a mother of none. That was her gift to God and to humanity.

The foundation of the new religious congregation gave Mother Teresa the space and impetus to become "Mother of the Poor," as

---

13. Cited in ibid., 23.
14. Jn 19:28.
15. Jn 4:9.
16. Cited in Spink, *Mother Teresa*, 24.
17. Cited in ibid., 38.

she came to be known. She chose to wear a white sari with three blue stripes on the edge, which dress was to become the habit of the Missionaries of Charity. Immediately she ventured into Motijhil, the slum close to the Loreto convent in Entally. Having received permission to open a slum school there, Mother Teresa started with twenty-one pupils on the first day, and the numbers kept swelling up until "the noise of the alphabet being repeated was a familiar sound in the muddy alleyways that divided up the row upon row of improvised hovels."[18] She taught the children, cleaned them, and fed them.

Mother Teresa was a mother not only to children but also to the sick, the dying, and the rejected. The Missionaries of Charity crossed religious borders in their work, extending their helping hand to Christians, Hindus, and Muslims alike. A story is told that once a group of Hindus protested against her work of looking after non-Christian poor because they saw it as a specious form of proselytism. The group stormed Nirmal Hriday (meaning a place of the Immaculate Heart) where the sisters took care of the sick and the dying. When the leader of the protesters went inside and saw the care the sisters were giving to the suffering and emaciated bodies, he returned to the protesters waiting outside and told them he was ready to evict the sisters, but on one condition: "that [the protestors] persuade their mothers and sisters to undertake the same service."[19] The protesters were cut to the heart and dispersed, for it dawned upon them that Mother Teresa and her sisters were doing what the biological mothers and sisters of the poor were failing to do.

Mother Teresa was a mother to the "apparently unlimited number of unwanted children who must otherwise fend for themselves on the streets of Calcutta, orphans, sick, crippled or mentally handicapped children whose parents found themselves unable to support them, children whose mothers had died in Nirmal Hriday, babies born to unmarried mothers who would never be accepted

---

18. Ibid., 35.
19. Ibid., 56.

back into their families."[20] She would rescue babies dumped in dustbins and drains or those abandoned on the city railway platforms. All these babies cried out for the love of a mother, and they found it in Mother Teresa, for "no child was ever refused a home . . . even if it meant that the babies slept three or more to a cot or were coaxed into life in a box heated by a light bulb."[21] Mother Teresa made all these unwanted children feel wanted and loved again.

She was aware that "being unwanted is the greatest disease of all."[22] Her account of the visit to one old people's home in Europe illustrates her point. This is what she saw in that home:

> I saw that in that home they had everything, beautiful things, but everybody was looking towards the door. And I did not see a single one with a smile on their face. And I turned to the sister and I asked, "How is that? How is it that these people who have everything here, why are they all looking towards the door? Why are they not smiling?" And she said: "This is so nearly every day. They are expecting, they are hoping that a son or daughter will come to visit them. They are hurt because they are forgotten."[23]

Mother Teresa noticed that if a mother loved her child, it did not matter whether she was poor; the child would still want to stay at home with her. There was, for instance, a case of a child who had been picked up from the streets and taken to one of the homes of the Missionaries of Charity. The sisters cleaned him, gave him fresh clothes and fed him. However, he ran away. The following day, someone brought him back to the sisters, but again he disappeared. When he was brought back the third time, one of the sisters was instructed to follow him and see where he went. When the child ran away the third time, the sister followed him and discov-

---

20. Ibid., 57–58.
21. Ibid., 59.
22. Cited in ibid., 87.
23. Cited in ibid., 169.

ered the following: "There under a tree was the mother. She had put two stones under a small earthenware vessel. She was cooking something that she had picked out of the dustbins. The Sister asked the child: 'Why did you run away from home?' And the child said: 'But this is home because this is where my mother is.'"[24]

Home is where mother is, Mother Teresa learned from the incident. It did not matter to the child whether the food the child's mother prepared was taken from dustbins; what mattered was that the food was cooked by his mother; "it was mother who hugged the child, mother who wanted the child. The child had its mother," Mother Teresa emotionally observes.[25]

Mother Teresa welcomed even those at the point of death, because what mattered to her was not simply the restoration of health to the sick but that they experience some love before dying.[26] She would instruct her sisters to love a dying child until he or she breathed his or her last. For her, there was no limit to giving love; one has to give "until it hurts."[27]

Trust in God's Providence

One of the keystones of Mother Teresa's motherhood was her trust in God's providence. When she decided to follow a more radical path in her response to the Lord's call to be of service to the poor, she left the Loreto nuns with only her ticket for Patna and five rupees. Though the Loreto Sisters would have been willing to provide her with more resources for her new adventure, she chose to put her trust in God's providence.[28] She was convinced that "Divine Providence is much greater than our little minds and will never let us down."[29]

In the work of the Missionaries of Charity, not much time was

---

24. Cited in ibid., 252.
25. Ibid.
26. Cf. ibid., 124.
27. Ibid., 216.
28. Cf. ibid., 32.
29. Cited in ibid., 49.

spent on planning or putting into place a complex infrastructure. Mother Teresa relates, "We do not make plans, we do not prepare an infrastructure. Everything is made according to the necessities of the poor … It is Divine Providence who guides us in the execution of the work and in the obtainment of means for it."[30] How different her approach was from that of the corporate world where every detail has to be planned and provided for!

Her trust in God's providence made her averse to fund-raising, though many organizations and governments would have been more than willing to help her with requisite resources. For instance, Cardinal Cooke of New York once offered to pay each sister of the Missionaries of Charity working in Harlem a monthly salary of five hundred dollars, but Mother Teresa turned down the offer and replied to the cardinal with a searching rhetorical question: "Do you think, Your Eminence, that God is going to become bankrupt in New York?"[31] She also dissuaded the Co-Workers of the Missionaries of Charity from fund-raising, because the sisters were receiving a lot of help even without asking for it.[32] And God worked many miracles for the sisters, meeting the needs of the poor in mysterious ways.[33]

Her work was greatly admired the world over. In 1979, for instance, she was awarded the Nobel Prize in recognition of her humanitarian service. She died in 1997 and was beatified in 2003. Mother Teresa was canonized by Pope Francis on September 4, 2016.

In his sermon on the occasion of the canonization of Blessed Mother Teresa, Pope Francis called her "a generous dispenser of mercy," for she committed herself to defending life and ceaselessly proclaimed the dignity of the smallest and weakest of society. She "bowed down before those who were spent, left to die on the side of the road, seeing in them their God-given dignity; she made her

---

30. Cited in ibid., 76.
31. Cited in ibid., 93.
32. Cf. ibid., 135.
33. Cf. ibid., 95.

voice heard before the powers of this world, so that they might recognize their guilt for the crime—the crimes!—of poverty they created." The pope added that he appreciated how difficult it would be for people to call her Saint Teresa, because "her holiness is so near to us, so tender and so fruitful that we continue to spontaneously call her 'Mother Teresa.'"[34] Like the little child who protested against her assuming the title "Mother" instead of "Ma," some people today prefer her to remain "Mother Teresa" instead of "Saint Teresa."

Conclusion

Mother Teresa is an outstanding example of spiritual motherhood, for she who did not have a child of her own ended up having thousands of men, women, and children who looked up to her for love and hope. By renouncing biological motherhood for the sake of the Kingdom,[35] she received a hundredfold of children in this world. She labored to supply for the lack of good motherhood in society, and her motherhood was inspired by the evangelical call to hearken to the cry of the little ones, the *anawim*, who thirst for love, acceptance, and care.

Prayer

Loving and compassionate God, you raised up Mother Teresa to serve the poor and to show to them your merciful face; grant, we pray, that we, too, may hear the cry of the vulnerable and the rejected in our society, so that, through our labor, they may rediscover their dignity as your sons and daughters. Through Christ our Lord. Amen.

---

34. Pope Francis, Homily, Canonization of Blessed Mother Teresa of Calcutta, https://w2.vatican.va/content/francesco/en/homilies/2016/documents/papa-francesco_20160904_omelia-canonizzazione-madre-teresa.html.

35. Cf. Mt 19:12.

Part IV

Motherhood as Theological Analogy

Theologians use analogy to speak about God. It is only through analogy that one can use finite reality to speak of infinite reality. In the Old Testament, God is called a "rock"[1] to highlight God's might and dependability. From the relational realm of human experience, God is described as "husband,"[2] "father,"[3] "king,"[4] and many other epithets.[5] The Kenyan theologian John Mbiti calls them "mental images," whose purpose is to aid the human understanding of God.[6] However, these metaphors and images do not exhaust humanity's knowledge and experience of transcendence. Our God is hyphenated, for God combines many facets: "God-mother, -father, -son, -daughter, -brother, -friend, -lover, -consoler, -comforter, -creator, -redeemer, -sanctifier . . . *at the same time and as the one and the same God*."[7] God dwells in inaccessible light. Theology as a rational discourse of faith has the responsibility to examine and bring to light the limitations of human language about God, for God is beyond male or female.[8]

When theological language loses its analogical (metaphorical) character, it degenerates into idolatry,[9] for, in truth, the divine reality expressed in the language of theology always goes beyond the words used to describe it. In fact, "concepts of God, no matter how sophisticated, are hardly the same as the reality deserving the title

---

1. Cf. Pss 18:46; 95:1.

2. Cf. Isa 54:5; Hosea 1-2.

3. Cf. Dt 32:6; Jer 31:9; Isa 63:16; 64:8.

4. Cf. Pss 5:2; 47:7; 95:3; 145:1.

5. Cf. Mary E. Mills, *Images of God in the Old Testament* (Collegeville, MN: Liturgical Press, 1998), 71–75.

6. Cf. John S. Mbiti, *Introduction to African Religion* (Nairobi: East African Educational Publishers, 1992), 53.

7. Agbonkhianmeghe E. Orobator, *Theology Brewed in an African Pot* (Maryknoll, NY: Orbis Books, 2008), 33; emphasis in original.

8. Leonardo Boff, *The Maternal Face of God: The Feminine and Its Religious Expressions*, trans. Robert R. Barr and John W. Diercksmeier (San Francisco: Harper & Row, 1987), 82.

9. Cf. Paul Ricoeur, *The Symbolism of Evil*, trans. Emerson Buchanan (New York: Harper & Row, 1967), 354.

'God.'"[10] Every concept or image used of God has both cataphatic (positive, affirmative) and apophatic (negative) dimensions, in the sense that God is "like" but also "unlike" the concept or image in question. The human vision of God on earth remains veiled.[11]

The limitedness of human language to express divine realities leads to the plurality of images and concepts predicated of the divine.[12] Litanies of divine attributes are an example of the plurality of images and concepts used to describe God. The plurality of metaphors and concepts used of God is a way to guard against idolatry. To literalize an image or to suppress its negative pole leads to idolatry, for God comes to be reduced to one image or concept.[13]

This section undertakes a theological reflection on "motherhood" as an attribute of God. Just as fatherhood is derived from God,[14] motherhood also flows from God and extends to the church and to the earth. Analogically, therefore, the church and the earth are also mothers.

10. John C. H. Laughlin, "Idolatry," in *The New Interpreter's Dictionary of the Bible*, vol. 3, ed. Katharine D. Sakenfeld et al. (Nashville, TN: Abingdon Press, 2008), 14.

11. Cf. 1Cor 13:12; Kevin W. Irwin, "Sacramentality: The Fundamental Language for Liturgy and Sacraments," in *Per Ritus et Preces. Sacramentalità della liturgia. Atti dell'VIII Congresso Internazionale di Liturgia* (Studia Anselmiana 150), ed. Pietro A. Muroni (Rome: Pontificio Ateneo S. Anselmo, 2010), 138; Nzuzi Bibaki, *Le Dieu-Mère. L'inculturation de la foi chez les Yombe* (Kinshasa: Editions Loyola, 1993), 49.

12. Cf. Anthony J. Gittins, "'Charged with the Grandeur of God': The Created World as a Path to Prayer," in *The Wisdom of Creation*, ed. Edward Foley and Robert Schreiter (Collegeville, MN: Liturgical Press, 2004), 90.

13. Cf. Sandra M. Schneiders, *The Revelatory Text: Interpreting the New Testament as Scripture* (New York: HarperSanFrancisco, 1991), 30.

14. Cf. Eph 3:15.

Chapter 19

God: Mother of Compassion

Introduction

In the 2012 British-American film version of the classic *Les Misérables*, the ex-prisoner turned mayor, Jean Valjean, goes out to find Cosette, a little orphaned girl entrusted to the care of a couple steeped in double-dealing. Valjean pays the couple for their pains and takes Cosette away. When she asks him if he will be like a papa to her, he responds in the affirmative and adds, "I will be father and mother to you." Obviously, motherhood is in this case understood symbolically. Though a man, Valjean commits himself to love Cosette with the depth of the love of a mother. In like manner, though God is Father, his love also embodies the characteristics of a mother.

The image of *God as mother* brings out an important dimension of the human experience of God. Mothers play a crucial role in the beginning of human life and in human development. One's life begins in the womb of the mother. A child is flesh of his or her mother's flesh, blood of her blood. After birth, one's first experience of the warmth of love and protection comes from the mother, who feeds her child at her breast. It is from one's mother that one learns the first smile. It is the mother who wipes her baby's first tears. It is the mother who, by embracing her dirty child, makes him or her understand that one's worth as a human being does not depend on external appearance. The role of a mother can therefore not fail to be an eloquent sacrament of God's love.

Yolanda Pierce, professor at Princeton Theological Seminary, grounds her belief that God is also a *mother* on her experience of motherly care at home:

> I was being raised in a household where I instinctively understood that the divine presence was manifest in the loving hands and arms of mothers, and most especially in the life of my grandmother who raised me ... I knew that if God was real, if God truly loved me as a parent loves a child, then God was also "Mother" and not only "Father."[1]

In a society where the number of single mothers is increasing, it is urgent to flesh out motherhood as a sacrament of God's love and care. The more one appreciates the motherhood of God, the more one takes cognizance of the inadequacy of the lopsidedly patriarchal image of God. It is remarkable to note that in Christian tradition, more men than women have spoken of God as a feminine principle. Therefore, this feminine image of God is not merely a product of "subjective, liberationist, human-centered theology."[2] It is further observed that while women are particularly drawn to the bridal imagery (underscoring the image of God as husband), men exude a greater attraction to God as a feminine and maternal figure. One of the explanations of this fascinating reversal is the desire for union with the divine, which union is presented with the metaphor of sexual union. The image of God as a mother allowed male mystics to conceptualize physical union with God either in the womb or at the breast. Theology and spirituality stand to gain much from paying attention to the motherly qualities of God.

The image of the motherhood of God, in fact, may yield more

---

1. Yolanda Pierce, "Why God Is a 'Mother,' Too," *Time* (May 11, 2013), http://ideas.time.com/2013/05/11/why-god-is-a-mother-too/.

2. Virginia R. Mollenkott, *The Divine Feminine: The Biblical Imagery of God as Female* (New York: Crossroad, 1983), 10.

theological dividend to men than women. As Mollenkott avers, "One reason so few men attend church regularly is that they are unconsciously repelled by being called toward intimacy with an exclusively masculine God."[3] Failure to articulate the maternal qualities of God may lead some, especially Catholics, to invest in Mary the qualities of divine motherhood. According to Charles Nyamiti, the suppression of the motherhood of God minimizes the maternal qualities of God and reduces the latter to a cold legislator, a "distant and severe judge, and—in case especially of many Catholics—the Virgin Mary then fulfills the function of a divinized Mother who consoles, protects, is near, bestows pardon ... —instead of ascribing all these qualities to God as well."[4]

God as Mother in Scripture

The image of God as mother is not an invention of modern or post-modern theologians. Rather, it goes all the way back to the Bible. The prophet Isaiah, for instance, encouraging the fainthearted in Israel in view of their social, political, and religious woes, speaks to them of a God who will comfort them as a mother comforts her child: "As a mother comforts her child, so I will comfort you; you shall be comforted in Jerusalem."[5] Just as a mother whispers words of consolation to her heartbroken child, God stoops down to speak to the heart of the despondent people of Israel, assuring them that tomorrow will be better. God will multiply blessings on Jerusalem, and the land will overflow with grain and peace.

Isaiah compares God's love to that of a mother, except that the love of God surpasses that of a mother, for God never forgets the people who belong to Him: "Can a woman forget her nursing child, or show no compassion for the child of her womb? Even these may forget, yet I will not forget you."[6] In biblical tradition, to

---

3. Ibid., 11.
4. Charles Nyamiti, "The African Sense of God's Motherhood in the Light of Christian Faith," *Africa Ecclesial Review* 23 (1981): 273.
5. Isa 66:13.
6. Isa 49:15.

"remember" is not a purely intellectual act of recalling; it implies to be present to someone with care, love, and solicitude. To "remember" means fidelity. God always remembers his people, especially in the hour of need.[7] God's love (remembering) surpasses that of a human mother because, while the latter can occasionally forget her babies, God never forgets his own children.[8]

In the so-called second Song of Moses (Deuteronomy 32), the people of Israel are chided for being forgetful of their Creator: "You were unmindful of the Rock that bore you; you forgot the God who gave you birth."[9] This text attributes to God the maternal characteristic of childbearing. Commenting on this verse, Carrie A. Miles argues that the "graphic depiction of God 'writhing in labor' for us presents an immediate and compelling picture of God's love and sacrifice on our behalf."[10] The God of compassion is a God of "motherly-womb-love."[11]

It is significant that the words *compassion*[12] and *womb*[13] have the same Hebrew root. The compassion of God for the suffering people is expressed with the image of a mother giving birth. The silent suffering of God on account of the travail of God's people is compared to the groaning of a woman in labor: "For a long time I have held my peace, I have kept still and restrained myself; now I will cry out like a woman in labor, I will gasp and pant."[14] These metaphors speak of the intensity of God's love that is especially extended to those oppressed by suffering in the world. God's travail gives birth to a new world order freed from suffering and turmoil.[15] The relation between *compassion* and *womb* shows that the love of

---

7. Cf. Gen 8:1; 19:29; 30:22; 1Sam 1:19; Jer 31:20; Lk 1:72.

8. Cf. Margaret Hebblethwaite, *Motherhood and God* (London: Geoffrey Chapman, 1984), 130.

9. Dt 32:18.

10. Carrie A. Miles, "God as Mother," *Sunstone* 124 (2002): 43.

11. Ibid.

12. *Rachum.*

13. *Rechem.*

14. Isa 42:14.

15. Cf. Mollenkott, *The Divine Feminine*, 15.

God is as strong as labor pains. In Moltmann's words, "God's compassion is creative and gives birth to new life."[16]

In his intercession for the people of Israel (Numb 11:12–13), Moses pleads with God not to be angry at the Israelites, for it was not Moses who conceived and gave birth to the people of Israel. Since it was God who conceived and gave birth to them, it is incumbent upon God to look after them like a nurse with a baby at the breast. It is God's responsibility to provide food for the famished people of Israel.

Hosea describes God's solicitude for Israel in a mixture of paternal and maternal imagery:

> When Israel was a child, I loved him, and out of Egypt I called my son. The more I called them, the more they went from me; they kept sacrificing to the Baals, and offering incense to idols. Yet it was I who taught Ephraim to walk, I took them up in my arms; but they did not know that I healed them. I led them with cords of human kindness, with bands of love. I was to them like those who lift infants to their cheeks. I bent down to them and fed them.[17]

In Jewish society, it was the mother who fed her children and taught them how to walk. The affectionate gesture of lifting an infant to one's cheek is also characteristic of a mother.[18]

Etymologically, the name *el Shaddai* used for God in the Old Testament can literally mean *the Breasted One*, just as a mountain (*shaddai*) has the shape of a breast. The word *shaddai* is derived from *shad*, meaning *breast*.[19] This image speaks of a provident God, the all-sufficient God, who nurtures people just as a mother

---

16. Jürgen Moltmann, *The Source of Life: The Holy Spirit and the Theology of Life*, trans. Margaret Kohl (Minneapolis: Fortress Press, 1997), 29.

17. Hos 11:1–4.

18. Cf. Miles, "God as Mother," 44.

19. This is one of the meanings discussed in *Theological Lexicon of the Old Testament*, ed. Ernst Jenni and Claus Westermann, trans. Mark E. Biddle (Peabody, MA: Hendrickson Publishers, 1997), 1307–8.

nurses her child. Significantly, the name *el Shaddai* is mentioned in contexts referring to the blessing of fertility.[20] For instance, it is God as *el Shaddai* whom Jacob invokes to bless Joseph with blessings of the "breast and of the womb."[21] Here, a remark by Elina Vuola is apt and merits to be quoted at length:

> What could be the most accurate symbol for life and giving life? Humankind has presented many such symbols, and often, understandably, they are taken from the shared human experience of reproduction and birth. One such symbol is the female breast, especially in its nursing capacity. However, even though it can be found as a metaphor for the God of life in the Old Testament, it has hardly occupied an important symbolic place in Christian theology. The closer we come to our own times, the less the breast is presented as the source of life, especially in Western popular imagery. The further back we go in history, the more often we find the breast—and especially breastfeeding—as a written and visual metaphor for life and for the sustenance of life, but also of human dependency and vulnerability.[22]

Since the breast is a symbol of motherhood, to speak of the divine nourishing breast is to speak of God as a mother. Womb, mother, and breast constitute synonymous parallelism.

God's motherhood is not confined to humanity, but rather extends to the rest of creation. Mollenkott discerns the divine motherhood motif in Acts 17:26 and 28, where, in his speech to the Athenian Council, Paul makes allusion to the saying that presents God as the one *in* whom we live, and move, and have our being. Mollenkott interprets the preposition *in* in a locative sense

---

20. Cf. Gen 17:1–22; 28:8–12; 43:14.

21. Cf. Gen 49:25.

22. Elina Vuola, "(The) Breastfeeding God," *Ecumenical Review* 65 (2013): 98.

and imagines the whole creation in the cosmic womb of God. She argues that "at no other time in human experience do we exist *within* another person."[23] God's womb has given birth not only to human beings but also to the whole natural world.

God as Mother in Christian Tradition

Daniel F. Stramara Jr.'s *Praying—with the Saints—to God Our Mother* contains a wealth of Christian writings that speak of God as a mother.[24]

In the second or early third century, Clement of Alexandria, speaking of God's love, affirmed that, in God's essence, God is Father, but in God's compassion, God became mother. By loving, God became feminine and begot the Son.[25] Stramara's translation of Clement's statement reads as follows:

> Behold the mysteries of love! Then you shall have a vision of the womb of the Father, whom the Only-Begotten declared. God in God's very self is love, and for love's sake became visible to us. And while the ineffable aspect of God is Father, the aspect that has loving sympathy for us manifests itself as Mother. The Father, by the act of loving, became feminine, and the great proof of this is the One whom God gave birth to from himself. Now the fruit that which is born of love is love.[26]

In Clement's thought, the motherhood of God consists in the act of giving birth or generating and in the act of loving. Clearly, the idea of the Father giving birth to the Son is theological metaphor, for the Son, as the Father, is without beginning.

---

23. Mollenkott, *The Divine Feminine*, 16.

24. Daniel F. Stramara Jr., *Praying—with the Saints—to God Our Mother* (Eugene, OR: Wipf and Stock, 2012).

25. Clement of Alexandria, *Qui dives salvetur* XXXVII, ed. J.-P. Migne, PG, vol. 9 (Paris, 1857), 641–42.

26. Stramara, *Praying*, 163.

The *Revelations of Divine Love*, also known as *Showings of Divine Love*, of Julian of Norwich (1342–1416) also articulates the motherhood of God. Her oft-quoted affirmation reads, "As truly as God is our Father, so truly is God our Mother."[27] On the basis of Exodus 3:14, in which God describes God's self as "I am who I am," Julian understands God not only as the "goodness of Fatherhood" but also the "wisdom and the kindness of Motherhood."[28] The motherhood of God is associated with the attributes of wisdom and kindness. Elsewhere, Julian attributes wisdom to the Son: "And thus, in our making, God almighty is our kindly Father: and God all-wisdom is our kindly Mother: with the love and goodness of the Holy Ghost."[29]

Edward Maitland (1824–97) similarly had a mystical vision of God as both Mother and Father. He writes, "This was . . . God as the Lord, proving by His duality that God is Substance as well as Force, Love as well as Will, feminine as well as masculine, Mother as well as Father."[30]

More recently, Pope John XXIII wrote about his experience in the seminary. In his diary, he speaks of his experience of God's love and compares it to the love of a mother:

> He [God] took me, a country lad, from my home, and with the affection of a loving mother he has given me all I needed. I had nothing to eat and he provided food for me, I had no books to study and he provided those also. At times I forgot him and he always gently recalled me. If my affection for him cooled, he warmed me in his breast, at the flame with which his Heart is always burning . . . He

27. Julian of Norwich, *Revelations of Divine Love* LIX, trans. James Walsh, Religious Experience Series, vol. 3 (St. Meinrad, IN: Abbey Press, 1974), 161.

28. Ibid.

29. Ibid., LVIII, 158–159. Stramara also develops the association between wisdom and motherhood, but he gives this attribute to the second Person of the Trinity. Cf. Stramara, *Praying*, 176ff.

30. Edward Maitland, *Anna Kingsford: Her Life, Letters, Diary, and Work*, vol. 1, ed. Samuel H. Hart (London: John M. Watkins, 1913), 130.

has preserved me from all ill, he has not allowed the sea to swallow me up . . . and he still cares for me without respite, day and night, more than a mother cares for her child.[31]

Though he addresses God as "he," the pope underlines God's maternal qualities, among which are often identified the following: affection, care, providence, protection, and fidelity.

God as Mother in African Traditions

In spite of the dominance of the male image of God in traditional African societies,[32] the ascription of motherhood to God is not lacking in traditional African religious consciousness. John Mbiti writes, "In a few African societies, God is also regarded as the Mother of people. This idea is found in the societies whose social organization is centered on the home and position of the mother."[33] Basing himself on the Igbo culture of Nigeria, Achebe highlights the importance of a mother as a source of consolation. Uchendu, one of the characters in *Things Fall Apart*, explains: "When a father beats his child, it seeks sympathy in its mother's hut. A man belongs to his fatherland when things are good and life is sweet. But when there is sorrow and bitterness he finds refuge in his motherland,"[34] because the mother is there to protect the child. It is not surprising, therefore, that the image of God as mother would have a place in the African religious imagination.

Granted, African tribal groups that explicitly describe God as a mother are not many; nonetheless, practically all African societies

31. Pope John XXIII, *Journal of a Soul*, trans. Dorothy M. White (London: Geoffrey Chapman, 1965), 90–91.

32. The image of God as "Father" is dominant in the collection of African prayers by John Mbiti. See John S. Mbiti, *The Prayers of African Religion* (Maryknoll, NY: Orbis Books, 1975).

33. John S. Mbiti, *Introduction to African Religion* (Nairobi: East African Educational Publishers, 1992), 53.

34. Chinua Achebe, *Things Fall Apart* (New Delhi, India: Allied Publishers, 2012), 122.

recognize maternal qualities of God. Charles Nyamiti enumerates some of the qualities of a mother as follows: "she is a being who surrounds the child with meticulous care, she caresses, nourishes, protects and shelters, she helps, she is patient and affective. Like all female beings the mother is fecund receptivity, warm tenderness, source and bearer of life, 'veiled gift,' interiority, profundity, intensity, refuge, she is always present, she welcomes and discovers what is delicate."[35] These qualities of a mother make motherhood a *sacrament* of God.

Some matriarchal societies in Africa conceive of God as Mother.[36] The southern Nuba and the Ovambo, for instance, call God the Great Mother, and when offering their prayers for a dying person they employ the female pronoun *she* to refer to God. They address God thus: "Our God, who has brought us into this world, may she take you."[37] According to Nzuzi Bibaki, it is difficult to meaningfully speak of God among the Yombe of the Democratic Republic of Congo without making reference to the maternal qualities of God. God the Mother is the God of compassion.[38] The name *Leza* or *Lesa* for God among the Bemba, Kaonde, Lamba, and Tonga, among others, is also said to derive from the verb *lesa*, to nurse or cherish, which actions designate what a mother does to her child and, by extension, what a chief does to the community.[39]

The motherhood of God is likewise clearly depicted in a prayer from the Boran of Kenya:

---

35. Nyamiti, "The African Sense of God's Motherhood," 270.

36. This does not mean that matriarchal societies in Africa do not have the image of God as "Father" or that the maternal image of God is absent from patriarchal societies in Africa.

37. Nyamiti, "The African Sense of God's Motherhood," 270; John S. Mbiti, *Concepts of God in Africa* (London: S.P.C.K, 1970), 92–93; John S. Mbiti, *African Religions and Philosophy* (Nairobi: East African Educational Publishers, 1969), 49.

38. Nzuzi Bibaki, *Le Dieu-Mère. L'inculturation de la foi chez les Yombe* (Kinshasa, Democratic Republic of the Congo: Editions Loyola, 1993), 186.

39. Cf. Mbiti, *Concepts of God in Africa*, 67.

O God, thou [hast] let me pass the day in peace,
Let me pass the night in peace,
O Lord who hast no Lord.
There is no strength but in thee.
Thou alone hast no obligation.
Under thy hand I pass the night.
Thou art my mother and my father.[40]

The prayer presents God as a source of protection from the evil forces operating at night. Such protection mirrors the qualities of a mother and a father. One can imagine God as a mother who holds her baby in a loving embrace to protect the child from the cold of the night.

In some African litanies of divine names, God is invoked as "mother of people" and "great nursing mother."[41] These attributes of God emanate from people's concrete experience of God's care and providence. The mother is the place of refuge and source of consolation for her children. The icon of a mother evokes paradise, the primordial home before the emergence of conflict and separation.[42]

Conclusion

While theological language, informed by Trinitarian theology, predominantly describes God as Father, references to God as Mother are not lacking both in Scripture and in the writings of Christian authors. As a mystery, God embodies an infinite range of characteristics and qualities that constitute part of the human experience, one of which is that of the love and care of a mother.

---

40. This prayer appears in Alward Shorter, "Divine Call and Human Response: Prayer in the Religious Traditions of Africa II," *The Way* 23 (1983): 238.

41. Cf. Agbonkhianmeghe E. Orobator, *Theology Brewed in an African Pot* (Maryknoll, NY: Orbis Books, 2008), 31, 35.

42. Cf. Nyamiti, "The African Sense of God's Motherhood," 273.

Prayer to God Our Mother

O God, when all was quiet, in your Wisdom you gave birth to the universe. You blessed it with fecundity just as you, O Lord, are fecund. Every morning you open your hand to give food to your creatures at the right time; every evening you lead the birds of the air and the animals of the forest to their resting place. Look with favor upon us, we pray, and grant us today our daily food. Quiet our troubled hearts with the soothing lullaby of your Spirit and grant us rest from all adversity, sorrow, and anxiety, for your love, O Mother, lasts from age to age. Amen.

Chapter 20

Jesus: The Gathering Mother

Introduction

If the description of God as Mother may sound befuddling to ears attuned to patriarchal vocabulary, even stranger will be the depiction of Jesus as a mother. The little-known medieval devotion to Jesus our Mother makes some theologians wince. And yet some theologians from the Patristic era identify qualities in Jesus Christ that are parallel to the characteristics of a mother. The maternal image of Jesus was particularly popular among Cistercian monks of the twelfth century (for instance, Bernard of Clairvaux, Aelred of Rievaulx, Isaac of Stella, William of St. Thierry, and others). The maternal image was at that time also applied to such male religious figures as bishops and abbots.[1]

Christ the Mother Hen

A well-known biblical reference to the portrayal of Jesus as a mother is the incident of Jesus's lament over Jerusalem. The episode is reported in Matthew 23:37 and in Luke 13:34. The New Revised Standard Version translates both verses as follows: "Jerusalem, Jerusalem, the city that kills the prophets and stones those who are sent to it! How often have I desired to gather your children

---

1. Cf. Caroline W. Bynum, *Jesus as Mother: Studies in the Spirituality of the High Middle Ages* (Berkeley: University of California Press, 1982), 110–11.

together as a hen gathers her brood under her wings, and you were not willing!"

In Matthew, this saying comes in the context of Jesus's indictment against the Pharisees and the Scribes on account of their hypocrisy. Matthew 23 is full of references to death: whitewashed tombs; bones of the dead; all manner of filth; tombs of prophets; graves of the righteous; shedding of the blood of the prophets, being sentenced to hell; killing and crucifying prophets, sages, and scribes; the righteous blood shed on earth; the blood of Abel; and the blood of Zechariah son of Barachiah.

There are three kinds of death alluded to in this passage: The first one is the existential or spiritual death of the Pharisees and the Scribes. On the outside, they look alive and comely but inside they are dead. The second type of death is martyrdom, that is, the death of the servants of God, the prophets, who are executed by those who do not accept God's word. By implication, Jesus will be killed because of his faithfulness to God. Jesus lays the blame of the murder of prophets squarely at the door of Jerusalem, which, by implication, stands for the religious establishment of the Jewish nation. The third type of death is eschatological, here presented as being sentenced to hell, which is the failure to inherit the Kingdom of God.

The children of Jerusalem (the people of Israel) find themselves torn between allegiance to two forces—that of the Pharisees and the Scribes (symbolized by death and disintegration), on the one hand, and, on the other, that of Jesus and the prophets (symbolized by life and gathering or integration). Jesus wants to gather the children of Jerusalem together under the wings of the Kingdom of God, but the religious authorities will not permit it.

Luke 13 is replete with antithetical images. On the one hand, there are images of death: the blood of the Galileans mingled with their sacrifices; the eighteen killed at the tower of Siloam; perishing; the barrenness of the fig tree; cutting down the tree; a crippled woman; failure to enter through the narrow door; rejection, weeping, and gnashing of teeth; Herod's threat to kill Jesus; and the killing of prophets in Jerusalem.

On the other hand, there are the images of life and vitality: repentance, grace period given to the barren tree, digging around the tree and putting manure on it, the healing of the crippled woman and her designation as daughter of Abraham, giving water to an ox, rejoicing, praising God, a mustard seed growing into a big tree in which birds of the air build nests, flour being leavened, eating at the table of the Kingdom of God, gathering of people from east and west in the Kingdom of God, casting out demons, and curing the sick.

In both accounts, Jesus compares himself to a hen so solicitous about her chicks that it gathers them under her wings in order to protect them from predators, as hens are wont to do. Christ's prophetic ministry is meant to save Jerusalem from destruction. Commenting on this verse, Donald A. Hagner writes, "The image of a mothering bird who gathers her young under her wings suggests such things as security, nurture, and well-being."[2] But since the city does not want to accept Jesus's saving presence, Jerusalem will be plundered. Having refused the protection of the mother, Jerusalem's children will become prey to destructive forces.

Death is associated with sin and resistance to repentance. Among those who resist God's work of salvation are the Pharisees and the Scribes. They are opposed to Jesus's healing ministry in the synagogue and ask Jesus to leave on the pretext that Herod wants to kill him. Jesus is doing everything possible to give life to the people of Israel. Like the gardener, he not only intercedes for the barren fig tree but also nurtures it with manure and water; like the farmer, he sows the seed of the word of God so that it may yield abundant harvest for the Kingdom of God; like the baker, he leavens the flour of human life with the yeast of the word of God so that humanity may increase and prosper. In other words, Jesus does everything to gather the daughters and sons of Israel into the Kingdom of God to rejoice therein with their fathers, Abraham, Isaac, and Jacob.

In the Bible, *gathering* is used as a metaphor for salvation. The

---

2. Donald A. Hagner, *Matthew 14–28*, Word Biblical Commentary, vol. 33B (Dallas, TX: Word, 2002), 680.

word features prominently in the Old Testament, especially in the prophetic tradition. Isaiah, for instance, uses it in the context of the hope for the restoration of the nation of Israel following upon the end of the exile. In Isaiah 43:1–14, God reassures the people of Israel that God will rescue them from the exile and lead them back home. God is described in this passage as creator, deliverer, and the Holy One of Israel. God says, "Do not fear, for I am with you; I will bring your offspring from the east, and from the west I will gather you."[3] Gathering is the work of the creator and deliverer. The Hebrew text uses the verb *qābaṣ*—gather, collect, assemble, bring together. In the Lucan and Matthean pericopes the verb used is *episynagagein*, a compound of *synagō*—literally meaning *I gather*. The term is used to describe God's salvific action in behalf of the exiled Israel. John L. McKenzie explains that "Yahweh will achieve the new creation of Israel by the ingathering of his people. However far they may have been scattered from their land, he will bring them back."[4]

Jesus apparently borrowed the image from the Second Book of Esdras, where God complains about Israel's rejection of God their creator and protector. God says, "Have I not entreated you as a father entreats his sons or a mother her daughters or a nurse her children, so that you should be my people and I should be your God, and that you should be my children and I should be your father? I gathered you as a hen gathers her chicks under her wings."[5] Since Israel has rejected God, God will cast them out of God's presence.

In his commentary on the six days of creation, St. Ambrose makes a veiled allusion to the image of a mother hen. Ambrose compares the devil to the partridge, a bird believed to steal the eggs of another partridge, but once they hatch and hear the voice of their true mother, they abandon the false mother and return to the par-

---

3. Isa 43:5.

4. John L. McKenzie, *Second Isaiah: A New Translation with Introduction and Commentary* (New York: Doubleday, 1968), 51.

5. 2 Esdras 1:28–30.

tridge that laid the eggs. The devil, likewise, steals the generations of God. While the evil one may succeed in bringing together those lacking in wisdom, the latter will return to Christ their mother, once they hear his voice, for Christ "embraces her young with an endearing mother's love. The Devil did not create the Gentiles, but he gathered them in. When Christ in His Gospel sent forth His message, they eagerly fled so as to be under the protection of the shadow of His wings."[6]

In his "Prayer to St. Paul," St. Anselm of Canterbury (1033–1109) prays to Christ the mother hen. In one section, he writes,

> And you, Jesus, are you not also a mother?
> Are you not the mother who, like a hen,
> gathers her chickens under her wings?
> Truly, Lord, you are a mother;
> for both they who are in labor
> and they who are brought forth
> are accepted by you . . .
> So you, Lord God, are the great mother.[7]

Jesus is the mother hen who gathers those who are generated in faith. In another section of the same prayer, St. Anselm, returning to the same image of Jesus as the mother hen, pleads with Jesus to revive him (St. Anselm), comparing himself to a dead chicken that will be revived by the warmth of the mother hen. The warmth of Jesus gives life to the dead, while Jesus's touch justifies sinners. Anselm asks Jesus to recognize again Jesus's dead son, "both by the sign of your cross and the voice of his confession. Warm your chicken, give life to your dead man, justify your sinner."[8] In this

---

6. Ambrose, *Hexameron* VI, 3, 13, trans. John J. Savage, The Fathers of the Church, vol. 42 (New York: Fathers of the Church, 1961), 234.

7. Anselm of Canterbury, "Prayer to St. Paul," in *The Prayers and Meditations of Anselm*, trans. Benedicta Ward (Middlesex, UK: Penguin Books, 1973), 153–54.

8. Ibid., 155–56.

segment of the prayer, Anselm makes veiled allusions to the resurrection. By his cross, Jesus gives life to those who were dead on
account of their sin.

The nurturing and protective maternal love of Jesus is also evident in Jesus's prayer of intercession for his disciples:

> Holy Father, protect them in your name that you have
> given me, so that they may be one, as we are one. While
> I was with them, I protected them in your name that you
> have given me. I guarded them, and not one of them was
> lost except the one destined to be lost, so that the scripture
> might be fulfilled . . . I have given them your word, and the
> world has hated them because they do not belong to the
> world, just as I do not belong to the world. I am not asking
> you to take them out of the world, but I ask you to protect
> them from the evil one.[9]

The dominant verb in this pericope is *protect*. While with the disciples, Jesus protects them so that none of them may be lost. Jesus's
solicitude for the disciples is reminiscent of the protectiveness of
the mother hen who gathers her chicks under her wings in order to
protect them from predators. Satan is the predator who wants to
steal Jesus's chicks. That is why Jesus asks that the Father may continue to protect the disciples so that they may remain united. Since
protection is a function of unity and unity implies being gathered
together, then, by way of syllogism, protection means gathering.
Jesus is aware that once the shepherd is gone, the sheep will be
faced with the spectre of dispersion.[10] Jesus keeps the disciples
united by means of his word. In other words, it is through the word
of God that the people of God are gathered and preserved in unity.
That is why the church is very concerned about unity of faith. The
enemy scatters the sheep by feeding them with a different word.

---

9. Jn 17:11–15.
10. Cf. Zech 13:7; Mk 14:27.

Christ: Mother of the Church

In one of his baptismal catecheses, John Chrysostom comments on the blood and water that flowed from the pierced side of Jesus. Chrysostom first interprets the pericope in a nuptial key. For him, the blood and water represent the church. Just as Eve was drawn from Adam's side while the latter slept, so is the church fashioned from the side of Christ as he sleeps on the cross. But later in the same discourse, the Antiochene bishop transposes the nuptial image into a maternal one: "As a woman nourishes with her own blood and milk the one she has given birth to, so does Christ constantly nourish with his own blood those he has generated."[11]

In Christian tradition, Jesus has sometimes been depicted as a pelican. The sixth stanza of Thomas Aquinas's hymn *Adoro te devote* reads as follows:

> O loving Pelican! O Jesus Lord!
> Unclean I am, but cleanse me in Thy Blood!
> Of which a single drop, for sinners spilt,
> Can purge the entire world from all its guilt.[12]

In ancient times, before Christianity, there was a legend, later reported in the *Physiologus* (a second-century Christian work written in Alexandria), which stated that, in time of famine, the mother pelican would strike her breast with its beak and feed her young with its own blood in order to protect them from starvation. In his *Divine Comedy*, Dante Alighieri applies the image of the pelican to Christ. Speaking of the beloved disciple, Dante writes,

---

11. John Chrysostom, *Catéchèses baptismales* III, 19, ed. Antoine Wenger, SCh, vol. 50 (Paris: Cerf, 1957), 162. Translation mine.

12. The Latin text runs as follows: *Pie pellicane, Iesu Domine, me immundum munda tuo sanguine; cuius una stilla salvum facere totum mundum quit ab omni scelere.* My translation: O pious Pelican, Lord Jesus, cleanse my impurity with your blood; whose drop [of blood] is capable of saving the whole world from every guilt.

> This is he, this, who on the breast reclined
> Even of our Pelican; 'tis he who bore
> The great charge from the cross to him consigned.[13]

In the first line, Dante makes reference to the Last Supper episode, where the beloved disciple is reported to have reclined next to Jesus.[14] The last two lines allude to the Golgotha scene where Jesus, hanging on the cross, gave Mary to the beloved disciple.[15] It is significant that Dante should single out these two events in the life of Jesus as *pelican* moments. At the Last Supper, Jesus gave his own body and blood as food and drink to the disciples, while on the cross he gave Mary to the beloved disciple. The pelican moments of Jesus can therefore be defined as those that involve his giving, his kenosis. William Saunders's commentary is apt: "The image of the pelican is a strong reminder of our Lord, who suffered and died for us to give us eternal life and who nourishes us on our pilgrim way with the Holy Eucharist."[16]

Julian of Norwich is also famous for calling Christ our mother. In one passage of her *Revelations of Divine Love*, she underscores Christ's quality of nourishing his children as a maternal characteristic: "The mother," she writes, "can give her child to suck of her milk. But our precious Mother Jesus, he can feed us with himself; and doth, full courteously and tenderly, with the Blessed Sacrament, that is the precious food of true life."[17]

Julian extends the discourse of Christ's motherhood to God's work of creation. She distinguishes the substantial (higher) part and the sensual (lower) part of our being. The distinction con-

---

13. Dante Alighieri, *Divine Comedy*, Paradiso, Canto XXV, 112–14, trans. Laurence Binyon (New York: Viking Press, 1969), 499–500.

14. Jn 13:23–24.

15. Jn 19:27.

16. William Saunders, "The Symbolism of the Pelican," *Catholic Herald* (November 20, 2003), http://catholicherald.com/stories/The-Symbolism-of-the-Pelican,3408; Patricia S. Klein, *Worship without Words: The Signs and Symbols of Our Faith* (Brewster, MA: Paraclete Press, 2000), 56.

17. Julian of Norwich, *Revelations of Divine Love* LX, trans. James Walsh, Religious Experience Series, vol. 3 (St. Meinrad, IN: Abbey Press, 1974), 164.

sist in that "our substance is that higher part which we have in our Father, God almighty."[18] And yet our substantial being is grounded and rooted in Christ, the second Person of the Trinity. Julian's idea is perhaps based on the teaching that Christians are the image of Christ.[19] But Christ also expressed his motherhood when he assumed our sensual (lower) nature so as to lead us to the Father. The incarnation was Christ's act of mercy, the mercy of a loving mother who wants to lead her children to their spiritual maturity. She writes,

> [Christ] is our Mother of mercy, in taking our sensuality
> . . . For in our Mother Christ, we have profit and increase;
> and in his mercy he re-formeth and restoreth us: and by
> the power of his passion, his death and his uprising, oned
> us to our substance. Thus worketh our Mother in mercy
> to all his beloved children who are docile and obedient to
> him.[20]

In her view, our substance is drawn from the Trinity as a whole, but our sensuality is only from the second Person. While we received our being from the Father, we received our reformation and our restoration from Christ the Mother of mercy.[21] Through the incarnation, the Son of God stoops down from heaven[22] and, like a mother, feeds her children and teaches them how to walk in the way of truth. By virtue of his incarnation, Christ's service to humanity became "nearest, readiest and surest; nearest: for it is most of kind; readiest: for it is most of love; surest: for it is most of truth."[23] In the new covenant, "all the fair working and all the sweet kindly offices of most dear Motherhood are appropriated to the second Person."[24]

Though a mother may sometimes allow her child to suffer, to fall

---

18. Ibid., LVIII.
19. Cf. Rom 8:29; 1Jn 3:2.
20. Julian of Norwich, *Revelations* LVIII.
21. Cf. ibid.
22. Cf. Ps 113:5–7.
23. Julian of Norwich, *Revelations* LX.
24. Ibid., LIX.

or to be distressed, Jesus "our heavenly Mother" can never allow that his children perish, because he loves them without end.[25] In his death, Christ bore his children to eternal life.[26] Just as a mother puts her child to rest on the mother's breast, the dying Christ leads his children home into his blessed breast. There shall they find eternal repose in the kingdom of the Father.[27]

Conclusion

Christ embraces the whole humanity and seeks to save the world from harm. He nourishes his children with his word, body, and blood so that they may have life and have it to the full.[28] Jesus forgives his sinful children and does not want any person to be lost. The image of *mother* captures powerfully Jesus's solicitude for his sheep. The Christology of *motherhood* is sure to enrich one's appreciation of the "breadth and length and height and depth"[29] of God's love made manifest in the history of salvation. Motherhood is indeed a "sacrament" of Christ's love.

Prayer to Christ Our Mother

O Christ, out of love for humanity, you embraced our lowly nature and came to dwell in our midst. On the cross you opened wide your arms to embrace the whole world, just as a mother hen gathers her chicks under her wings. You feed us with your own body and blood so that we may have life within us; you suckle us at the breast of your word so that we may grow strong and become your disciples. Grant, we pray, that we may follow you faithfully and love you deeply, for you are our Mother, our Home, our Hope. Amen.

---

25. Cf. ibid., LXI.
26. Cf. ibid., LXIII.
27. Cf. ibid., LX.
28. Cf. Jn 10:10.
29. Eph 3:18.

Chapter 21

Holy Spirit: Mother of Newness

Introduction

The role of the Holy Spirit in the lives of Christians has in recent times received unprecedented attention, especially with the emergence of Pentecostalism in its different manifestations (neo-Pentecostalism and Charismatic Renewal movements, to mention but a few), which underscores the personal experience of the Holy Spirit as a manifestation of spiritual rebirth also known as baptism of the Spirit. In their worship, communities belonging to the Pentecostal movement have a special predilection for palpable manifestations of the Spirit, such as speaking in tongues, joyful praise, healing, and prophecy, among others.[1]

The Holy Spirit in Popular Imagination

In popular imagination, the Holy Spirit is seen as a bird or tongues of fire. These images are informed by the description of the descent of the Holy Spirit during Jesus's baptism (Mt 3:13–17; Mk 1:10; Lk 3:21–22; Jn 1:32) and at Pentecost (Acts 2:2–3). Other symbols of the Spirit include water, anointing, fire, cloud, light, the seal, the

---

1. Cf. Ludovic Lado, *Catholic Pentecostalism and the Paradoxes of Africanization: Processes of Localization in a Catholic Charismatic Movement in Cameroon* (Leiden, the Netherlands: Brill, 2009), 14–15.

hand, and the finger.[2] It is also possible that the neuter pronoun (*it*) often used for the Holy Spirit is partly informed by the fact that in Greek the word *pneuma* is neuter. The *thingification* of the Holy Spirit affects the adorability of the Holy Spirit as the third Person of the Trinity.[3] It is easier to ask the Father to send the Holy Spirit (conceived as a force or energy) than to pray to the Holy Spirit. Sometimes the Spirit is referred to as *he*, the language of which is probably influenced by the masculine gender of the Latin *spiritus*. As the Theological-Historical Commission for the Great Jubilee of the Year 2000 confesses, "To speak of the Holy Spirit is not easy. While the terms 'Father' and 'Son' applied to the first two persons of the Holy Trinity recall something 'personal' and very familiar, the word 'Spirit' alludes above all to biblical language, to 'breath' and 'wind.'"[4] In its attempt to capture the personal operations of the Spirit, the commission employs the masculine pronoun to refer to the Holy Spirit.

In contemporary theology, nonetheless, one occasionally hears of the Holy Spirit as a feminine principle. For instance, in his book *The Divine Mother*, Donald Gelpi refers to the Holy Spirit as *she* through and through. In his commentary on Rhabanus Maurus's (c.780–856) hymn *Veni Creator*, Raniero Cantalamessa observes that the feminine gender of the noun *spirit* in Semitic languages partly influenced ancient Christian writers who developed a rich doctrine of the Holy Spirit as *mother*. This maternal image of the Holy Spirit throws into the foreground such characteristics of the Spirit as tenderness and gentleness. However, because of the Gnostic abuse of this doctrine, mainstream church doctrine gradually distanced itself from the maternal image of the church. Cantalamessa finds the neglect of this fertile image regrettable since of the

---

2. Cf. CCC nn.694–700.

3. Cf. Donald L. Gelpi, *The Divine Mother: A Trinitarian Theology of the Holy Spirit* (Lanham, MD: University Press of America, 1984), 215–16.

4. The Theological-Historical Commission for the Great Jubilee of the Year 2000, *The Holy Spirit, Lord and Giver of Life*, trans. Agostino Bono (New York: Crossroad, 1997), 12.

three persons, the Holy Spirit is the one that is least characterized as masculine both in revelation and in language. Though church writers avoided any systematic treatment of the motherhood of the Holy Spirit, they still made use of this title when speaking of the functions of the paraclete.[5]

The understanding of the Holy Spirit as mother has not yet entered the mainstream of theological imagination and tends to raise eyebrows when used. According to Anne Claar Thomasson-Rosingh, feminist theologians seem more preoccupied with debunking the images of God as Father and Son than with exploiting the fertile feminist themes in pneumatology.[6] One of the possible reasons why theologians shy away from exploring the maternal image of the Holy Spirit is that this field is littered with the landmines of heresy, for in the early centuries this was one of the battlegrounds between Gnostic-Christian theology and orthodox theology.

The Holy Spirit as Mother in Apocryphal and Gnostic Writings

There are many references to the maternal character of the Holy Spirit in various apocryphal and Gnostic writings of the early centuries. Some of them are veiled allusions to the third Person of the Trinity while others are quite explicit. For instance, the *Apocryphon of John*, a second-century Sethian[7] Gnostic Christian text,

---

5. Raniero Cantalamessa, *Come, Creator Spirit: Meditations on the Veni Creator,* trans. Denis and Marlene Barrett (Collegeville, MN: Liturgical Press, 2003), 14; Francis Brown, ed., *The Brown-Driver-Briggs Hebrew and English Lexicon* (Peabody, MA: Hendrickson Publishers, 1997), 924; Jürgen Moltmann, *The Spirit of Life: A Universal Affirmation,* trans. Margaret Kohl (Minneapolis: Fortress Press, 1992), 157.

6. Anne C. Thomasson-Rosingh, *Searching for the Holy Spirit: Feminist Theology and Traditional Doctrine* (London: Routledge, 2015), 2–3.

7. Sethianism was a Gnostic group that attributed its gnosis (spiritual and secret knowledge) to Seth, third son of Adam and Eve and to Norea, Noah's wife. Their teaching was heavily influenced by Platonism, especially in its conception of creation as a series of emanations of God.

speaks of God as the Father, the Mother, and the Son. John the brother of James has a vision in which God speaks to him: "I am the one who is with you forever. I am the Father, I am the Mother, I am the Son."[8]

The apocryphal *Gospel of Philip*, dating to the third century, captures the maternal image of the Spirit from the point of view of the feminine gender of the word *spirit*. Making reference to the creation of Adam, the writer sustains that the breath of God given to Adam became his mother: "The soul of Adam came into being by means of a breath, which is a synonym for Spirit. The spirit given him is his mother. His soul was replaced by a spirit."[9] The text adds that Adam came into existence from two virgins, namely, the Spirit and the earth. Christ, the second Adam, was thus born of a virgin in order to rectify the fall of Adam.[10] Earlier in the text, the writer contests the belief that Mary conceived by the Holy Spirit. Those who say this, the writer argues, are in error and do not know what they are saying, for it is impossible that a woman should conceive by a woman.[11] The implication is that the Holy Spirit is a feminine principle. Stanley M. Burgess interprets this as meaning that the virgin of whom Christ was born is the Holy Spirit.[12]

Another apocryphal *Gospel of the Hebrews* reports Jesus calling the Spirit, "my Mother." Origen quotes this line in his commentary

8. *The Apocryphon of John* II, 1, 2, trans. Frederik Wisse, in *The Nag Hammadi Library in English*, ed. Marvin W. Meyer (New York: Harper & Row, 1977), 99.

9. *The Gospel of Philip* II, 70, trans. Wesley W. Isenberg, in *The Nag Hammadi Library in English*, 142.

10. Ibid., 143.

11. Ibid., II, 55, in *The Nag Hammadi Library*, 134.

12. Stanley M. Burgess, *The Holy Spirit: Ancient Christian Traditions* (Peabody, MA: Hendrickson Publishers, 1984), 43. The idea that the Son was born of the Spirit approximates the Trinitarian doctrine of the fourth-century African philosopher and theologian Marius Victorinus, who, in his treatise against Arius, argues that the Holy Spirit is the mother of the Logos both in heaven and on earth: in heaven because the Spirit is the generating power of the Father's intelligence, and on earth, because Mary conceived of the Holy Spirit. Cf. Gelpi, *The Divine Mother*, 217–18.

on John. Origen's argument is that when Jesus says that those who sin against him will be forgiven, but those who blaspheme against the Holy Spirit will not be forgiven, this does not mean that Jesus is lower than the Holy Spirit. Origen affirms that, if all things were made through the word, then the Spirit was also made through the word. Consequently, it is illogical that Jesus should call the Spirit his mother. Origen writes, "If anyone should lend credence to the Gospel according to the Hebrews, there the Savior Himself says, 'My mother, the Holy Spirit took me just now by one of my hairs and carried me off to the great mount Tabor,' he will have to face the difficulty of explaining how the Holy Spirit can be the mother of Christ when it was itself brought into existence through the Word."[13] In his attempt to debunk the inferiority of the Son to the Holy Spirit, Origen ends up subordinating the Holy Spirit to the Son.

The image of the Holy Spirit as mother is also found in the spiritual homilies attributed to Macarius the Egyptian (c. 345–410).[14] In the nineteenth century, a monk of Mount Athos, Neophytes Kavsokalivites, conducted research that showed that these homilies are not to be attributed to Macarius the Egyptian, but rather to a Symeon of Mesopotamia who lived in northeast Syria in the middle of the fourth century. He was a member of a heretical group of ascetics called the Messalians.[15]

In Homily 28, Pseudo-Macarius compares the darkness that prevailed on the face of the earth after the sin of Adam and before the coming of the last Adam (Christ) to the darkness that covered

---

13. Origen, *Commentary on John* II, 6, trans. Allan Menzies, ANF, vol. 10 (Grand Rapids, MI: Wm. B. Eerdmans, 1978), 329.

14. Not to be confused with Macarius the Alexandrian (c. 295–394), in charge of a monastic school in the Nitrian desert.

15. George A. Maloney, *Intoxicated with God: The Fifty Spiritual Homilies of Macarius* (Denville, NJ: Dimension Books, 1978), 7. The Messalians were a heretical sect that emerged in Mesopotamia in around 360 and survived up to the ninth century. They emphasized the power of prayer and dismissed sacraments as useless. Their theological mainstay was the doctrine of the indwelling of the Spirit.

Egypt for three days before the exodus. The darkness impaired the sense of sight, so much that a son could not see his father nor could a brother see his brother. Likewise, from the time Adam sinned, darkness covered the soul of humanity so much that "man did not see the true Heavenly Father and the good and kind mother, the grace of the Spirit and the sweet desired Brother, the Lord, and the friends and relatives, the holy angels with whom He was rejoicing, dancing and celebrating."[16] In this familial metaphor of the relationship between humanity and the powers of heaven, God is Father, Jesus is Brother, the Spirit is Mother, and the angels are relatives and friends.

Salvaging the Motherhood of the Holy Spirit

The Gnostic teaching on the motherhood of the Holy Spirit is not without heretical underpinnings in that the Holy Spirit as a mother appears to be turned into a hypostasis, thereby creating the triad Father, Mother, and Son in the Godhead. However, as the foregoing chapters suggest, the motherhood of God is not confined to a single Person of the Trinity, but rather extends to all of them. Affirmation of the motherhood of the Spirit does not necessarily change the three Persons of the Trinity into God the Father, God the Son, and God the Mother, an image Moltmann finds more agreeable than "the ancient patriarchal picture of God the Father with two hands, the Son and the Spirit."[17] There are some maternal characteristics in the operations of God the Father, God the Son, and God the Spirit, just as there are paternal qualities in the three Persons. The feminine qualities of God the Spirit (tenderness, loving care, and gentleness) shine forth more clearly in women than in men, while the presence of the Spirit in men tends to take on masculine features such as power, strength, and courage.[18] Articulating the maternal ministrations of the Spirit is, therefore, not slipping back

---

16. Macarius (pseudo), Homily XXVIII, 4, in *Intoxicated with God*, 166.

17. Jürgen Moltmann, *The Source of Life: The Holy Spirit and the Theology of Life*, trans. Margaret Kohl (Minneapolis: Fortress Press, 1997), 37.

18. Cf. Cantalamessa, *Come, Creator Spirit*, 15.

into Gnostic heresies, but rather an attempt to more adequately understand the operations of the Holy Spirit.

Holy Spirit the Comforter

One of the maternal operations of the Holy Spirit is the ministry of comforting. This maternal image of the Spirit is based on a conflation of John 14:26 and Isaiah 66:13. Isaiah speaks of God as one who comforts, as a mother comforts her child, while John talks about the promise of the Holy Spirit, the paraclete, the comforter. By transposing the notion of comfort as a maternal function onto the Holy Spirit, the latter comes to be seen as a mother figure. As Jürgen Moltmann puts it, "If the Holy Spirit is the Comforter, as the Gospel of John understands the Paraclete to be, then she comforts 'as a mother comforts' . . . In this case the Spirit is the motherly comforter of her children."[19]

Holy Spirit and Regeneration

Another biblical foundation of the image of the Holy Spirit as mother is the Christian idea of regeneration or rebirth. In John 3, the conversation between Jesus and Nicodemus revolves around the question of rebirth as a prerequisite for entry into the Kingdom of God. Jesus tells Nicodemus: "Very truly, I tell you, no one can enter the kingdom of God without being born of water and Spirit. What is born of the flesh is flesh, and what is born of the Spirit is spirit."[20]

While in Eastern cosmology, later adopted by the Pythagoreans, *rebirth* was understood as a cyclic return of phenomena through reincarnation, Christian rebirth catapults those regenerated onto a new realm of existence. In other words, the prefix *re-* in *rebirth* no longer means return to life, but rather acquires the valence of

---

19. Moltmann, *The Source of Life*, 35.
20. Jn 3:5–6.

radical newness.[21] The radical newness of those born of the Spirit is symbolized by the distinction between *flesh* and *spirit*. The Spirit reconfigures reality into new being.

The Spirit of the Resurrection

The motherhood of the Holy Spirit is also affirmed from the standpoint of the resurrection of Christ understood as birth to a radically new life. According to Jürgen Moltmann, the point of departure for Christian regeneration is the resurrection of Christ. Scripture says that the Spirit of the Lord raised Christ from the Lord.[22] Through the resurrection, Christ became a new creation; he did not simply return to his former life. Therefore, the Spirit of the Lord regenerated Christ and gave him a life that was radically new. But the rebirth of Christ at the resurrection is

> the beginning of the rebirth of the whole creation.... Believers are possessed by the Spirit of the resurrection, and through it are born again to a well-founded hope for eternal life. A coherent process issues from the rebirth of Christ from death through the Spirit, by way of the rebirth of mortal human beings through the Spirit, to the universal rebirth of the cosmos through the Spirit.[23]

The Holy Spirit is therefore the agent of both the resurrection of Christ and the regeneration of creation. As 1 Peter 1:3 says, through the resurrection of Jesus Christ from the dead, those who believe in Christ are born to new life and hope. Titus 3:5–7 adds that those who are regenerated in virtue of the Holy Spirit through Jesus Christ are constituted heirs in hope of eternal life. In this regard, the cornerstone of the theology of regeneration is Easter

---

21. Jürgen Moltmann, *The Spirit of Life: A Universal Affirmation*, trans. Margaret Kohl (Minneapolis: Fortress Press, 1992), 145.

22. Rom 8:11.

23. Moltmann, *The Spirit of Life*, 152–53.

theology, because the Spirit that regenerates Christians is the very Spirit that raised Christ from the dead.[24]

It is in the resurrection of Christ and regeneration of creation that the roles of Christ and of the Holy Spirit interpenetrate in a preeminent way. To be justified is to be regenerated. Justification is Janus-headed: the forgiveness of sin is backward looking, while the new creation of life and the rebirth to a new life and hope are forward looking.[25]

Since the new life is lived *in* the Spirit, then the Spirit is the medium, rather than the object, of the new experience. It is from this standpoint that Moltmann makes the following lapidary statement:

> If these experiences are thought of as re*birth* or as being *born* again, this suggests a singular image for the Holy Spirit ... *the image of the mother.* If believers are "born" again from the Holy Spirit, then the Spirit is "the mother" of God's children and can in this sense also be termed a "feminine" Spirit.[26]

The connection between Christian regeneration and the resurrection means that the fruits of the Holy Spirit enjoyed by those who have been born of the Spirit are essentially connected to the Easter experience. The fruits of the Spirit speak of *life*: love, joy, peace, patience, kindness, goodness, faithfulness, gentleness, and self-control.[27] These are the fruits of the new life of the resurrection. Opposed to these are the works of death: sexual immorality, impurity, sensuality, idolatry, sorcery, hostility, strife, jealousy, anger, dispute, dissension, and drunkenness, among others.[28]

The trials and tribulations of the world turn human beings into

---

24. Ibid., 146.
25. Ibid., 149.
26. Ibid., 157.
27. Gal 5:22–23.
28. Gal 5:19–21.

grieving spirits. But once one is reborn in the Spirit, one acquires a new perspective on the world and lives joyfully even in the midst of difficulties. Though one is in the world, one is no longer of the world. Life in the Spirit is founded on hope that generates peace in the midst of tumult and uncertainty. Spiritual regeneration is "the rebirth of the full and undivided *love of life.* The total Yes to life and the unhindered love of everything living are the first experiences of the Holy Spirit. That is why from earliest times Yahweh's *ruach* has been called the source or well of life (*fons vitae*)."[29]

Conclusion

The importance of the Holy Spirit in the history of salvation cannot be overemphasized. Like a mother, the Spirit generates children of God by breathing in them the breath of the Risen Lord. Like a mother, the Holy Spirit teaches the Pentecost language of love to the children of God, empowering them to call God Abba, Father. Like a mother, the Spirit comforts the children of God when they are engulfed by trials and tribulations. In darkness, despair, and gloom, the Holy Spirit whispers sounds of hope to the children of God, making them exclaim, "Our God reigns!" Just as the mother of the Maccabean sons inspired her sons with courage and determination to witness to God, the Holy Spirit fills the people of God with the courage and wisdom to witness to Christ in the tribunals of the present age. In the age to come, the divine womb of the Holy Spirit will deliver the groaning creation to a new life saved from corruption and decay. All these maternal qualities of the Holy Spirit make it plausible for Christians to relate to the Holy Spirit as a mother.

Prayer to Holy Spirit Our Mother

Holy Spirit, our life-giving Mother, at creation you transformed chaos into cosmos; through the prophet Ezekiel you taught us that you can bring life back to the scattered bones of our shattered hopes and dreams;

---

29. Cf. Moltmann, *The Source of Life*, 85; emphasis in original.

through the resurrection you renew all things in Christ; hear the cry of your children in the furnace of suffering and extinguish the flames of temptation with the dew of your consolation so that they may be re-created and renewed in hope. Amen.

Chapter 22

Earth: Nurturing Mother

Introduction

The concept of *motherhood* goes deeper than the rational or conscious sphere of existence and plunges into what psychologists call archetypes. The notion of the *archetype* is arguably one of the most significant contributions of psychotherapy to human knowledge, though the concept can be traced all the way back to Plato's conception of the *idea* as something preexistent to all phenomena, the prototype of all that exists.[1] Simply defined, an archetype is the collective part of the unconscious that is universal, impersonal, and common to all individuals irrespective of one's spatial or temporal placement. The archetypes precede cultural conditioning and constitute the dwelling place of *primordial images* one finds in myths, folklore, rites, dreams, and symbols. It is at the level of archetypes that humanity discovers its fundamental unity. In the words of Jung, "There is an *a priori* factor in all human activities, namely the inborn, preconscious and unconscious individual structure of the psyche. The preconscious psyche—for example, that of a new-born infant—is not an empty vessel into which, under favorable conditions, practically anything can be poured."[2] Jung holds that it is a mistake to imagine that the psyche of a newborn child is a *tabula*

---

1. Cf. Carl G. Jung, *The Archetypes and the Collective Unconscious*, trans. Richard F. C. Hull (London: Routledge & Kegan Paul, 1959), 75.
2. Ibid., 77.

rasa, an empty slate on which to write cultural norms and knowledge.[3]

One of the archetypes is that of a *mother* and belongs to the class of personified archetypes.[4] Other examples of personified archetypes are the shadow, the wise old man, the maid, and the child. There are four main characteristics of archetypes: first, they are numinous, that is, they have a spiritual or divine quality; second, archetypes are *given*, they are not a product of human rationality or social construction; third, archetypes are symbolic: through them, that which is unconscious is brought to consciousness. A symbol "intimates, suggests, excites. Consciousness is set in motion and must employ all its functions to assimilate the symbol, for a merely conceptual assimilation proves totally inadequate."[5] In other words, archetypes open up new levels of consciousness. The fourth quality of archetypes is ambivalence: they cannot be reduced to a single meaning; archetypes embody many and sometimes opposite meanings.[6]

Earth as Personification of Motherhood

The figure of speech called *personification* operates on a symbolic level and is not arbitrary. Just as a symbol embodies some of the qualities of the object it symbolizes, the earth serves as a personification of the archetype of a mother because the earth exudes some characteristics of the primordial phenomenon of motherhood. Therefore, the designation of earth as mother is not simply a matter

---

3. Cf. ibid., 66.

4. The second class of archetypes, called "archetypes of transformation," is not personified. Examples are journeys, death, and rebirth. All of them denote movement from one state of being to another, a phenomenon anthropologists would call "rites of passage."

5. Erich Neumann, *The Great Mother: An Analysis of the Archetype*, trans. Ralph Manheim (Princeton, NJ: Princeton University Press, 1963), 17.

6. Cf. Joan C. Engelsman, *The Feminine Dimension of the Divine* (Wilmette, IL: Chiron Publications, 1987), 13–18.

of poetry but rather a conscious meditation of that which lies in the collective unconscious.

In his "Canticle of the Creatures," St. Francis of Assisi affectionately describes the earth as mother:

> Praise be to you, my Lord, through our Sister, Mother Earth, who sustains and governs us, and who produces various fruit with colored flowers and herbs.[7]

According to Francis, the earth is mother because, just as a mother looks after her children, the earth sustains us with her products. She produces fruit, flowers, and herbs. Pope Francis, who cites Francis of Assisi's canticle, adds that the earth is our mother because we were made from the dust of the earth and that "our very bodies are made up of her elements, we breathe her air and we receive life and refreshment from her waters."[8] In other words, just as a child is made out of the flesh and blood of his or her mother, the human body is constituted by elements of the earth. Here, the pope is alluding to the second creation account in Genesis 2, which narrates that God made humanity out of dust. Thus, the notion of motherhood, in this case, points to the question of the primordial origin of humanity. The earth is the womb from which humanity originates.[9]

This aspect of the motherhood of the earth reflects what Neumann calls the "elementary character" of the archetypal feminine, namely, its tendency "to hold fast to everything that springs from it and to surround it like an eternal substance. Everything born of it belongs to it and remains subject to it."[10] From this standpoint, the

---

7. Francis of Assisi, "Canticle of the Creatures," in *Francis of Assisi: Early Documents*, vol. 1, ed. Regis J. Armstrong et al. (New York: New City Press, 1999), 113–14.

8. Pope Francis, Encyclical Letter *Laudato Si': On Care for Our Common Home*, no. 2 (Rome: Vatican Press, 2015), 3.

9. Cf. Malidoma P. Somé, *The Healing Wisdom of Africa: Finding Life Purpose through Nature, Ritual, and Community* (New York: Jeremy P. Tarcher, 1998), 232.

10. Neumann, *The Great Mother*, 25.

independence (from the earth) of living things is relative and non-essential. In its positive manifestation, the elementary character of the archetypal feminine is preoccupied with birthing, nourishing, and protecting her children. Its symbol is a vessel.[11] In mythical symbolism, the archetypal feminine is artistically represented as the great many-breasted mother, "ruler and nourisher of the animal world."[12]

The metaphor of earth as mother can also be found in the writings of the Fathers of the Church. In his expositions on the six days of creation, St. Ambrose describes the contribution of the earth to the growth of plants in the following terms: "The pliable sod receives, then a grain of wheat; the scattered seed is controlled by the use of the hoe and mother earth cherishes it in firm embraces to her breast."[13] The nurturing power of the earth is presented using maternal images of embrace and breast (breastfeeding). Later in the same book, Ambrose speaks of the joy of the farmer at harvest thusly: "When she smiles on him, fertile Mother Earth pours forth her offspring, so that she never incurs a loss to her creditors."[14] The harvest is compared to the process of childbearing.

Earth as Mother in Traditional African Societies

The symbolic motherhood of the earth is based on the experience of human dependence on the resources of the earth. This imagery would ring true especially for agricultural societies that have a more immediate relation to the earth than one does in urban settings where many things are offered or encountered in a processed form. It is no wonder, then, that some traditional African societies revered the earth as mother. The Yoruba of Nigeria, for instance, honored the earth as "our Mother" because "at birth we rest on her, at death we are placed in her womb, and at every meal the ancestors

---

11. Cf. ibid., 120.

12. Ibid., 126.

13. Ambrose, *Hexameron* III, 8, 34, trans. John J. Savage, The Fathers of the Church, vol. 42 (New York: Fathers of the Church, 1961), 93.

14. Ibid., 8, 35.

who dwell in her are honored with a few drops of drink poured on the ground."[15]

Similarly, the Akan of Ghana praise the earth in these words: "O earth, earth, at birth we depend upon you. At death we repose on you."[16] This praise for the earth singles out two key moments (archetypes of transformations) in human life: birth and death. Both moments are marked by dependence on the earth. The creation myth of some African communities recounts that human beings were made in the ground and then brought out through a hole. Others simply say that God made human beings out of clay.[17] The Ashanti, belonging to the family of the Akan, designated the earth as *Asase Ya*, that is, "Old Mother Earth." She is the "Great Mother," the "giver of birth."[18]

A Malagasy prayer, though it does not explicitly refer to earth as mother, spells out the maternal characteristics of the earth, especially that of nourishing her children:

> Have mercy upon me, O Earth! It is upon thee that I dwell, it is thou that givest to me my food and the water that I drink, it is thou that givest me clothes. Be merciful towards me, O Earth! Thou takest from me the wife without whom I cannot live, thou takest from me the children that are my joy, takest my friends that are dear to me, and takest even my father and mother.[19]

In this prayer, the one praying presents the earth not only as the dwelling place, the home, but also as the provider of food, water, and clothes. The earth is the resting place for the dead. These

---

15. Noel Q. King, *African Cosmos: An Introduction to Religion in Africa* (Belmont, CA: Wadsworth, 1986), 14.

16. Cited in ibid., 22.

17. Cf. John S. Mbiti, *Introduction to African Religion* (Nairobi: East African Educational Publishers, 1992), 83.

18. Lawrence E. Y. Mbogoni, *Human Sacrifice and the Supernatural in African History* (Dar-es-Salaam, Tanzania: Mkuki na Nyota, 2013), 25.

19. Cited in Mbiti, *The Prayers of African Religion*, 87.

descriptions of the earth spell out the manifestation of the Great Mother archetype as a *mater*, who "conceives a child, supports it in her womb, and finally brings it forth into the world at birth. After birth she is the nurturing and caring mother. As a result, the child perceives her as the all-enveloping source of life."[20] At the same time, the above-cited prayer makes allusion to the negative pole of the *mater*, that is, devouring her own children. It is never the great mother who dies; it is always the child. From this negative perspective, the mother's body is a coffin, a cauldron, or a grave.[21] As Carl Jung observes, the negative side of the mother archetype "may connote anything secret, hidden, dark; the abyss, the world of the dead, anything that devours, seduces, and poisons, that is terrifying and inescapable like fate."[22] That is why the Malagasy orant pleads with mother earth not to devour his or her loved ones. Indeed, archetypes are ambivalent.

The earth as mother welcomes back *home* her children when their physical life is over. The earth can be compared to a mother who gives birth to a child, nurtures it, and sees it go out to play; but when evening comes, the child comes back home to rest and to enjoy the mother's warm embrace. When plants and animals reach the end of their sojourn on earth, they return to their mother who welcomes them with the warm embrace of decomposition. They become one with her again, just as they were one with her before their birth. The fact that the word *humility* is related to *humus* suggests that to be humble requires the capacity to recognize the earth as the origin of things. The expression *down to earth* also implies going back to one's foundations, lowly though they may be.

In addition to the *mater* dimension of its motherhood, the earth also takes the manifestation of the *anima*, youthful and transformative in character. This is the dimension of the mother archetype responsible for the transformation of matter.[23] From this vantage

---

20. Engelsman, *The Feminine Dimension of the Divine*, 20.
21. Cf. ibid., 21.
22. Jung, *The Archetypes and the Collective Unconscious*, 82.
23. Cf. Engelsman, *The Feminine Dimension of the Divine*, 21.

point, the mother is the agent of innovation, for she brings about new combinations of substances. The womb, for instance, is the seat where the woman's egg and the man's seed are transformed into a differentiated human body. Similarly, the earth is the womb in which seeds are transformed into plants that may eventually yield a hundredfold. Such a qualitative and quantitative transformation is the work of the earth in its *anima* dimension of the mother archetype. The very mystery of the resurrection is a transformation worked in the womb of the earth. In his teaching on the resurrection, Jesus said, "Very truly, I tell you, unless a grain of wheat falls into the earth and dies, it remains just a single grain; but if it dies, it bears much fruit."[24] To rise to a new and more glorious life, one has to die and be buried in the womb of the earth. The earth does not simply *devour* her children, but rather recycles them into something nobler: dead leaves are turned into manure; rainwater sinks into the earth and shoots up as fresh springs; dead human bodies rise to immortality.

Respecting Mother Earth

In many societies, one is expected to treat one's own mother with respect and kindness. In fact, some of the strongest taboos in African traditions revolve around one's relation to one's mother. For instance, beating up or insulting one's own mother would bring unspeakable curses upon the perpetrator of such violence. In addition, children are expected to protect their mothers from any form of shame, because the shame that falls upon the head of the mother falls even with greater force upon the children. Violating a mother in front of her children brings pain and shame not only to the mother but also to the children.

The earth as *our mother* deserves to be respected and protected. Over the centuries, especially after the onset of the industrial age, the relationship between humanity and the earth has been characterized by wanton exploitation, instrumentalization, and domina-

---

24. Jn 12:24.

tion. In the quest for material well-being, humanity has robbed the earth of her beauty and dignity. The earth has become an immense depository of toxic wastes. Unfortunately, such toxic deposits affect the lives of the poor, who cannot afford clean living environments.[25]

A proper relation to the earth requires what John Paul II called "ecological conversion,"[26] which implies, among other things, learning to consume less and to share more equitably the resources of the earth, because all are sons and daughters of the same mother. The Shona expression *mwana wevhu*, son or daughter of the soil, can become a clarion call for solidarity, recognizing all creatures as children of the earth. This would imply not to breach the boundaries God has put in place in creation, for the origin of sin, inequality, natural disasters, and conflict in society is the tendency of human beings to go beyond such demarcations. For instance, God prescribed boundaries for the sea and said to it, "Thus far shall you come, and no farther, and here shall your proud waves be stopped."[27] When human activity leads to the erosion of these limits, natural disasters erupt. The sin of Adam and Eve emanates from their disregard for the boundaries God set to their food chain.[28]

The numinous valence of the archetype of the motherhood of the earth has historically led some communities, such as the Igbo of Nigeria, to revere the earth as a goddess. That is why the earth-human relation was surrounded with rituals and taboos.[29] From the Christian point of view, however, the earth is a creature: "In the beginning ... God created the heavens and the earth."[30] Calling the earth mother does not mean deifying it, but rather recognizing the earth as a channel or medium of God's providence.

---

25. Pope Francis, *Laudato Si'*, nos. 2–12.

26. Cf. ibid., n.5.

27. Job 38:11.

28. Cf. Gen 3:1–7.

29. Cf. Chinua Achebe, *Things Fall Apart* (New Delhi, India: Allied Publishers, 2012), 26.

30. Gen 1:1.

Conclusion

Calling the earth our mother, as does St. Francis of Assisi and numerous cultures and traditions, underscores the earth's importance and dignity as the provider of resources needed for existence. It also underpins the fundamental unity not only of humanity but also of the whole creation, for we all have the same mother. This means that the human relationship to the nonhuman world can no longer be that of objectivism and instrumentalism, but rather that of intersubjectivity and solidarity or, as Martin Buber put it, a relationship of "I-Thou," not "I-It."[31] At the same time, respect for the earth as mother should not degenerate into idolatry, for the earth is not a goddess but a fellow creature that also enters into the economy of sacramentality.

A Prayer for the Earth[32]

All-powerful God,
you are present in the whole universe
and in the smallest of your creatures.
You embrace with your tenderness all that exists.
Pour out upon us the power of your love,
that we may protect life and beauty.
Fill us with peace, that we may live
as brothers and sisters, harming no one.
O God of the poor,
help us to rescue the abandoned
and forgotten of this earth,
so precious in your eyes.
Bring healing to our lives,
that we may protect the world and not prey on it,
that we may sow beauty,
not pollution and destruction.

---

31. Martin Buber, *I and Thou*, trans. Walter Kaufmann (New York: Charles Scribner's Sons, 1970), 53–85.

32. Pope Francis, *Laudato Si'*, no. 246.

Touch the hearts
of those who look only for gain
at the expense of the poor and the earth.
Teach us to discover the worth of each thing,
to be filled with awe and contemplation,
to recognize that we are profoundly united
with every creature
as we journey towards your infinite light.
We thank you for being with us each day. Amen.

Epilogue

The art and literature of every culture depict the immense joy of a mother clasping in her hands a fragile bundle of life. The tears of childbearing turn into the tears of joy. That is why, in spite of the pain of childbearing, many women are ready to go back to the labor ward to experience once more the indescribable consolation of bringing to light a living being. The joy of the mother grows as the child grows in stature and in spirit. The mother looks on with great satisfaction and sense of wonder as the child takes the first step without the mother's physical support. She listens with gratitude as the child pronounces the first syllable of the human language that goes beyond verbal communication and mediates the dialogue of hearts. The mother's words gradually become the child's, just as the mother's milk builds up the child's body.

One can see a mother's joy when her own children play and talk as brothers and sisters; when they defend one another, knowing that blood is thicker than water; when they share the little food and pass on the cup of water, because they know that their mother loves them all and does not want any of them to go to bed on an empty stomach; when they support one another, especially the weak—intellectually, economically, and spiritually; when they learn to forgive one another, aware that the bonds they share are stronger than the centrifugal forces bent on tearing them apart.

These joys notwithstanding, one cannot ignore the crisis facing motherhood in modern society. The contemporary media report numerous cases of baby-dumping, mostly because of the mother's fear of not being able to fend for the child. And we face a constant paradox that while some women reject the children God has given them, others are unable to bear children.

There is also the question of the social stigma attached to barrenness. To resolve this problem, some women are tempted to run to self-styled healers promising to grant the fruit of the womb to struggling couples. Such *healers* often exploit the victims and compromise the moral integrity of those in need of help. While it is important to pray for the gift of biological motherhood, it is also good to remember that the Christian tradition presents cases of motherhood that flourishes without biological children. Mother Teresa, though a mother of none, became a mother of thousands because she responded to the physical and spiritual needs of the poor. Many women have tasted the joy of bringing up someone's child, for nurturing is as marvelous an experience of motherhood as is birthing. There are many children who have no significant memories of their biological mothers but still enjoy the tender love of a mother.

Another challenge mothers face these days is to nurture the faith of their children. The explosion of information, both religious and scientific, sometimes undermines the authority of mothers in their role as cultivators of the faith in the homestead. It is not uncommon for children to abandon the faith of their mothers and seek consolation elsewhere. This is the pain suffered by mothers both in developed and developing countries. It was the pain suffered by St. Monica when her son Augustine abandoned the faith and sought refuge in Manichaean philosophy. In my ministry as a priest, I have encountered mothers who were in tears over their children's religious indifference or rebellion.

The division of one's own children is yet another sword that pierces mothers' hearts in modern society. Quarrels over inheritance have, in some families, sundered relations between or among siblings. A mother weeps when her own children take one another to court because material goods have become more important than the bonds of children of the same womb.

The suffering of one's child breaks the heart of a mother. One can imagine the depth of sorrow Mary suffered when she stood at the foot of the cross and watched her son bleed to death. One cannot fathom the agony of the mother of the seven Maccabean brothers who stood by as her sons, one by one, were mutilated and roasted to death. One cannot plumb the depth of pain suffered by the widow of Nain when she lost her only son. In our day, one cannot comprehend the anguish of a mother who loses her children to war and disease. The pain of such mothers is the pain God suffers when greed gives rise to conflict and bloodshed. Motherhood thrives best in peace.

From a sacramental perspective, the human experience of motherhood points to an important aspect of God's relation to the world. The joy of childbirth represents, albeit in a limited manner, the joy of God at creation. The love of a mother for her child is a sign of God's infinite love for God's people. The sorrow of a mother at the suffering and death of a child speaks of the pain God suffers when one of God's sons or daughters suffers and dies, especially spiritually. Motherhood is an important theological locus.

For sons and daughters, the love of a mother is a sacrament of the love of God. The bond between mother and child is so strong that it cannot easily be severed. In many languages, when one is hurt, one spontaneously invokes *mother*—understandably so—since mother is closest to her child. It is consoling and reassuring to realize that God is closer to God's children than a mother is to her baby.

Bibliography

Achebe, Chinua. *Things Fall Apart*. New Delhi, India: Allied Publishers, 2012.

Acholonu, Rose. "Women in the African Novel and the Quest for Human Rights." In *Beyond the Marginal Land: Gender Perspective in African Writing*. Edited by Chioma Opara, 97–100. Port Harcourt, Nigeria: Belpot, 1999.

Alexander, Desmond. "The Old Testament View of Life after Death." *Themelios* 11 (1986): 41–46.

Amat, Jacqueline, ed. *Passion of Perpetua and Felicity*. SCh, vol. 417. Paris: Cerf, 1996.

Ambrose of Milan. *Cain and Abel*. In *Hexameron, Paradise, and Cain and Abel*. Translated by John J. Savage, 359–437. Fathers of the Church, vol. 42. New York: Fathers of the Church, 1961.

———. *On [the Death of] Emperor Theodosius*. Translated by Roy J. Deferrari. In *Funeral Orations by Saint Gregory Nazianzen and Saint Ambrose*. The Fathers of the Church, vol. 22. New York: Fathers of the Church, 1953.

———. *Traité sur l'Evangile de s. Luc*. Edited by Gabriel Tissot. SCh, vol. 45. Paris: Cerf, 1956.

Anselm of Canterbury. *The Prayers and Meditations of Anselm*. Translated by Benedicta Ward. Middlesex, UK: Penguin Books, 1973.

Augustine. *Confessions*. Translated by Richard S. Pine-Coffin. Middlesex, UK: Penguin Books, 1961.

———. *Letters: 83–130*. Translated by Wilfrid Parsons. The Fathers of the Church, vol. 18. New York: Fathers of the Church, 1953.

———. *Sermons 273–305A*. In *The Works of Saint Augustine: A*

Translation for the 21st Century, vol. 3. Translated by Edmund Hill. New York: New City Press, 1994.

———. *Tractates on the Gospel of John*. Translated by John W. Rettig. The Fathers of the Church, vol. 78. Washington, DC: Catholic University of America Press, 1988.

Bâ, Mariama. *So Long a Letter*. Translated by Modupé Bodé-Thomas. Nairobi: Heinemann, 1981.

Beasley-Murray, George R. John. *Word Biblical Commentary*, vol. 36. Dallas: Word, 2002.

Bellis, Alice O. *Helpmates, Harlots, and Heroes: Women's Stories in the Hebrew Bible*. Louisville, KY: Westminster John Knox Press, 2007.

Bibaki, Nzuzi. *Le Dieu-Mère. L'inculturation de la foi chez les Yombe*. Kinshasa, Democratic Republic of the Congo: Editions Loyola, 1993.

Black, Allen. *Mark. The College Press NIV Commentary*. Joplin, MO: College Press, 1995.

Boff, Leonardo. *The Maternal Face of God: The Feminine and Its Religious Expressions*. Translated by Robert R. Barr and John W. Diercksmeier. San Francisco: Harper & Row, Publishers, 1987.

Bovon, François, and Helmut Koester. *Luke 1: A Commentary on the Gospel of Luke 1:1–9:50*. Minneapolis: Fortress Press, 2002.

Bronner, Leila L. "The Resurrection Motif in the Hebrew Bible: Allusions or Illusions?" *Jewish Bible Quarterly* 30 (2002): 143–54.

Brown, Peter. *Augustine of Hippo: A Biography*. London: Faber and Faber, 1967.

Brown, Raymond E. *The Birth of the Messiah: A Commentary on the Infancy Narratives in Matthew and Luke*. New York: Doubleday, 1979.

———. *The Gospel according to John*, vol. 2. Basingstoke, UK: Pickering & Inglis, 1983.

Brown, Raymond E., Karl P. Donfried, Joseph A. Fitzmyer, and John Reumann, eds. *Mary in the New Testament: A Collabora-*

tive Assessment by Protestant and Roman Catholic Scholars. Philadelphia: Fortress Press, 1978.

Brueggemann, Walter. "From Hurt to Joy, from Death to Life." *Interpretation* 28 (1974): 3–19.

———. *Ichabod toward Home: The Journey of God's Glory.* Grand Rapids, MI: Wm. B. Eerdmans, 2002.

Burgess, Stanley M. *The Holy Spirit: Ancient Christian Traditions.* Peabody, MA: Hendrickson Publishers, 1984.

Butler, Alban. *The Lives of the Fathers, Martyrs, and Other Principal Saints,* vol. 7. New York: P. J. Kenedy & Sons, 1886.

Bynum, Caroline W. *Jesus as Mother: Studies in the Spirituality of the High Middle Ages.* Berkeley: University of California Press, 1982.

Caesarius of Arles. *Sermons.* Translated by Mary Magdalene Mueller. The Fathers of the Church, vol. 31. New York: Fathers of the Church, 1956.

Cantalamessa, Raniero. *Come, Creator Spirit: Meditations on the Veni Creator.* Translated by Denis and Marlene Barrett. Collegeville, MN: Liturgical Press, 2003.

Cogan, Mordechai. *I Kings: A New Translation with Introduction and Commentary.* New Haven, CT: Yale University Press, 2008.

Congar, Yves. *The Meaning of Tradition.* Translated by A. N. Woodrow. San Francisco: Ignatius Press, 2004.

Chrysostom, John. *Catéchèses baptismales.* Edited by Antoine Wenger. SCh, vol. 50. Paris: Cerf, 1957.

———. *Commentary on Saint John the Apostle and Evangelist.* Translated by Thomas A. Goggin. Fathers of the Church, vol. 33. New York: Fathers of the Church, 1957.

———. *Homilies on Genesis, Homilies 18–45.* Translated by Robert C. Hill. The Fathers of the Church, vol. 82. Washington, DC: Catholic University of America Press, 1990.

———. *Homilies on Genesis: Homilies 46–67.* Translated by Robert C. Hill. The Fathers of the Church, vol. 87. Washington, DC: Catholic University of America Press, 1992.

———. *Homilies on Hannah.* Translated by Robert C. Hill. Old

Testament Homilies, vol. 3. Brookline, MA: Holy Cross Orthodox Press, 2003.

———. *Homilies on Ephesians.* Translated by Gross Alexander. NPNF, series 1, vol. 13. New York: Christian Literature, 1889.

Clement of Alexandria. *Stromata.* Edited by Alain le Boulluec. SCh, vol. 428. Paris: Cerf, 1997.

Collins, Adela Y., and Harold W. Attridge. *Mark: A Commentary.* Minneapolis: Fortress Press, 2007.

Culpepper, R. Alan. *The Gospel of Luke.* The New Interpreter's Bible, vol. 9. Nashville: Abingdon Press, 1995.

Cyprian. *The Lord's Prayer.* Translated by Roy J. Deferrari. The Fathers of the Church, vol. 36. New York: Fathers of the Church, 1958.

Cyril of Jerusalem. *Procatechesis.* Translated by Anthony A. Stephenson. The Fathers of the Church, vol. 61. Washington, DC: Catholic University of America Press, 1969.

Daniélou, Jean, and Henri Marrou. *The Christian Centuries,* vol. 1: *The First Six Hundred Years.* Translated by Vincent Cronin. London: Darton, Longman, and Todd, 1964.

Davies, William D., and Dale C. Allison. *A Critical and Exegetical Commentary on the Gospel According to Saint Matthew,* vol. 3: *Commentary on Matthew XIX–XXVIII.* Edinburgh: T&T Clark, 1997.

Day, Dorothy. *The Long Loneliness: The Autobiography.* New York: HarperOne, 1952.

———. *Selected Writings.* Edited by Robert Ellsberg. Maryknoll, NY: Orbis Books, 1992.

Demoustier, Adrien. *Les Exercices Spirituels de s. Ignace de Loyola. Lecture et pratique d'un texte.* Paris: Editions Facultés Jésuites, 2006.

Drijvers, Jan W. *Helena Augusta: The Mother of Constantine the Great and the Legend of Her Finding of the True Cross.* Leiden, the Netherlands: Brill, 1992.

Eichrodt, Walther. *Theology of the Old Testament,* vol. 2. Translated by John A. Baker. London: SCM Press, 1967.

Elliot, James K. "Does Luke 2:41–52 Anticipate the Resurrection?" *Expository Times* 83 (1971): 87–89.

Ellis, Edward A. *The Gospel of Luke*. The New Century Bible Commentary. London: Marshall, Morgan & Scott, 1974.

Elm von der Osten, Dorothy. "Perpetual Felicity: Sermons of Augustine on Female Martyrdom (s. 280–282 auct. [Erfurt 1])." *Studia Patristica* 49 (2010): 203–9.

Engelsman, Joan C. *The Feminine Dimension of the Divine*. Wilmette, IL: Chiron Publications, 1987.

Eusebius. *The Life of Constantine*. In *Eusebius Pamphilius: Church History, Life of Constantine, Oration in Praise of Constantine*. Edited by Philip Schaff. Translated by Arthur C. McGiffert. Grand Rapids, MI: Christian Classics Ethereal Library, 1890.

Farina, William. *Perpetua of Carthage: Portrait of a Third-Century Martyr*. Jefferson, NC: McFarland Publishers, 2009.

Fessard, Gaston. *La dialectique des Exercices Spirituels de Saint Ignace de Loyola*. Études Publiées souls la Direction de la Faculté de Théologie S.J. de Lyon-Fourvière, vol. 53. Paris: Editions Montaigne, 1956.

Gallares, Judette A. *Images of Faith: Spirituality of Women in the Old Testament*. Maryknoll, NY: Orbis Books, 1992.

Galot, Jean. *Who Is Christ? A Theology of the Incarnation*. Translated by Angeline Bouchard. Rome: Gregorian University Press, 1980.

Gelpi, Donald L. *The Divine Mother: A Trinitarian Theology of the Holy Spirit*. Lanham, MD: University Press of America, 1984.

Goldstein, Jonathan A. *II Maccabees: A New Translation with Introduction and Commentary*. New Haven, CT: Yale University Press, 2008.

Grimshaw, Allan D. "Genocide and Democide." In *Stress of War, Conflict and Disaster*. Edited by George Fink, 281–301. San Diego, CA: Elsevier, 2010.

Haenchen, Ernst. *John 1: A Commentary on the Gospel of John Chapters 1–6*. Translated by Robert W. Funk. Philadelphia: Fortress Press, 1984.

Hagner, Donald A. *Matthew 14–28*. Word Biblical Commentary, vol. 33B. Dallas, TX: Word, 2002.

Hamilton, Victor P. *The Book of Genesis: Chapters 1–17*. Grand Rapids, MI: Wm. B. Eerdmans, 1990.

———. *The Book of Genesis: Chapters 18–50*. Grand Rapids, MI: Wm. B. Eerdmans, 1995.

Harrington, Daniel J. "The Gospel According to Mark." In *The New Jerome Biblical Commentary*. Edited by Raymond E. Brown et al., 596–629. London: Geoffrey Chapman, 1990.

Hebblethwaite, Margaret. *Motherhood and God*. London: Geoffrey Chapman, 1984.

Hertzberg, Hans W. *I & II Samuel*. Translated by John S. Bowden. Kent: SCM Press, 1964.

Hicks, Jane E. "Moral Agency at the Borders: Rereading the Story of the Syrophoenician Woman." *Word & World* 23 (2003): 76–84.

Hilary of Poitiers. *Sur Matthieu*. Edited by Jean Doignon. SCh, vol. 258. Paris: Cerf, 1979.

Iersel, Bas M. F. van. *Mark: A Reader-Response Commentary*. London: T&T Clark, 2004.

Jeansonne, Sharon P. *The Women of Genesis: From Sarah to Potiphar's Wife*. Minneapolis: Fortress Press, 1990.

Jenkins, Philip. *The New Faces of Christianity: Believing the Bible in the Global South*. Oxford: Oxford University Press, 2006.

Jerome. *Commentary on Matthew*. Translated by Thomas P. Scheck. The Fathers of the Church, vol. 117. Washington, DC: Catholic University of America Press, 2008.

———. *Letters*. Translated by William H. Fremantle. NPNF, series 2, vol. 6. New York: Christian Literature, 1893.

Julian of Norwich. *Revelations of Divine Love*. Translated by James Walsh. Religious Experience series, vol. 3. St. Meinrad, IN: Abbey Press, 1974.

Jung, Carl G. *The Archetypes and the Collective Unconscious*. Translated by Richard F. C. Hull. London: Routledge & Kegan Paul, 1959.

King, Noel Q. *African Cosmos: An Introduction to Religion in Africa*. Belmont, CA: Wadsworth, 1986.

Lado, Ludovic. *Catholic Pentecostalism and the Paradoxes of Africanization: Processes of Localization in a Catholic Charismatic Movement in Cameroon*. Leiden, the Netherlands: Brill, 2009.

LaKelly Hunt, Helen. *Faith and Feminism: A Holy Alliance*. New York: Atria Books, 2004.

Laurentin, René. *Jésus au Temple: Mystère de Pâques et foi de Marie en Luc 2. 48–50*. Paris: J. Gabalda, 1966.

Lietzmann, Hans. *A History of the Early Church*, vol. 3: *From Constantine to Julian*. Translated by Bertram L. Woolf. London: Lutterworth Press, 1961.

Loyola, Ignatius. *The Spiritual Exercises*. Translated by George E. Ganss. Anand, India: Gujarat Sahitya Prakash, 1993.

Luz, Ulrich. *Matthew 8–20*. Translated by James E. Crouch. Minneapolis: Fortress Press, 2001.

Luz, Ulrich, and Helmut Koester. *A Commentary on Matthew 1–7*. Minneapolis: Fortress Press, 2007.

Maloney, George A. *Intoxicated with God: The Fifty Spiritual Homilies of Macarius*. Denville, NJ: Dimension Books, 1978.

Mbiti, John S. *African Religions and Philosophy*. Nairobi: East African Educational Publishers, 1969.

———. *Concepts of God in Africa*. London: S.P.C.K., 1970.

———. *Introduction to African Religion*. Nairobi: East African Educational Publishers, 1992.

———. *The Prayers of African Religion*. Maryknoll, NY: Orbis Books, 1975.

Mbogoni, Lawrence E. Y. *Human Sacrifice and the Supernatural in African History*. Dar-es-Salaam, Tanzania: Mkuki na Nyota, 2013.

McCarter, P. Kyle. *I Samuel: A New Translation with Introduction, Notes, and Commentary*. New Haven, CT: Yale University Press, 2008.

McKenzie, John L. *Second Isaiah: A New Translation with Introduction and Commentary*. New York: Doubleday, 1968.

Meier, John P. *A Marginal Jew: Rethinking the Historical Jesus,* vol. 1: *The Roots of the Problem and the Person.* New York: Doubleday, 1991.

Miles, Carrie A. "God as Mother." *Sunstone* 124 (2002): 43.

Mills, Mary E. *Images of God in the Old Testament.* Collegeville, MN: Liturgical Press, 1998.

Mollenkott, Virginia R. *The Divine Feminine: The Biblical Imagery of God as Female.* New York: Crossroad, 1983.

Moltmann, Jürgen. *The Source of Life: The Holy Spirit and the Theology of Life.* Translated by Margaret Kohl. Minneapolis: Fortress Press, 1997.

———. *The Spirit of Life: A Universal Affirmation.* Translated by Margaret Kohl. Minneapolis: Fortress Press, 1992.

Munonye, John. *The Only Son.* London: Cox & Wyman, 1966.

Neumann, Erich. *The Great Mother: An Analysis of the Archetype.* Translated by Ralph Manheim. Princeton, NJ: Princeton University Press, 1963.

Nolland, John. *Luke 1:1–9:20.* Word Biblical Commentary, vol. 35A. Dallas, TX: Word, 2002.

Nyamiti, Charles. "The African Sense of God's Motherhood in the Light of Christian Faith." *Africa Ecclesial Review* 23 (1981): 269–74.

Origen. *Commentaire sur l'Evangile selon Matthieu.* Edited by Robert Girod. SCh, vol. 162. Paris: Cerf, 1970.

———. *Commentary on John.* Translated by Allan Menzies. ANF, vol. 10. Grand Rapids, MI: Wm. B. Eerdmans, 1978.

———. *Homélies sur Samuel.* Edited by Pierre Nautin and Marie-Thérèse Nautin. SCh, vol. 328. Paris: Cerf, 1986.

Orobator, Agbonkhianmeghe E. *Theology Brewed in an African Pot.* Maryknoll, NY: Orbis Books, 2008.

Ott, Martin. *African Theology in Images.* Kachere Series, vol. 12. Blantyre: Christian Literature Association in Malawi, 2000.

Peterson, Amy R. *Perpetua: A Bride, a Martyr, a Passion.* Lake Mary, FL: Relevant Books, 2004.

Pope Francis. *Encyclical Letter Laudato Si': On Care for Our Common Home.* Rome: Vatican Press, 2015.

Pope John XXIII. *Journal of a Soul.* Translated by Dorothy M. White. London: Geoffrey Chapman, 1965.

Plummer, Alfred. *A Critical and Exegetical Commentary on the Gospel According to S. Luke.* London: T&T Clark International, 1896.

Quasten, Johannes. *Patrology,* vol. 3: *The Beginnings of Patristic Literature from the Apostles Creed to Irenaeus.* Allen, TX: Christian Classics, 1995.

Perkins, Pheme. "The Gospel According to John." In *The New Jerome Biblical Commentary.* Edited by Raymond E. Brown et al., 942–85. London: Geoffrey Chapman, 1990.

Pierce, Yolanda. "Why God Is a 'Mother,' Too." *Time* (May 11, 2013). http://ideas.time.com/2013/05/11/why-god-is-a-mother -too/.

Prange, Victor H. *Luke.* Milwaukee, WI: Northwestern Publishing House, 1988.

Robinson, John. *The First Book of Kings.* Cambridge: Cambridge University Press, 1972.

Ross, Allen P., and John N. Oswalt. *Genesis, Exodus.* Cornerstone Biblical Commentary, vol. 1. Carol Stream, IL: Tyndale House Publishers, 2008.

Schnackenburg, Rudolf. *The Gospel According to St. John,* vol. 1: *Introduction and Commentary on Chapters 1–4.* Translated by Kevin Smyth. New York: Herder and Herder, 1968.

Schneiders, Sandra M. *The Revelatory Text: Interpreting the New Testament as Scripture.* San Francisco: HarperSanFrancisco, 1991.

Shorter, Alward. "Divine Call and Human Response: Prayer in the Religious Traditions of Africa II." *The Way* 23 (1983): 231–43.

Somé, Malidoma P. *The Healing Wisdom of Africa: Finding Life Purpose through Nature, Ritual, and Community.* New York: Jeremy P. Tarcher, 1998.

Speiser, Ephraim A. *Genesis: Introduction, Translation, and Notes.* New Haven, CT: Yale University Press, 2008.

Spink, Kathryn. *Mother Teresa: A Complete Authorized Biography.* San Francisco: HarperSanFrancisco, 1997.

Stramara, Daniel F. *Praying—with the Saints—to God Our Mother.* Eugene, OR: Wipf and Stock, 2012.

Swete, Henry B. *The Gospel According to St. Mark: The Greek Text with Introduction, Notes, and Indices.* London: MacMillan, 1898.

Tertullian. *A Treatise on the Soul.* Translated by Peter Holmes. ANF, vol. 3. Grand Rapids, MI: Wm. B. Eerdmans, 1978.

———. *On Fasting.* Translated by Sidney Thelwall. ANF, vol. 4. Grand Rapids, MI: Wm. B. Eerdmans, 1979.

Thomasson-Rosingh, Anne C. *Searching for the Holy Spirit: Feminist Theology and Traditional Doctrine.* London: Routledge, 2015.

Turner, David L., and Darrel L. Bock. *Matthew and Mark.* Cornerstone Biblical Commentary, vol. 11. Carol Stream, IL: Tyndale House Publishers, 2005.

Vasko, Peter F. *Our Visit to the Holy Land.* Jerusalem: Mount Olives Press, 2000.

Verecundus Iuncensis. *Commentarii super cantica ecclesiastica.* Edited by Roland Demeulenaere. CCL, vol. 93. Turnhout, Belgium: Brepols, 1976.

Viviano, Benedict T. "The Gospel According to Matthew." In *The New Jerome Biblical Commentary.* Edited by Raymond E. Brown et al., 630–74. London: Geoffrey Chapman, 1990.

Vuola, Elina. "(The) Breastfeeding God." *Ecumenical Review* 65 (2013): 98–113.

Wénin, André. *D'Adam à Abraham ou les errances de l'humain: Lecture de Genèse 1, 1–12, 4.* Paris: Cerf, 2007.

Westermann, Claus. *Genesis 12–36: A Commentary.* Translated by John J. Scullion. London: S.P.C.K., 1981.